FACING THE NEW WORLD

Jewish Portraits
in Colonial and Federal America

FACING THE NEW WORLD

Jewish Portraits in Colonial and Federal America

Richard Brilliant

With an Essay by Ellen Smith

Research assistance provided by Elizabeth Lamb Clark

The Jewish Museum, New York
Under the auspices of The Jewish Theological Seminary of America

Prestel   Munich · New York

This book has been published in conjunction with the exhibition *Facing the New World: Jewish Portraits in Colonial and Federal America*, presented at The Jewish Museum, New York, September 21, 1997–January 11, 1998, and at The Maryland Historical Society, Baltimore, February 19, 1998–May 24, 1998.

Facing the New World: Jewish Portraits in Colonial and Federal America has been supported by grants from The Skirball Foundation, the Maurice Amado Foundation, The Morris S. and Florence H. Bender Foundation, The Bank of New York, Erica Jesselson and Family, the Roy J. Zuckerberg Family Foundation, and Carol and Arthur Goldberg.

Exhibition Curator: Richard Brilliant
Exhibition Consultant: Ellen Smith
Research Curator: Elizabeth Lamb Clark
Project Director: Kathryn Potts
Catalogue Editor: Sheila Friedling

Library of Congress Cataloging-in-Publication Data
  Facing the new world : Jewish portraits in colonial and federal
  America / Richard Brilliant [exhibition curator] : with an essay by
  Ellen Smith.
  Includes bibliographical references and index.
  ISBN 3-7913-1863-2
  1. Jews--United States--Portraits--Exhibitions. 2. Portraits,
  Jewish--United States--Exhibitions. 3. Jews--United States--Biography.
  4. Portrait painting--United States--Exhibitions. 5. United States--Biography--
  Portraits--Exhibitions. I. Brilliant, Richard. II. Smith, Ellen
  III. Jewish Museum (New York, N.Y.) IV. Maryland Historical Society.
  E184.J5F34   1997
  973'.04924'0092--dc21   97-33276

Cover image: Detail of *Solomon Isaacs* by John Wesley Jarvis. Oil on canvas; 28 ¼ × 26 ⅛; 71.76 × 67.64 cm. The Jewish Museum, New York. Museum purchase; gift of Mr. and Mrs. Jacob Shulman and the J.E. and Z.B. Butler Foundation, by exchange; with funds provided by the estate of Gabriel and Rose Katz; and gift of Kallia H. Bokser, by exchange, 1996-6.

Prestel-Verlag
Mandlstrasse 26, D-80802 Munich, Germany
Tel (89)381709-0; Fax (89)381709-35
16 West 22 Street, New York, NY 10010
Tel. (212) 627-8199; Fax: (212) 627-9866

Prestel books are available worldwide.
Please contact your nearest bookseller or write
to either of the above addresses for infomation
concerning your local distributor.

Copy–edited by Susan Dixon

Color separations by Repro Ludwig
Printed by Holzer, Weiler
Bound by Conzella

Printed in Germany on acid-free paper
ISBN   3-7913-1863-2

Contents

Lenders to the Exhibition

Abby Aldrich Rockefeller Folk Art Center,
    Williamsburg, Virginia
American Jewish Historical Society, Waltham,
    Massachusetts, and New York, New York
The Baltimore Museum of Art
Brooklyn Museum of Art
The Chrysler Museum of Art and the
    Moses Myers House, Norfolk, Virginia
Cincinnati Art Museum
Congregation Shearith Israel, New York,
    New York
Delaware Art Museum, Wilmington
The Detroit Institute of Arts
E. Norman Flayderman
Gibbes Museum of Art/Carolina Art Association,
    Charleston, South Carolina
Indiana University Art Museum, Bloomington
The Jewish Museum, New York
Kenneth and Sandra Malamed Trust, Los Angeles,
    and Bernard and S. Dean Levy, Inc., New York,
    New York
The Maryland Historical Society, Baltimore
Massachusetts General Hospital, Boston
The Metropolitan Museum of Art, New York
The Montclair Art Museum, New Jersey
Museum of the City of New York
Emily da Silva Solis Nathan
The New-York Historical Society
The Newport Historical Society
Museum of American Art of the Pennsylvania
    Academy of the Fine Arts, Philadelphia
Redwood Library and Athenaeum, Newport,
    Rhode Island
Rosenbach Museum and Library, Philadelphia
Henry Hendricks Schulson
Ruth Hendricks Schulson
Cipora O. and Philip C. Schwartz
Joan Sturhahn
The Toledo Museum of Art
Wadsworth Atheneum, Hartford, Connecticut
Warner House Association, Portsmouth,
    New Hampshire

Foreword

Joan Rosenbaum

HELEN GOLDSMITH MENSCHEL DIRECTOR
THE JEWISH MUSEUM

THE FIRST JEWS ARRIVED in this country in 1654, when twenty-three Jewish refugees from Brazil landed in New Amsterdam. During the seventeenth and eighteenth centuries, they were joined by more immigrants, many of them descendants of Jews expelled from Spain and Portugal, and others with origins in Western and Central Europe. The early American Jews encountered a new society in which they would build productive lives as merchants, traders, shippers, and property owners. Despite incidents of anti-Semitism and, at first, the denial of full civil rights, they experienced a high level of religious, political, and personal freedom. By the time of the Revolution, many American Jews had risen to positions of prominence in colonial society, and a large number played a role in the struggle for American independence. Especially during the Federal period, some American Jews were involved in public life—in politics, law, and the military. By 1830, there were as many as 4,000 Jews living in the New Republic; and the Sephardic communities who had been the first to arrive in the colonies were increasingly outnumbered by Ashkenazic immigrants from Central Europe and the German lands.

Facing the New World: Jewish Portraits in Colonial and Federal America offers new insights into this little-known but fascinating chapter of American Jewish life, culture, and history. As with many other exhibitions at The Jewish Museum, this exhibition and accompanying publication integrate art and Jewish history, interpreting the portraits within the framework of a particular historical period, place, and aesthetic context. The portraits are thus viewed simultaneously as art objects, self-representations, and social documents.

The early American Jews depicted in these portraits were typically leading members of their communities—men of affairs and women of good families. Among these early

Jewish families, who enjoyed the freedom to move within both Jewish and gentile circles during the colonial and Federal periods, were the Hays and Touro families of Newport and Boston; the Gomez, Levy-Franks, Hendricks, Phillips, and Seixas families of New York; the Gratz and Levy families of Philadelphia; the Etting, Gratz, and Cohen families of Baltimore; and the Myers family of Norfolk. As one way to assert their belonging in American society, these American Jews commissioned the leading artists of the day to create portraits that they displayed prominently in their homes.

Facing the New World is the first comprehensive museum exhibition to examine early American Jewish portraiture from approximately 1700 to the early 1800s. It includes important public portraits as well as more intimate portrait miniatures by distinguished American painters such as Gilbert Stuart, Thomas Sully, John Wesley Jarvis, Charles Willson Peale, and Ralph Earl. There are also portraits by unknown folk artists and some comparative paintings of non-Jewish subjects, including a work by Joshua Johnson, an accomplished African-American painter active in the Baltimore area. Also shown are examples of early American drawings, silhouettes, ritual objects, and decorative arts.

Facing the New World features two groundbreaking and complementary essays. "Portraits as Silent Claimants: Jewish Class Aspirations and Representational Strategies in Colonial and Federal America," by Richard Brilliant, guest curator of the exhibition and an authority on portraiture, discusses the European models of representation that artists drew upon in their portraits of Jewish sitters, examining how the self is represented by means of various social and cultural roles and images—the "beauty," the military hero, the prominent man of affairs, the husband-wife pair. Exploring family and regional groupings that demonstrate the evolution of imagery and modes of self-representation over time, Richard Brilliant reveals how the Jewish individuals and families who commissioned artists to paint their portraits chose to identify publicly as belonging to a prominent merchant class rather than to a distinctive ethnic group.

Ellen Smith's essay, "Portraits of a Community: The Image and Experience of Early American Jews," explores the tension between Jewish self-representation in the portraits and the social reality of early American Jewish life. Drawing on surviving letters, business records, and domestic and religious objects, she gives us a lively and well-illustrated overview of early American Jewish history, the texture of daily and family life, the development of Jewish religious life and identity, and the Jewish community's relationships with the larger society.

Facing the New World shows a range of remarkable men and women, and also gives us the fascinating stories behind the portraits. To name just a few, there are Bilhah Abigail Levy-Franks, whose correspondence provides a rare and vivid picture of early-eighteenth-century life in New York City; Colonel Isaac Franks, who fought in the Battle of Long Island under the command of George Washington and gave his home in Germantown for President Washington's use; Gershom Mendes Seixas, *hazzan* or leader of worship at Congregation Shearith Israel in New York City, Revolutionary patriot, and one of thirteen clergyman who participated in the inauguration of George Washington as President; Rebecca Gratz, philanthropist, educator, and society "beauty" who founded the first Hebrew Sunday School and orphan home, and is said to be the model for the Jewish heroine Rebecca in Sir Walter Scott's novel *Ivanhoe;* and Uriah P. Levy, who became a commodore in the U.S. Navy and later purchased and restored Jefferson's estate at Monticello. With their detailed cross-references, the catalogue entries and essays enhance our understanding of the complex network of family relationships among the sitters, and the range of family, business, religious, and regional connections that characterized the early American Jewish community.

This exhibition is traveling to The Maryland Historical Society in Baltimore. We are pleased that they have lent so many important works and that they have joined the exhibition tour. It is especially fitting that Baltimore is a venue for the exhibition given the significance of its Jewish community during the colonial and Federal periods. Among the portraits in the exhibition representing members of the Baltimore Jewish community, there are nine paintings of the distinguished Etting/Gratz family, including that of Solomon Etting, a director of the Baltimore and Ohio Railroad, America's first railroad, and the first Jew elected to the Baltimore City Council in 1826. The Cohen family is represented by three portraits, including that of Mendes Cohen, the world traveler and banker.

The original idea for *Facing the New World* emerged from a conversation between the leadership of the American Jewish Historical Society and The Jewish Museum to mount a joint exhibition of the Society's early American portraits. As the scale and context of the exhibition have grown, the Society's collection has remained at the core of the exhibit, and the Society remains the single largest lender to it. The Jewish Museum gratefully acknowledges the generosity of the American Jewish Historical Society in sharing its materials and its academic expertise with The Jewish Museum. In particular we would like to thank Justin L. Wyner, President, and Michael Feldberg, Ph. D., Director of the American Jewish Historical Society, for their strong institutional commitment and faith in the relationship between our two institutions.

Although the management of the exhibition was initiated by Eric Zafran, formerly Deputy Director for Curatorial Affairs at The Jewish Museum, at an early stage Kathryn Potts, Assistant Curator for Traveling Exhibitions, stepped in to take over direction of the project; and she quickly and deftly absorbed the content issues, administrative challenges, and lending needs of a project that had an unusually short timetable. Kathryn's competent management, fine curatorial skills, and good nature have kept this project on track. Under her direction, the exhibition has materialized as the beautiful, highly illuminating, and thoughtful exhibition that was envisioned. I am most grateful for her fine work, as it provided the opportunity for the Museum to benefit from the collective contributions of all who were involved: in particular, the highly informed scholarship and creativity of guest curator Richard Brilliant; the invaluable knowledge and guidance of exhibition consultant Ellen Smith; the generosity of the funders; and the extraordinary cooperation of lenders to the exhibition.

The exhibition and catalogue have been supported by a number of funders, to whom we express our deepest appreciation. I extend initial thanks to the Museum's Board of Trustees whose support of the institution's mission and operations through generous yearly contributions has served to encourage an ambitious exhibition program, including scholarly endeavors such as *Facing the New World*. Direct support for the costs of research, consultants, loans, the catalogue, exhibition design, installation, and video has come from The Skirball Foundation, the Maurice Amado Foundation, The Morris S. and Florence H. Bender Foundation, The Bank of New York, Erica Jesselson and Family, the Roy J. Zuckerberg Family Foundation, and Carol and Arthur Goldberg. I thank all of these donors for their belief in the importance of this project and their confidence in the Museum's work. I also thank Sue Davis, Director of Restricted Funding, for her excellent administration of the fundraising process.

There are thirty-two lenders to the exhibition from all over the country noted on p. *vii*. Not surprisingly, the collections for the most part reside in the states that were part of the original American colonies, with the largest number of works borrowed from the landmark collection of the American Jewish Historical Society in Waltham, Massachusetts, and New York, New York, and from The Maryland Historical Society in Baltimore. There are many interesting facts related to the lending institutions and individuals. We are particularly fortunate to have had the cooperation of two historic houses that were once the homes of early American Jews represented in our exhibition: the Moses Myers House in Norfolk, Virginia, now under the auspices of The Chrysler Museum of Art; and the Deshler-Morris House in Philadelphia, formerly the home of Colonel Isaac Franks. The generosity of these institutions has made it possible for our audience to view important portraits that are rarely seen outside of their unique contexts. In addition, Congregation Shearith Israel in New York, established in the late seventeenth century and the owner of the portrait of Mordecai Manuel Noah, is the original congregation of many colonial Jewish families. Four descendants of colonial families are lenders—Emily da Silva Solis Nathan, Henry Hendricks Schulson, Ruth Hendricks Schulson, and Joan Sturhahn.

I am most grateful to Richard Brilliant for his extraordinary work in conceptualizing *Facing the New World* and interpreting the complex and revealing portraits; and I express great appreciation to Ellen Smith for contributing her intimate knowledge of the colonial period, including vital information about the background of the sitters and the history of their communities. Many thanks also to the catalogue editor, Sheila Friedling, who jumped into the project with zeal, determination, and tremendous skill. Renewed thanks to Kathryn Potts and to all of those individuals who, in sharing responsibility for *Facing the New World,* have formed a formidable team—staff, consultants, trustees, donors, and lenders. Congratulations on creating an exhibition and catalogue that will serve as a highly informative and truly fascinating point of reference for those who wish to appreciate, study, and identify with the Jewish, American, and deeply human values embedded in this admirable endeavor.

Acknowledgments

IN 1995 THE AMERICAN JEWISH Historical Society approached The Jewish Museum with a proposal to create a small exhibition that would highlight the Historical Society's important collection of colonial portraits. Although there was enthusiastic support for this project from the start, the curatorial staff of The Jewish Museum proposed instead to mount a more comprehensive exhibition of colonial and Federal portraits of early American Jews. This exhibition would not only provide the first opportunity to see a large and diverse group of these portraits exhibited together for the first time, but also would consider the artworks in the context of their time and pay special attention to the predicament of the American Jewish community as it struggled to establish itself in the colonies and the New Republic.

To organize an exhibition of this nature and scope, The Jewish Museum turned to Richard Brilliant, Anna S. Garbedian Professor in the Humanities at Columbia University and an authority on portraiture. Professor Brilliant literally shaped this exhibition, having conceived of both the exhibition and catalogue as a kind of visual essay or rhetorical argument on the subject of early American Jewish portraiture. He has had a hand in every aspect of this project, from the selection of paintings to the exhibition design to his illuminating and comprehensive catalogue essay. Although he wears many different professional and personal "hats," he has been incredibly generous with his time, critical insights, and expertise. We are greatly indebted to him, and hope that he is as pleased with the results of his curatorial endeavors and scholarship as we are.

Since the story of the early American Jews was to be a central focus, we invited Ellen Smith, Curator of the American Jewish Historical Society, to join us in the initial planning and development of the exhibition. Her knowledge, experience, and advice were crucial to the project. In addition to writing an important essay that considers the portraits in the context of early American Jewish life and material culture, she prepared entries for the catalogue as well as instructive Appendix material, and was instrumental in developing the historical context and interpretive plan for the exhibition as well as its audio-visual component. As the representative of the American Jewish Historical Society, she also handled a myriad of curatorial and administrative details related to the loan of paintings and decorative arts from the Society. She has played a critically important and creative role in this exhibition, and we thank her for her efforts.

Also part of the original team was Elizabeth Lamb Clark, who served as Research Curator for the exhibition and traveled around the country to examine paintings and conduct her research. Later she would turn her attention to the task of writing the bulk of the catalogue entries—fifty-nine to be exact. This she did in a few short months, all the while demonstrating grace under the pressure of very tight deadlines. In the entry writing, we were also very fortunate to have the collaboration of Joellyn Wallen Zollman, a graduate student at Brandeis University and colleague at the American Jewish Historical Society. She has written fifteen catalogue entries, provided valuable historical research for the catalogue, collaborated in preparing the Chronology, and managed many details related to loans from the American Jewish Historical Society. Charlotte Emans Moore also contributed expert catalogue entries; she came to the project in its final stage and we are very grateful for her help.

I think it is fair to say we would not have a catalogue if it were not for Sheila Friedling, our editor. She managed all aspects of the catalogue editing and production, and was integral to its conceptualization. She is an intelligent and sensitive editor, and a wonderful colleague. She is the heart and soul of this book, and also its greatest supporter. It is a pleasure to thank her. We were also extremely fortunate to have Michael Rizzo as our exhibition designer. He has created an installation that reads with great clarity and is beautiful to look at. David Barquist, Associate Curator at the Yale University Art Gallery, advised us on the decorative arts components of the exhibition and helped plan an historically accurate exhibition design. Michael McLoughlin of Thwaite Productions created a highly informative and engaging script for the audio-visual presentation.

In the initial planning, Eric Zafran, formerly Deputy Director for Curatorial Affairs at The Jewish Museum, served as project director, helping to develop a concept into an exhibition. He visited many of the private and institutional collections to make the initial selection of paintings and managed much of the exhibition organization during the first phase of this project. He also shared his insights on the project and was generous with suggestions and advice. During the early phase of the project we also held a number of planning meetings to determine the thematic focus and scope of the exhibition. In addition to the exhibition staff already mentioned, I would like to thank the following individuals for participating in these meetings and for offering their expertise: Ken Ames, Lynne Breslin, Eric Goldstein, and Barry Kessler.

We are also indebted to our colleagues at The Maryland Historical Society, in particular to Director Dennis Fiori and Curator Nancy Davis for their enthusiasm and support for bringing the exhibition to Baltimore. Thanks also to Sarah Harman, Jeannine A. Disviscour, and Heather Ersts Venters of The Maryland Historical Society who coordinated the presentation of the exhibition there.

This catalogue was designed and produced by our co-publisher Prestel-Verlag. We would like to acknowledge the entire staff of Prestel-Verlag, including Michael Maegraith, Cilly Klotz, Julia Fuchshuber, James Bloom, Daniela Petrini, and Susan Dixon.

This exhibition and catalogue are the result of more than two years of planning and research, and numerous individuals at other institutions have generously contributed their assistance to this project. Along with my other project colleagues, I wish to thank: Anne Motley at the Abby Aldrich Rockefeller Folk Art Center; Dawne Bear and Libby Finkelstein at the American Jewish Historical Society; Sona Johnston at the Baltimore Museum of Art; Jonathan Sarna at Brandeis University; Linda Ferber at the Brooklyn Museum of Art; Elizabeth Ardrey, and Catherine Jordan at The Chrysler Museum; Barbara Gibbs and John Wilson at the Cincinnati Art Museum; William H. Gerdts at the City University of New York; Nancy Miller Batty and Stephen T. Bruni at the Delaware Art Museum; Nancy Rivard Shaw at The Detroit Institute of Arts; Angela Mack at the Gibbes Museum of Art; Shalom Sabar at the Center for Jewish Art at The Hebrew University of Jerusalem; Kathleen Foster at the Indiana University Art Museum; Ann Appelbaum and Annette

Botnick at The Jewish Theological Seminary of America; Bernard Levy, S. Dean Levy and Frank Levy at Bernard and S. Dean Levy, Inc.; Allison Rimm at the Massachusetts General Hospital; Carrie Rebora at The Metropolitan Museum of Art; Gail Stavitsky at the Montclair Museum of Art; Harriet Collins at the Moses Myers House; Barbara Ball Buff and Alison Eisendrath at the Museum of the City of New York; Jeannine Falino, Erica Hirshler, and Shelley Langdale at the Museum of Fine Arts, Boston; Ellen G. Miles at the National Portrait Gallery; Margaret Tamulonis at The New-York Historical Society; M. Joan Youngken at the Newport Historical Society; Sylvia Yount at the Pennsylvania Academy of the Fine Arts; John Ravenal at the Philadelphia Museum of Art; Maris Humphreys at the Redwood Library and Athenaeum; Elizabeth Fuller at the Rosenbach Museum and Library; Alan Singer and Susan Tobin at Congregation Shearith Israel; Cindy Shapiro at Sotheby's; David W. Steadman at The Toledo Museum of Art; Dilys Winegrad at the University of Pennsylvania; Melvin Urofsky at the Virginia Commonwealth University; Elizabeth Kornhauser at the Wadsworth Atheneum; and Joyce Volk at the Warner House Association.

Warm thanks are also due to the following individuals for their support: Morton C. Bradley, Maury A. Bronson, Judith Eisenberg, Michael Heidelberg, Kathleen Madden, Carl J. Mastandrea, Ken Moser, Edgar and David Nathan, John Parnell, Ruth and Herman Schulman, David Sultan, John D. Woolfe, and Roy J. Zuckerberg.

At The Jewish Museum, there were numerous individuals who worked to make this exhibition a reality. In particular, I would like to thank Margie Weinstein, Exhibition Assistant, who helped in innumerable ways during this project. Her intelligence, expertise, and enthusiasm have made her an invaluable colleague. Exhibition Assistant Jessica Keuskamp also played an important role in coordinating large numbers of photographic requests for this book, obtaining the reproduction rights for all works, and overseeing the in-house photography and duplication of photographic materials. Curatorial Affairs Intern Mara Gerstein provided research and editing support for the catalogue.

Ruth Beesch, Deputy Director for Program, guided us through the final stages of the catalogue production and the installation of the exhibition. Judith Siegel, Director of Education, Media, and Public Programs, gave indispensable advice on the exhibition interpretive plan and design. Associate Registrar Lisa Mansfield coordinated the shipment of all the loans for the exhibition in New York and also the presentation in Baltimore. Sue Davis, Director of Restricted Funding, secured the funding for the exhibition, without which this project would not have been possible. Special thanks are due to Alessandro Cavadini, Audio-Visual Co-ordinator, for producing the video that accompanied the exhibition.

Anne Scher, Director of Public Relations, coordinated the publicity for the exhibition. Aviva Weintraub, Manager of Public Programs, created a special public program to complement the exhibition. Grace Rapkin and Marcia Saft also helped in our marketing and community outreach efforts. Many colleagues in the Curatorial Division were generous with advice and support, including: in the Departments of Fine Arts, Norman Kleeblatt, Susan and Elihu Rose Curator of Fine Arts; Mira Goldfarb Berkowitz, former Curatorial Assistant; and Irene Zwerling Schenk, Research Associate; in the Judaica Department, Vivian Mann, Morris and Eva Feld Chair of Judaica; Sarah Lawrence, Andrew W. Mellon Fellow in Judaica; Denny Stone, Andrew W. Mellon Fellow in Judaica; and Sharon Wolfe, Curatorial Assistant and Program Manager for Core.

Debbie Schwab, Director of Retail Operations, Robin Cramer, Director of Product Development and Merchandising, and Sara Abraham, Buyer, designed and selected products for sale in the Museum's Cooper Shop. Thanks also to Thomas Dougherty, Deputy Director of Finance and Administration, Samantha Gilbert, Administrator, Donna Jeffrey, Controller, Jane Dunne, former Deputy Director for Administration, and Jack Salzman, former Deputy Director for Education, Media, and Public Programs, who provided advice and assistance at different stages in this project.

Finally, I would like to acknowledge our Director, Joan Rosenbaum, who endorsed this project from its inception and who inspired us to create this memorable exhibition.

Kathryn Potts
PROJECT DIRECTOR

RICHARD BRILLIANT

Portraits as Silent Claimants:
Jewish Class Aspirations and Representational Strategies
in Colonial and Federal America

If I am not for myself, who will be?
And I, by myself, what am I?

      HILLEL, *Pirke Avoth*

Hath a Jew not eyes? Hath a Jew not hands, organs, dimensions, senses,
affections, passions?
Fed with the same food, hurt by the same weapons, subject to the same diseases,
healed by the same means, warmed and cooled by the same winter and summer,
as a Christian is?

      SHAKESPEARE, *Merchant of Venice*

THE SMALL COMMUNITY of Jews in America, perhaps numbering no more than four thousand persons in 1830, seemed to take the spirit of Shylock's words most seriously, at least with respect to their efforts at self-representation through painted portraits. Indeed, despite the small size of the Jewish population, many substantial portraits of Jews survive from the colonial period and early Republic, often painted by the leading artists of the day who, apparently, did not discriminate among their Jewish and gentile patrons in their selection of suitable images. The very existence of these Jewish portraits bears witness to the importance placed upon the deliberate confection of their faces and their fashionably clothed bodies as conventially, and recognizably, "American."

Of course, the sociopolitical content of the designation "American" was only coming into being during the eighteenth and early nineteenth centuries, as people of very diverse origins were slowly assimilated into a distinctive, yet open, society, which was constantly recruiting new members. For Jews who could afford it, commissioned portraits of themselves and of their wives and children constituted a significant affirmation of their right to belong. To commission portraits,

and then collect and display them in suitably furnished houses in Boston, Newport, New York, Philadelphia, Baltimore, Norfolk, Richmond, Charleston, and Savannah, represented a visual claim by these early American Jews to membership in the propertied class of merchant-traders, shippers, and bankers, to which by occupation and wealth they properly belonged, even if they remained Jews by religion. This propertied class, with its roots in Dutch and English colonial society, together with the plantation magnates of the South, dominated American life for decades. Their control was challenged by the "democrat" Andrew Jackson and his supporters in the 1820s and 30s, by the strong demographic shift away from the eastern cities toward the West, and by the displacement of trade by industry as the prime source of new, and great, wealth.

Because Jews were closely tied to the old mercantile ways of acquiring wealth and prestige, their participation in these profound changes in the complexion of American life was marginal, even as their numbers increased. The conventions of Jewish portraiture, developed over the course of a century, remained tied to an eighteenth-century bourgeois imagery of restrained sobriety, thereby maintaining the effective distancing of its subjects from the viewer; and they emphasized the descriptive character of the likeness, soon to be undermined in the 1840s by the advent of photography.

Thus the shape of the exhibition emerges from, and is consistent with, historical reality and Jewish experience in colonial and post-colonial America, a discrete episode in the familiar search for representative self-imaging through the artifice of portraiture, which met the aspirations of its Jewish patrons to become known and, then, remembered as participants in contemporary American society. The transition from the awkwardness of Duyckinck's *Mr. and Mrs. Moses Levy*, c. 1720–28 (Plate 1, cats. 1, 2), still closely dependent on harsh, late Baroque conventions of the seventeenth century, to the gentle, proto-Victorian sensibility of Dunlap's *Mr. and Mrs. Moses Judah* (Plate 15, cats. 86, 87), almost a century later, demonstrates very clearly the persistence of the gendered roles, even as the formulae for the representation of husband and wife changed. In the portrayal of these marital pairs—and paired portraits of worthy husband and equally worthy wife are common throughout this period—no overt attempt has been made to suggest the Jewishness of the subjects, either by including some elements of an allegedly distinguishing physiognomy—"Jewish looks"—or by an identifying attribute, drawn from the world of ceremonial objects, usually found in Jewish homes but not in these portraits.

Whether or not colonial Jews actually looked different from everybody else, the apparently deliberate separation of the ethnic or religious "self," as one basis of identity, from the public "self" of the counting house or the world of commerce, another source of identity, may be taken as a symptom of accommodation, or assimilation, to the norms of class. Membership in that merchant class was not wholly subject to these religious and ethnic factors, even if admission to the full prerogatives of the class remained somewhat restricted in practice because of these same factors. Anti-Semitism existed even in the commercial world; and Jews not only suffered from its expression both economically and socially, but in most pre-Revolutionary colonies and in the later states their political rights were circumscribed until well after the Revolution and the creation of the United States. Appearing to be like the others, full-fledged members of the propertied class, was a means of becoming or being like these others, a member of an undifferentiated economic elite. It would seem as if an acceptably Americanized body, the face attached to it, and the clothes worn by it would be sufficient to signify that class membership. The Jewish "self" inside that body was not only concealed thereby from the secular environment but could also be reserved to exposure in the home, that traditional locus of Jewish life, or in the synagogue.

Strangely, the portraits themselves often exhibit, perhaps unintentionally, a tension between the assumed burden of a confected social self—present in the painted image—and the semi-private function of the original display of the painted portrait itself. For the most part, this display occurred in the home as an attribute of propertied gentility, especially in those semi-public rooms—the parlor and the dining room—that conceivably might be visited by an outsider, even another propertied Jew. Here, a Jewish merchant or banker could be comfortably perceived, even positively acknowledged, as a Jew, when defined by his actions, by the presence of ritual objects in his home, and by his names. The Myers family portraits (Plate 11, cats. 69–71), preserved in the Moses Myers House in Norfolk, Virginia, exemplify the dichotomy between the absence of ethnic or religious markers in their painted portraits and the "Jewish" domestic context in which they were displayed. Such people asserted, in good American fashion, their association with the secular world "outside" through the medium of the family portraits hanging on the walls, portraits comparable to those of his gentile compatriots, such as the Griffins (cats. 77, 78), which formerly hung in similar places on their walls. Indeed, an assemblage of such family portraits, the ostensible manifestation of worthy ancestors, could augment substantially the impression of a distinguished lineage and serve to reveal generations of membership in the "right" class.

Jewish identity in the colonial period and early Republic was not a singular entity. Jews had emigrated into North America from Portugal and Brazil, from the Dutch and British colonies in the Caribbean, from Holland and England more or less directly, from the German states, and to a limited extent from Eastern Europe and the Mediterranean rim. The majority were of Sephardic origin, their primacy slowly giving way in the late-eighteenth century to the Ashkenazim in New York and elsewhere. Jewish families frequently intermarried among the available Jewish groups of diverse origin, given the relative paucity of suitable matches, the small population, and the desire to marry within the faith, if possible. This intermarriage among different Jewish groups, coupled with the movement of prominent families from one city to another in pursuit of economic opportunity, helped break down the difference of origin or region, opening up the Jewish communities on the cities of the Eastern seaboard to constant exchange, especially among the well-to-do for whom exchange itself was a traditional pattern of doing business. Given the social pressure to marry and raise a family, choices were limited, leading some to move beyond the Jewish community entirely to find marriage partners in the proper class, as did Phila Franks (cat. 8), who married a Delancey, and members of the Levy family (cats. 18–25).

In effect, in the hundred years encompassed in this exhibition, a progressive convergence of Jewish and American culture took place. It resulted not so much in an overall, homogeneous society, but rather compatible regional variants, reflecting the social and artistic practices of each locale—New England, the Middle Atlantic, and the South—and the particular configuration of the local elite. And yet, perhaps because of the fragile state of the artistic enterprise in early America, or the prevalence of itinerant limners with modest training, or the influence of the few leading portrait painters —such as Thomas Sully, Gilbert Stuart, the Peales, John Wesley Jarvis, and before them the eighteenth-century masters, Gerardus Duyckinck, John Wollaston, and Ralph Earl—portraiture was the product of an active, often unequal, negotiation between the clients' awkward demands and the shaping of those demands by the few artists available.

It was the artists themselves who absorbed the prior conventions of elite portraiture, largely derived from English models known to them not principally through original works of art but through mezzotints. These image makers promulgated the pictorial models in general circulation, sometimes particularizing them for individual clients but more often relying on formulae, and not just for their own convenience. Their models conveyed the social aspirations of their clients. The formulae themselves were status-ridden composites of meaningful, readily intelligible signs, already familiar to their audience, and for that very reason much in demand.

That familiarity was acquired through progressive indoctrination, a by-product of the rapid secularization of the Jews in America during the eighteenth century, because colonial society was much more open to them than the European societies from which they had come. Although European traditions of portraiture were well-developed and ultimately would provide models for American artists and their patrons, usually through their English intermediaries, Jewish access to portraits and portrait artists, as well as their employment, had been extremely limited. In a sense, Jews appreciated personal

achievement, as well as the possession of a distinctive lineage, but their celebration was memorialized in language, in written texts, and in oral presentations, not in works of visual art, such as painted portraits. Lack of custom, a lingering inhibition about the use of figured images, insufficient desire or opportunity, all combined to prevent the adoption of commemorative or celebratory portraits. This obstacle, combining inexperience in the visual arts and a reluctance to take advantage of them, stood in the way of Jewish portraits, even when the so-called middle classes of Western Europe and Britain sought to commission portraits of themselves as a mark of their rising status vis-à-vis the old aristocracy. For European Jews the past was incorporated in a verbal rather than a visual tradition; for Americanized Jews, late-comers to an increasingly secularized, bourgeois society, the adoption of the portrait practices of the mercantile class they sought to enter determined their subsequent behavior.

Commissioning a painted portrait, or several of them, was a highly charged act. It must be seen as a very significant gesture, a tangible affirmation of the desire to belong, to exhibit the trappings of class membership in the new American society, and a privileged society at that. As a result, the portrait types and functions of their display, already present in gentile society, were adopted wholesale. Ironically, that same gentile society in colonial America was itself rather new to the practices of portraiture, either as subjects or as patrons. They, too, incurred a dependency on the few available artists to create, or promulgate, a repertory of satisfactory, if derivative, images. It was not originality these new patrons of portraiture sought but conformity to established models, models that would convey the right kind of image of themselves; and those colonial Jews who could, followed suit. The transaction between artist and patron in colonial America must have been very one-sided at first, but eventually learned expectation and growing experience tended to balance that relationship, as the patrons became more knowledgeable and the portrait artists more reputable.

In considering the portraits in this exhibition, from the grim awkwardness of the early eighteenth century, evident in the Levy and Franks portraits (Plate 1, cats. 1–3, 5, 7, 8), to the solid, even graceful confidence of *Harmon Hendricks* (cats. 79, 80) or *Abraham Rodriguez Brandon* (cat. 81), or to the fashionable beauty of *Rebecca Gratz* (Plate 7, cats. 39, 40), the search for a particularly "Jewish" semiotic, some partly hidden sign of ethnic or religious identification, has proven to be extremely difficult to discern. Comparisons with contemporary portraits, reliably identified as gentile, that is non-Jewish—for example, Blackburn's *Mary Warner* (cat. 6), or Wollaston's *Mr. and Mrs. Reade* (cats. 9, 10), or Moulthrop's *Mr. and Mrs. Job Perit* (cats. 51, 53), or the *Griffins* (cats. 77, 78), reveal profound formal and iconographic correspondences with their "Jewish" counterparts. There seems to be no particular sign of the gentiles being gentile, other than being themselves, or of the Jews being Jewish, other than seeming to look gentile, and therefore American, in their portraits. All of them, Jew and gentile alike, appear to be members of a certain American economic class, at least in terms of that class's confirmatory self-imagery.

The question of what constitutes "Jewishness" in the portraits of Jews of the colonial period and early Republic may be either irrelevant or unfounded, when, apparently, neither the portrait artists in selecting their distinctive modes of representation nor their Jewish subjects in adopting particular attitudes of self-representation sought to indicate in some overt way that the portrait offered to the viewer an image of an individual recognizably Jewish in feature or dress. This absence of ethnic particularity seems to be a central issue when assessing the meaning of these portraits of early American Jews, identifiable as such only by factors extrinsic to the paintings themselves. Jewish identification was established by the circumstances of birth, by religious association, by surname, and in the perception of "others." Such an identification was surely important in construing Jewish identity, but it constituted only a part of Jews' sense of self, divided, again in the American way, between private matters and public associations. The portraits intentionally functioned as semi-public documents, mediating between the home and the world of affairs, but semi-public also implies semi-private. Yet, there is no trace of any specifically Jewish element in the portraits; the Menorah may be on the sideboard in the dining room, and may have been used appropriately, but it does not appear in the portraits hanging on the wall above. Jewish attributes of this kind remain invisible, as if they had been erased, having given way to the irresistible demands of class designation or being deliberately suppressed. Given the consistency of this somewhat self-effacing imagery, one must take these portraits as emissaries to a world indifferent or hostile to attempts to proclaim ethnic distinction.

Beginnings: Models, Manners, Modes

The effort to conform is present at the very beginning of American Jewish portraiture, when already established patterns of (self-)representation were fully assimilated. Portraits of husband and wife, both Jewish and Christian, provide a continuous imagery of preferred choice, indicating the strong connection between public and private society as well as the importance of women in colonial life as legitimate, even essential subjects of portrayal. The paired portraits of *Moses Raphael Levy* (Plate 1, cat. 1) and his second wife, *Grace Mears Levy* (cat. 2), c. 1720–28, present people "of parts," leading members of New York Jewish society. The paintings have been attributed to Gerardus Duyckinck, a local limner who worked, uncomfortably, in a late Baroque style, incorporating stiff, formal poses, topical references to the different spheres of his subjects' activity—maritime trade and domestic tranquillity—and an inclined orientation of the figures towards one another, complemented by outward gestures, suggesting that together they constitute a couple and a pair of pendant pictures. The comparable pair of *Bilhah Abigail Levy Franks* and *Jacob Franks* (cats. 3, 5), possibly by the same artist, exhibit the softening of color and contour that marks the tentative entrance of the rococo, an effect that also touches *Anna Cruger* (cat. 4), a contemporary non-Jewish subject. The Franks couple reverses the Levy arrangement, evidence that the left/right order was fortuitous and not canonical. These early-eighteenth-century pictures all follow the same compositional models, even to details of pose, dress, hairstyle, placement of arms and expression—or lack thereof. Gender differences are observed, marked, and displayed, but without subtlety.

Portraits of *David and Phila Franks* (Plate 2, cat. 7) and of *Phila Franks* alone (cat. 8) represent the genealogical succession of the Franks family, one of several such generational assemblies in the exhibit. Their affected poses, images striving to express gracefully the upper class at leisure, all the more impressive in young people, directly follow prototypical imagery derived from a more elegant sensibility, realized by Joseph Blackburn in his famous family portrait (c. 1755) of *Isaac Winslow and His Family* (Fig. 1), Boston gentry depicted in a contemporary, light English manner, or in his portrait of *Mary Warner*, 1761 (cat. 6). The Blackburn pictures represent a higher level of artistic achievement, a more successful evocation of the imagery of the English gentry that established the norms of such portraiture; but the young Franks pictures adopt the same conventions, if less successfully.

Fig. 1 *Isaac Winslow and Family,* by Joseph Blackburn, 1752–1774. Oil on canvas, 54 ½ × 79 ½ in.; 138.4 × 201.9 cm. Courtesy Museum of Fine Arts, Boston, Abraham Shuman Fund.

There was more than one mid-century English model available to colonial artists. If Blackburn adopted the imagery and compositions developed for the portraiture of the English gentry and applied those models to his Boston patrons, John Wollaston followed a more sombre, Hogarthian "plain" manner, suitable for urban worthies—business people and professional. His paintings of the New Yorkers *Mr. and Mrs. Joseph Reade,* c. 1749–52 (cats. 9, 10), exemplify that tradition, perhaps ultimately more applicable to an urban elite, whose distinction arises from personal achievement rather than an aristocratic lineage, an excellent model for the aspirant Jewish patron. The great similarity between the gentile *Mrs. Reade* and the portrait of the Jewish *Rachel Levy Seixas,* 1750 (Plate 3, cat. 11), attributed to Wollaston, is due not just to the same authorship but, also, to the same intentions of representing "quality" on the part of both artist and sitter.

"Quality" can be considered an attribute of character, social position, and artistic accomplishment. Ralph Earl's slightly old-fashioned "man of fashion," *Benjamin S. Judah,* signed by the artist in 1794 (Plate 4, cat. 12), is a quality work in all those respects. Set in elegant surroundings, the slight figure of Judah is surrounded by the trappings of wealth, derived from his very successful mercantile business. Although Earl, the painter of distinguished Americans, is usually more restrained, this New York notable appears, richly dressed, his right hand resting on a bill of exchange, and beyond the open window a generalized landscape, unburdened by any overt sign of his occupation as an international trader. Those who look for such things might find in his extravagant costume and in his prominent nose signs of a sensibility or affiliation foreign to New England Yankees, but then Judah was a New Yorker with a different attitude about wealth and its display.

His image is surely at odds with the portrait of *Israel Israel* (cat. 13), an American patriot and Revolutionary soldier, portrayed by an unknown, lesser artist in a "primitive" manner. Israel Israel and his wife, Hannah Erwin (cat. 14)—after marriage, Mrs. Israel Israel—may have had a Jewish name, but she was a Quaker and, although he had a Jewish father, his mother was Christian and he, himself, was baptized when very young. In this case, as in many others, the question "What are the identifying features of a Jewish portrait?" joins the equally difficult question, "Who is a Jew?" Alterity—that is, the perceived distinction that separates one class of persons, or any particular individual, from "others"—seems to have been all but obliterated in these eighteenth-century portraits, as if to all outward appearances Jew and gentile could not be physically distinguished.

Families: Private and Public; Resemblances and Relationships, Physiognomical and Nominal

In the development of family portraits, whether of more than one family member depicted within a single work of art or the representation of several family members in a series of portraits, American Jews of wealth and social standing again followed the custom of their gentile contemporaries. Portraits and their subjects served as agents of memory, recalling to the mind's eye family members, ancestors, no longer present except through the reiterative imagery of their likenesses. These portraits were often copied and distributed among family members as the family itself proliferated and dispersed, yet maintained its generational associations. The coalescence of subject and audience, intense, even intimate in the original taking of a likeness from life survived as a form of family, or generational, history, even if rarely exposed to the public at large. Perhaps it was enough to know that the pictorial record existed, proof of the family's on-going presence in America.

The silhouette of *Mrs. Simon Nathan and Her Son*, c. 1824 (cat. 15), sister and nephew of *Gershom Mendes Seixas* (cat. 37), exemplifies a well-established motif of family structure, represented by the matron seated, her son standing respectfully before her, as well as the very popular folk-art tradition of the silhouette cut-out. However, silhouette portraits are by their very nature intimate in scale, private in intention, and reserved for a very small circle of potential viewers. Their domestic public also adopted the small-scale portrait, the per-

sonal, intimate index of a precious likeness, rendered in pen-and-ink sketches of varying dimensions or in the oval format of the portrait miniature, sometimes fetishized by enclosing hair clippings of the subject on the back (cat. 52). So the silhouette of *Mrs. Simon Nathan and her Son* would have complemented the miniature portraits of herself and her husband, *Simon Nathan*, c. 1820 (cats. 16, 17), locked away in some cabinet for private contemplation or placed in the more private rooms of the home.

Similar histories are likely for the portrait drawings of *Samson Levy, Jr.* and his mother, the gentile *Martha Lampley Levy*, 1802 (cats. 18, 19), larger in scale but intimate in purpose. One must see them now as a grand, more complicated expression of social ambition, extended to the Sully portraits of the same *Samson Levy, Jr.*, and his wife, *Sarah Coates Levy*, 1808 (cats. 20, 21). Samson Levy, Jr., appears with a partly open book in his hand, as if caught in the momentary act of reflecting on the text, the gesture of a literate intellectual, perhaps; but he converted to Christianity, as did another Levy, Judge Moses Levy of Philadelphia, whose Episcopalian connection did not shield him from anti-Semitic slurs. Judge Levy and his wife (cats. 23, 22) sired Henrietta Levy and Martha Levy (cats. 24, 25), the very image of "proper ladies of good family," as (re)presented by Thomas Sully, a portraitist much favored by such families. Not only fashionable artists but more humble limners of the time took to family portraiture. Joshua Johnson, a Baltimore artist, possibly trained in the ateliers of the famous Peale family, undertook an ambitious group portrait of *Mrs. Thomas Everette and Her Children*, 1818 (cat. 26), brother and sister, awkwardly active in a dark landscape that is strangely detached from them as if it were only a pictorial convention, exactly the kind of convention that governed the portraiture of Jews and gentiles alike.

The sanitizing of portrait imagery, so commonly encountered in these works, may, on occasion, give way to the exploration of the salient features of an individual's physiognomy in the hands of a gifted artist. The portraits of *Jacob Rodriguez Rivera*, 1774 (cat. 29), attributed to Gilbert Stuart, and of his daughter and grandson, *Sarah Rivera Lopez and Joshua*, 1775 (Plate 6, cat. 30), more securely placed in the artist's oeuvre, are strikingly individualistic portraits of these members of a distinguished Sephardic family of Newport, Rhode Island. In examining such portraits in the search for distinguishing "Jewish" or "Sephardic" characteristics, an effort that can be extended, as well, to the portraits of *Jacob da Silva Solis* (cats. 31, 33), *Aaron Rodriguez Rivera* (cat. 36), or *Gershom Mendes*

Seixas (cat. 37), the attempt to isolate aquiline (hooked) or prominent noses, curving eyebrows, and even sallow skin as "Jewish" features rather than personal, physical idiosyncrasies, subject to depiction, must be met with some skepticism. The mixing up of families through marriage—for example, *Mr. and Mrs. Jacob da Silva Solis,* c. 1811 (cats. 33, 32), she a New York Hays, he a Sephardic Jew from London—conflated bloodlines, just as the artists imposed their own manners and modes of vision upon their portraits. Thus the portrait of *Samuel Hays,* another member of this distinguished Jewish family, 1802 (cat. 34), very closely resembles the drawing of *Leonard Bleecker,* 1795 (cat. 35), both by James Sharples, in almost every respect except for the detailing of their faces, required for identification.

Whether or not some degree of stereotyping existed in the depiction of persons in their respective roles, the American presence, a strongly unifying force, is felt throughout, no less so in the portrait of *Rabbi Seixas,* c. 1770 (cat. 37), bare-headed and wearing the clerical collar of a Protestant minister.

Role Playing: Beauties, Handsome Officers, Worthy Burghers

Role playing here alludes to a series of secular categories in which American Jews placed themselves, assuming in the process more of a public face or posture than the domestic face characteristic of family portraits. One such image is surely that of the "beauty", the representation of young Jewish women in accordance with the current standards of feminine pulchritude, an instance of reaching out beyond the Jewish community with a freedom of expression for her sex that was very unconventional. Thus the portraits of *Miriam Etting Myers,* 1804 (cat. 38), a young Baltimore beauty and especially those of the famous Philadelphian *Rebecca Gratz* in the early 1830s (Plate 7, cats. 39, 40) are remarkable extensions of their physical presence into a more public situation of viewing— real or implied—even if Rebecca Gratz refused to marry outside of her faith. This belle of Philadelphia society, recognized as a beautiful and virtuous woman by her contemporaries,

enjoyed the translation of her reputation into fiction when Walter Scott used her as the model for his beautiful and faithful "Rebecca" in *Ivanhoe.*

Jews were also military and political figures of some distinction, given the opportunities offered by the Revolutionary War, the War of 1812, and the politics of the new Republic. *Stephen Decatur,* c. 1815–20 (cat. 42), *Major Mordecai Myers,* c. 1813 (Plate 8, cat. 43), *Commodore Uriah Phillips Levy,* c. 1816 (cat. 44), and *Colonel Isaac Franks,* 1802 (cat. 45) are largely cut from the same cloth. *Mordecai Manuel Noah* (Plate 9, cat. 46), an active supporter of James Madison in the War of 1812, and a New York politician, newspaper publisher, diplomat, and world traveler, as well as a philanthropist in Jewish causes, was involved in both military and political spheres during his career, enough to be subjected to caricature (cat. 47), symptomatic not merely of a public presence but, also, of a public response.

Perhaps the most persistent image remained that of the worthy burgher, an outgrowth of the imagery and perceptions of the eighteenth- and nineteenth-century efforts first to belong and then to maintain the fact of belonging. The Gratzes of Philadelphia, the Baltimore Ettings, the New York Harts, the Cohens and Alexanders of the South, the Myerses of Norfolk, the Hendrickses and Brandons of New York, the Touros of Newport—emigrants, merchant-traders, and their prosperous descendants—repeatedly presented themselves as persons of substance, worthy of respect. The representation of "handsome" men (cats. 57, 71, 79, 83) may be the male counterpart to the "beauty", but by and large the sobriety of the propertied-class imagery prevailed.

Again and again, the interchange between Jewish and non-Jewish portraits can be observed: the portrait of *Shinah Solomon Etting,* 1792 (cat. 50), vividly realized and fashionably, if modestly dressed, may be compared with that of *Mrs. Job Perit,* 1790 (cat. 51) who holds a portrait miniature in her hand, exactly of the type represented in this exhibition. The pairing of husband and wife continues, such as the *Harts* (cats. 55, 56). However, the portrait of their son, *Nathan Hart,* 1817 (cat. 57) reveals a new spirit, reflecting the novel imagery, derived from Romanticism, of the brooding youth, fashionably dressed, of course, that looks for its inspiration to the non-Jewish world.

Generations: Continuity and Change

Jewish portraits are not insulated from stylistic developments, although they tend to remain relatively conservative in appearance. Yet, a degree of contemporaneity seems to have been necessary to buttress the assertion of "belonging." Thus, the portraits of *Mr. and Mrs. Joshua Isaacs* (cats. 58, 59) or of their daughter, *Frances Isaacs* (cat. 60), may look back into the eighteenth century for models, but Frances married *Harmon Hendricks* (cat. 80), whose portrait painted some twenty years later represents an entirely different mode of pictorial construction and self-presentation. From *Jacob Cohen's* miniature (cat. 61), the image of an elegant dandy, to those of the *Ettings* (cats. 64, 65), painted by James Peale in 1794, to the impressive series of Myers portraits (cats. 69–71), painted by Gilbert Stuart and Thomas Sully during the first decade of the nineteenth, one sees a movement toward a heightened immediacy of presence, a greater naturalism. The formulaic conventions seem to have been replaced by others, no less indicative of the sitters' status but more personal, more specific in the depiction of their appearance, as if the stress of self-assertion had been alleviated by a growing confidence in their position, in their sense of belonging.

Jarvis's portraits of *Rachel Gratz Etting* and her husband, *Solomon Etting,* c. 1810–12 (Plate 12, cats. 73, 74) possess a lively directness in their manner, a substantiality not just of their position but of their very person–a vibrant charisma that brings the images beyond the shadow land of role playing. Jarvis also brings this attitude to his authoritative portraits of *Solomon Isaacs* (Plate 13, cat. 76), *Harmon Hendricks* (cat. 80), and *Abraham Brandon* (cat. 81). But this more physically powerful imagery is not solely a feature of John Wesley Jarvis's personal manner, because it also informs the Waldo and Jewett portrait of the same *Harmon Hendricks,* c. 1820 (cat. 79), an early copper magnate, as well as their portraits of the non-Jewish *Mr. and Mrs. George Griffin,* c. 1827 (cats. 77, 78). The world of upper-middle-class society in the Eastern cities of the United States has changed and with it the Jews who lived in that society and took an increasing part in it. In New York City, at least, the presence of German Jews would be increasingly felt in the 1830s and 40s, when August Belmont, the Rothschild agent in the city, would become a leader of New York Society, even as he was reviled as a Jew and social climber.

> The figure of Rebecca might indeed have been compared with the proudest beauties of England .... Her form was exquisitely symmetrical and was shown to advantage by a sort of Eastern dress, which she wore according to the fashion of females of her nation. Her turban of yellow silk suited well with the darkness of her complexion. The brilliancy of her eyes, the superb arch of her eyebrows, her well-formed aquiline nose, her teeth as white as pearl, and the profusion of her sable tresses, which, each arranged in its own little spiral of twisted curls, fell down upon as much of a lovely neck and bosom as a simarre of the richest Persian silk .... permitted to be visible.
>
> WALTER SCOTT, *Ivanhoe,* chapter 7 (1820)

Scott's admiring description of his "Rebecca" was intended to refer, as well, to Rebecca Gratz (Plate 7, cats. 39, 40), a description that was touched with the oriental exotic, often present in nineteenth-century English literature. Possibly an aspect of the phenomenon of "orientalism," it seemed to surface as a disguise in the portrait of *Mendes I. Cohen,* 1832 (Plate 14, cat. 84), something consciously assumed as a costume reflecting his Egyptian experience, whose function as an ethnic marker at this late stage of Americanization seems problematic, especially when compared with *Mrs. Israel I. Cohen's* forthright portrait of approximately the same date (cat. 85).

No, the immediate future of Jewish portraits in the early Republic does not lie in exoticism but rather in conformity to a new social paradigm, a proto-Victorian settlement of the sexes in their gendered roles, anticipated fully in William Dunlap's *Mr. and Mrs. Moses Judah* of 1818 (Plate 15, cats. 86, 87). Quieter, more comfortably settled in their bourgeois lifestyle, Mr. and Mrs. Moses Judah need no longer assert their class membership; they belong—or think they do—and only time will tell whether they were mistaken in their belief, in their confidence.

See Appendix for a Selected Bibliography of Early American Potraiture.

ELLEN SMITH

Portraits of a Community:
The Image and Experience of Early American Jews

Your Pictures Are quite an Acceptable Pres[en]t you will make my Compliments of thanks to Mrs. Franks for those
of her Family & allsoe to Mast[e]r & Miss Franks the whole Family Was in raptures Your Father walks abouth the
Parlour with Such Pleasure a Viewing of them As is not to be Expresst Most of your Acquaintance knew Your Picture
but I will ingeniously Own I dont find that Likeness but it was designed for you & that Pleases me to have it .[1]

NAPHTALI FRANKS WAS twenty-four years old and had been living in England for nearly seven years when, in 1739, his mother, Bilhah Abigail Levy Franks, wrote him her joyful thanks for the receipt in New York City of his painted portrait. Perhaps remembering Naphtali as a child, Abigail did not readily recognize her oldest offspring in his portrait. Perhaps thrilled to see an adult visage in his son and business partner, Naphtali's father Jacob Franks exhibited joy beyond expression. The portrait was hung in the family parlor—a private, domestic space where the family could have intimate contact with the image of the absent son and brother. Abigail would never see him again. For the rest of her life, the portrait of Naphtali through his letters and the portrait of her son on her parlor wall were all she had of him.

As with many of the comments in her surviving correspondence, Abigail Franks made astute observations about portraiture and its function in colonial and early American society. The image served in lieu of her absent son. As portraits continued to be exchanged, they became keepers of memory and images of family continuity for generations to come. Portraits were ways of meeting people with whom face-to-face contact could not take place. They were intimate private objects, commissioned for personal, not public, display.

Four separate letters in the Levy-Franks family correspondence of 1733–48 discuss portraits.[2] In July, 1733, Abigail thanked Naphtali for the "Picture" of Isaac Franks, Jacob Franks's older brother in England. Just as Abigail felt Naphtali's portrait did not do full justice to the original,

"every one that knows [Isaac] Tells me it falls Short of the Originall." In June of 1734, Abigail reported to Naphtali that "Your brother Moses Picture is don to be Sent Mrs. Salomons [Jacob Franks's youngest sister]." Ever the critic, Abigail confesses "Its not flatered my [step]mother would Not have me Send it being She does Not think it well don but I would not goe to the charge of a Nother."[3] Other intended Franks family portraits of Abigail and her daughter Richa never materialized. But lest Naphtali go without an image of his mother, she reminds him that his uncle Asher Levy [Abigail's younger brother] has a portrait of her, and since Asher is "not in England I had rather you Should have it." In 1741, Abigail wrote Naphtali to "thank Miss Franks for the Snuff box and Picture She Sent Me." This was likely Phila Franks, daughter of Jacob's older brother Isaac, Naphtali's first cousin, and soon to be his bride. Knowing Abigail's love both of snuff and family portraits, Phila won a place early in her future mother-in-law's heart.[4]

Abigail also recognized that beyond triggers of memory and affection, portraits were conscious constructions—commissioned by the sitter and "designed for" him or her. Naphtali's own choices of self-representation therefore pleased Abigail, even if they did not match her images of him. And the personal connection, the joy, the "raptures" that portraits brought to a family permanently separated across the Atlantic Ocean gave them value beyond any commercial or personal exchange undertaken.

From the earliest days of European settlement in North America, portraits were brought over, and, soon after, made.[5]

From the earliest days of Jewish settlement in North America, painted portraits became part of Jewish culture. Astounding numbers of them were made. Hannah London documented 185 portraits and miniatures in 1927 and documented 113 miniatures in 1953.[6] The American Jewish Historical Society collection alone contains 48 pre-1830 portraits. The 87 paintings in this exhibition were selected from among several hundred identified in public and private collections. Additional portraits, whose present whereabouts are unknown, are believed still to exist.[7] The sheer volume of surviving portraits of early American Jews speaks to the important role they played in colonial Jewish culture, though they were expensive, and only the wealthier families could usually afford them.

Painted portraits realize a complex of interactions and decisions among the sitter, the artist, and the notion of the audience for whom the painting is intended. Whereas most early Jewish settlers in North America emigrated from European Jewish communities where portraits seem not to have been part of the Jewish cultural norm, in the American colonies, beginning in the first half of the eighteenth century, Jewish families began to imitate the tradition of commissioning portraits that pervaded the non-Jewish mercantile culture around them.[8] The portraits—painted by the same artists and based on the same models, mezzotint books, and colonial tastes—therefore looked like the portraits of non-Jewish sitters of the era. Nor was this conventional presentation—this act of self-representation—accidental. Early American Jews intended to be seen as looking like the broader community. The portraits declared the sitters' desires to be seen, and to be seen as looking like everyone else. Early American Jewish portraits were visual declarations that this small band of North American Jews were a part of, rather than apart from, the colonial, mercantile society in which they lived.

But colonial and early American Jewish identity was complex, and painted portraits are only part of the picture colonial and early American Jews drew of themselves. A broad array of individual and community self-portraits were consciously constructed by the early American Jewish community. Letters and correspondence reveal less formal, more intimate profiles, of individuals. Naming patterns reinforced family connections through traditional Jewish practices, as painted portraits connected families in less traditional ways. Business records, wills, and religious and institutional documents all reveal aspects of the communities' aspirations and character. All these portrait forms, too, are self-referential and self-descriptive, conscious self-profiles for their contemporaries

and future generations. The types of Jewish community and identity they describe change over time and with place. But the constancy of the great experiment of early American Jewry—establishing a functional equilibrium between being Jewish and being part of the larger colonial and early American society—informs the complex portrait of the Jewish community during their first two centuries in America.

Jews first settled in North America in 1654. But the society they brought with them had been formed in Europe, and shaped again by a sojourn in Brazil. Exiled from Spain in 1492, and forced to convert and practice "underground Judaism" in Portugal less than a decade later, many Jews, and forced Jewish converts, emigrated to Holland, and through the Dutch West India Company, on to Brazil. For twenty-four years there they enjoyed economic, social, and religious freedoms unparalleled in their recent European experience. When Brazil fell to Portugal in 1654, the Jews again set sail—this time for Holland, England, the Dutch West Indies, and the small Dutch community of New Amsterdam on the mouth of the Hudson River in North America.

From the beginning, Jewish identity in the Americas was complicated. Early Jews in the colonies were refugees or trans-Atlantic traders, not intentional pilgrims; they were strangers and sojourners in many strange lands. Their stays in the colonies were often impermanent and transient, moving from city to city, and between nations, as business dictated.

Jewish colonists also emigrated from many countries, bringing with them differing religious traditions and even languages. Spanish and Portuguese Sephardic Jews, whose religious and common native language was Portuguese, were joined in almost equal numbers by Central European, German, English, and Yiddish-speaking Ashkenazic Jews, whose numbers surpassed the Sephardim by 1720.[9] The standard "solution" to pluralistic pre-Revolutionary American Judaism was to establish a single synagogue-community in each location with a sufficient Jewish population. Sephardic liturgy and ritual predominated, but the congregations themselves were more usually dominated by Ashkenazim.

Business interests, which generally brought all Jews west to the New World, oriented them back to the east, to England, Europe, Africa, and the Caribbean. A national "home" identity could thus be varied and unstable. Upon what, then, could colonial Jewish identity be based? In the national and religious amalgam—the portable religious crazy-quilt that defined pre-Revolutionary American Jewry—there was no stable or standard norm. European models of origin were varied and far away. And American religious and cultural patterns—pluralistic, nearby, and alluring—presented many challenges to the basic foundations of traditional Jewish identity.

Jews arriving in New Amsterdam had already begun undergoing the process that would in many ways define the social and religious history of American Jewry: the elongated experiment of building, preserving, and transmitting Jewish community in a new environment, of reconciling Jewish tradition and American realities.

The Levy-Franks portrait series captures these dilemmas and ambiguities of colonial American Jewish identity as they were lived. Two great portrait series survive of the family: a series of seven paintings of three generations of the clan, and a lively series of letters exchanged between Abigail Franks and her son Naphtali between 1733 and 1748.

The painted portraits, still in their original frames, are the oldest surviving portraits of colonial American Jews, and the oldest family-series portraits to survive in all of American painting. Probably executed in the mid-1730s, and attributed by present scholars to Gerardus Duyckinck, the paintings look to English aristocratic models for their costume, background, and pose.[10] Patriarch *Moses Raphael Levy* (cat. 1) and his son-in-law *Jacob Franks* (cat. 5) are both portrayed as English gentlemen, following customary English portrait and print models. The paintings are virtually mirror images of each other: the two men and occasional business partners wear nearly identical coats, blouses, and wigs. They lean on similar props, are draped in comparable blue curtains, and gesture similarly toward one another—perhaps subtly reinforcing their own familial and business links, though, of course, they are painted to hang next to, and gesture toward, their respective wives. Moses is painted with two ships in the background, an overt symbol of his mercantile enterprises, but the contemporary conventions of the pose and props are so common that Jacob's mercantile status is instantly read into his portrait as well.

Similarly, the portraits of *Grace Mears Levy*, Moses's second wife (cat. 2), and *Bilhah Abigail Levy Franks* (cat. 3), wife of Jacob Franks, and oldest child of Moses and his first wife, Richea, display many of the conventions of English portraiture of that period. Again nearly mirroring one another, with only color of costume and drapery reversed, the images likewise imitate other portraits of the era, and, more importantly, their English sources. A 1728 portrait of *Mrs. Joseph Hallett* (Fig. 1), for example, serves as a nearly direct model (but reversed) for Grace Mears Levy and Phila Franks. *Mrs. Hallett*, in

turn, is based on an English mezzotint version of the *Countess of Ranelagh* by John Smith, after a painting by Sir Godfrey Kneller.[11] Three portraits of the Franks children (two exhibited here) likewise emulate English models and replicate the clothing and posing of their parents, Jacob and Abigail Franks.[12]

To read the Levy-Franks portrait series, then, is to receive visual signals and confirmation that this is a well-established, mercantile family, consciously placing themselves within the representational conventions of English portraiture and the emerging English bourgeois class, and part of a broad range of early eighteenth-century colonial American portraits that represent men and women and children in similar costumes and poses. There is no symbol, no gesture, no background, no prop, that identifies these people as Jews. Seven known times the Levy-Franks family commissioned images of their clan, and seven times they chose to be represented as successful English-style merchants with aristocratic pretensions. Their portraits in paint evaporated any overt signal that Jewishness formed part of the identity put on display in the Levy and the Franks homes.

All these portrait conventions and prototypes fit the colonial Jewish self-image. The Levy-Franks portraits accurately represent the family's understanding of its members as successful merchants, familial partners, and European bourgeoisie. These were not mere aspirations; they were painted strokes of reality. More importantly, those realities were painted to present no tension, no raw conflict, with the rest of their identity. The Levy-Franks family of the portraits, Jews or not, were comfortable as American colonials.

Still, the portraits present only half of the picture. The tensions embedded in forging a Jewish colonial identity were real, and found expression in other material forms.

The Levy-Franks family lived in an early eighteenth-century New York City inhabited by successful and long-established Dutch and English mercantile families. Their neighborhood in Dock Ward housed some of the city's most prominent families. Approximately 8,500 people lived in New York in 1731; about 10,000 in 1737. Among them, only 20 Jews were recorded in 1734.[13] The Jewish community owned a synagogue building, Shearith Israel, on Mill Street, dedicated in 1730, and a burial ground off Chatham Square, purchased in 1728. But the community was tiny, fragile, and transient.

If the Levy-Franks portraits are confident expressions of the social status and place of the family in America, their letters to their oldest son, Naphtali, in England, are not. In

Fig. 1 *Mrs. Joseph Hallett,* artist unknown, c. 1728. Oil on canvas, 49 ½ × 40 ½ in.; 125.73 × 102.87 cm. The New-York Historical Society.

more melancholy and ambiguous gaze in the correspondence. Abigail and Jacob probably never saw their adult children after their departure, nor any of their English grandchildren.

Abigail's letters are also an extended conversation on the fit and fate of Judaism in colonial New York. The Levy and Franks families were active members of Shearith Israel and supported Jewish causes throughout the colonies. They practiced traditional Judaism, honoring the Sabbath, keeping kosher, and keeping the Jewish holidays. Abigail urged Naphtali in England to keep up with his "morning Dev[otio]ns," and cautioned him to avoid non-kosher food, warning him off even his uncle's table.[15] She rejoiced in the Sabbath and made sure her daughters and sons received instruction in Hebrew.[16] Jacob addressed Jewish interests in his letters, even conducting business correspondence in Yiddish and Hebrew as the occasion demanded.[17]

But Abigail also worried for the future of Judaism in America, and for the future of her children as Jews. In the open air of colonial America, and likely under the influence of the broad range of English philosophers and novelists she read, she yearned for a modernized Judaism. "I Must Own I cant help Condemning the Many Supersti[ti]ons wee are Clog'd with & heartly wish a Calvin or Luther would rise amongst Us," she mused in 1739.[18] On the ground, she was scathing in her critique of the New York Jewish community, calling its ladies "a Stupid Set of people," and despairing about the pool of Jewish suitors available for her daughters.[19] When David Gomez, of the powerful, successful, and, to some degree, rival New York Jewish family, showed interest in daughter Richa, Abigail dismissed him as "a Stupid wretch." Even "if his fortune was much more and I a begar noe child of Mine … Should Never have my Consent And I am Sure he will never git hers."[20]

deeply intelligent prose, Abigail ponders the future of her family as Jews in the colonial environment, and puzzles whether its best interests ultimately reside in Europe or colonial America.

Abigail treasures the broad freedom to achieve and mingle in the colonies. Critical of England's rigid class structure— "You will not allow any thing right but wath has the Advantages of being bred amongst you"—she worries that Naphtali has accepted it too easily. She revels in the openness of New York ("It Gives me a Seceret pleasure to Observe the faire Charecter Our Familys has in the place by Jews & Christians").[14] Nevertheless, the Franks family in America never achieved the financial stability of the Franks and Levy families in England; and, one by one, Jacob and Abigail sent their children to England in order to prosper. The confident look toward England expressed in the portraits assumes a

But the cost was high. With a limited pool of Jewish marriage prospects, Abigail's disdain for most of them, and the entire Franks family's desire to be part of the larger New York community, it was perhaps inevitable that two of her children would take non-Jewish spouses. Oldest daughter Phila (cat. 8) was the first. In the fall of 1742 Phila secretly married Oliver

Delancey, son of a prominent and successful New York Huguenot merchant family. For six months they kept the match secret, but in the spring of 1743 Phila announced the deed and went to live with her husband. Abigail never recovered. Letters to Naphtali spoke of her sense of betrayal and of her pain.[21] It was not to be the last hurt she would feel. Son David (Plate 2, cat. 7) married Margaret Evans, the Christian daughter of one of Abigail's close friends, and settled in Philadelphia. Her younger children seem never to have married at all. Even sons Naphtali and Moses, who married their English first cousins (both named Phila Franks), watched as all of their own grandchildren left the Jewish faith. Of Jacob and Abigail Franks's more than two dozen grandchildren, not one of them appears to have passed on Judaism to his or her descendants.[22]

The Franks family thus defended America even as they looked to England for models of financial success and social status; and they defended their Judaism even as they sought to adapt and belong to the larger colonial American society. The self-portraits they left us suggest they never fully belonged in either place. The confident, English-gazing portraits belie the anxieties of maintaining that posture while enduring as Jews. Their colonial identity and their Jewish identity strained under the pressures of colonial and Christian realities. Neither their commissioned portraits in paint, nor their self-portraits in words, are complete one without the other. The conscious self-representations of the Levy-Franks family—constructed images of self created in paint and in ink—reflect the full palette of desires, demands, and loyalties that competed in forming a colonial Jewish identity.

But other paths were taken by other colonial Jews. The Gomez family (see cat. 63) were contemporaries of the Franks family in New York, more successful in business, more adapted as Jews to the colonial environment. Descended from Isaac Gomez, an exile from Spain, the family had emigrated to New York by the late-seventeenth century; and by the mid-eighteenth century, they were the wealthiest Jewish family, and among the wealthiest New York families, of their era.

Like most of the colonial Jewish families, the Gomezes were traders, merchants, investors in real estate, and owners of shipping fleets. They consciously expanded their trading networks through judicious marriages: in the first American generation into Sephardic families from Jamaica, Barbados, and Curaçao; and in the second through a series of first-cousin marriages that consolidated their wealth and the connections that linked family, business, and religion. This religious

and economic stability, resulting from a strategy of intermarriage among themselves and other North American Sephardic families, was complemented by their economic focus on North America. Whereas the Franks family functionally existed in New York in the shadow of the family's English enterprises, the Gomez family cast their financial lot with the land to which they emigrated. They struck deep roots, were active in the community's religious affairs, and occupied the most prominent seats and offices in Shearith Israel for nearly a century. Having secured—even ensured—Jewish identity within the home, the family, and the religious community, the potential dangers of the marketplace and gentile world to Jewish identity and survival were significantly lessened. The Gomezes thrived both as colonial Americans and as Jews.

Fig. 2 *Etrog Holder of the Gomez Family of New York,* maker unknown, late 18th c. Silver and blue glass. Engraved on front: "E/BG/R/MG;" engraved on back: "C/BG" 4 × 3 ¾ × 2 ¾ in.; 10.2 × 9.6 × 7 cm. American Jewish Historical Society, Waltham, Massachusetts, and New York, New York.

Their adaptability is winsomely portrayed in a silver mustard pot owned by the Gomez family in New York (Fig. 2). Commissioned for the family and imported from England, the piece is a fine example of late-eighteenth-century silver, with its cabriole feet, hinged lid, engraved Gomez-family initials, and blue glass insert to hold condiments. But in the New World, the piece took a new identity. Removed from access to

European-made Jewish ritual objects, the Gomezes adapted the mustard pot to necessary Jewish ritual use, employing it as an *etrog* holder—a covered receptacle to protect the *etrog*, or citron, one of the four plants and fruits used in worship during the Jewish fall harvest festival of Sukkoth. The pot descended through six generations of the Gomez family with the attributed use intact, serving in its way as a portrait of the values and determination of the Gomezes to simultaneously thrive as Americans and survive as Jews.

Other objects likewise are material expressions of the efforts of colonial Jews to declare and preserve their Judaism. Headstones in Jewish cemeteries declare a variety of Jewish virtues, and attest to the literal survival of the Jewish people.[23] Synagogue architecture blended local architectural exteriors with Jewish architectural interiors.[24] Jewish books were common in early American Jewish households, even if they consisted mostly of prayer books and family Bibles. Jewish books also began to appear in translation, reinforcing an emerging, if problematic, American-Jewish culture. Isaac Pinto, *hazzan* (religious leader) of Shearith Israel, despaired that Hebrew was not well-understood by colonial Jews of the mid-eighteenth-century, and subsequently produced *Prayers for Shabbath, Rosh-Hashanah, and Kippur* (1765/6) in English (Fig. 3).[25]

But the central, and most sacred, printed object in any Jewish community is the Torah scroll, the hand-written parchment upon which the Five Books of Moses are written in Hebrew, and set sections of which are read and studied both communally and privately each week. The earliest known Torah in America arrived in New Amsterdam in 1655, borrowed from a synagogue in Amsterdam, but returned in 1663 as the original New Amsterdam community dispersed. Torah scrolls were acquired by communities, large and small, throughout the colonial era: Lancaster and Reading in Pennsylvania had them, as did the Jewish communities of Savannah, Newport, Charleston, Philadelphia, and New York. But Torah scrolls were also held privately, and their importance both to Jewish and family identity is indicated by their unique mention and dispensation in wills, even though no other Jewish objects are discussed. Lewis Gomez of New York, for example, bequeathed to his oldest son Mordecai in his 1740 will "one pare of Silver Adornments [*rimonim*—silver ornaments for the top of Torah scrolls] for the five Books of Moses." In 1750, Mordecai willed both the *rimonim* and the Torah to his oldest surviving son, Isaac. David Gomez, another of Lewis's sons, likewise inherited a Torah and *rimo-*

nim through his wife's family, which he then bequeathed in 1769 to his brother Isaac. Isaac specifically bypassed his oldest, unmarried, and female child, Esther, in his 1770 will, leaving the Torah and its accoutrements to his oldest surviving son, Mattathias. In 1784 Mattathias bequeathed them to his oldest son, Isaac.[26] Rachel Luis, one of four women whose wills survives, left money "to buy a Shefer Tora [Torah Scroll] for the use of the Kall Kados [Holy Congregation] of Sherith Ysraell in New York."[27] No other objects—not portraits, not plate, not furnishings—receive the unique attention in writing and succession as do these central objects of Jewish identity.

Jewish self-consciousness declares itself in a variety of other objects as well. *Ketubbot*, traditional Jewish wedding contracts, continued to be prepared in the colonies, and a few survive from these earliest years. Rebecca Hendricks, like most young girls of her era, learned needlework, and made samplers to practice her skills. One of her samplers survives, a neat counted-thread cross-stitch on twenty-count linen. Text for colonial samplers commonly derives from biblical phrases and aphorisms. But Rebecca picked a unique text, one that reflected a sense of herself not only as a colonial young lady of breeding, but also as a Jew. In neatly spaced letters, her embroidery (Fig. 4) reproduces verses 1–14 of the Seventy-eighth Psalm, including the phrases "He commanded our fathers that they should make them known to their children.... That they might [not] forget the works of God but keep his commandments" (Ps. 78: 5, 7).

The most ancient sign of Jewish identity within the Jewish community is the circumcision of its males, as commanded to Abraham by the Lord in Genesis. Traditionally taking place on the eighth day after a boy is born, circumcision seems to have been widely maintained throughout the colonial era.[28] Two circumcision sets, in the collections of the American Jewish Historical Society, survive from early America: one from the Sheftall family of Georgia, and one from the Seixas family of New York. The Seixas set includes a silver circumcision clip that bears the maker's mark of New York's Myer Myers (Fig. 5), one of the most important and skilled of all colonial silversmiths, and a Jew.

Nevertheless, actual early American Jewish ritual objects, or records of their manufacture, sale, and use, are extremely rare. Jacob Franks ordered a set of *etz hayyim*, wooden rollers for Torah scrolls, in 1743, but it is an unusual surviving example relating to the acquisition and use of Jewish objects.[29] In the late-eighteenth century, Moses and Rachel Hays of Boston commissioned at least nine pieces of silver from Paul Revere

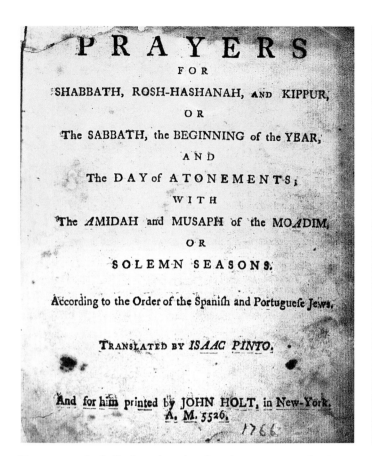

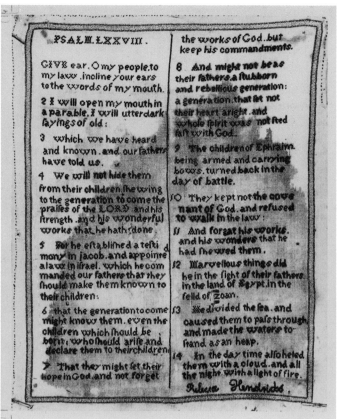

Fig. 3 *Prayers for Shabbath, Rosh-Hashanah, and Kippur …*, translated from the Hebrew by Issac Pinto. New York: John Holt, 5526 [1765/6]. Title page, 7 ½ × 5 ¼ in; 19 × 13.3 cm. American Jewish Historical Society, Waltham, Massachusetts, and New York, New York.

Fig. 4 *Sampler of the Seventy-Eighth Psalm,* by Rebecca Hendricks (1740–1844), late 18th c. Linen with cotton thread, 10 ¼ × 8 in.; 26.5 × 20.4 cm. American Jewish Historical Society, Waltham, Massachusetts, and New York, New York. Gift of Mrs. Louisa Salomon Hendricks.

(Fig. 6), but none of them seems to have been for religious use.[30] Myer Myers manufactured only a few known Jewish ritual objects, though he had a significant Jewish clientele. All this may suggest that Jewish ritual forms were either brought by families when they emigrated, or like the Gomez *etrog* holder (Fig. 2), adapted from existing domestic forms. In any event, the private possession and use of traditional Jewish ritual objects may have been limited in early America.

The objects that do survive, like the portraits themselves, are primarily domestic or synagogue pieces—material expressions of Jewish identity and practice nevertheless confined to the private spaces of home and Jewish worship. Public expressions of Jewish identity and self-representation also existed, although they tend to lack a tangible quality. Naming patterns declared Jewish identity openly. While surnames are notoriously unreliable ways to identify Jews in colonial America, traditional Jewish first-naming patterns—naming children after deceased relatives—continued long after the Revolution,

and resisted more fashionable gentile naming trends. For example, the names Bilah, Richea, Rebecca, and Shinah endure into the mid-nineteenth-century over four generations of the Etting-Myers-Cohen family. Perla, Rebecca, and Levi remain given names in the Sheftall family through the early national period.[31] Wills, normally formulaic colonial legal documents, occasionally revealed insistence on public declaration, and even accommodation, to Judaism. Among forty-one surviving eighteenth-century New York City wills made out by Jews, sixteen bequeathed money to Jewish organizations, including the synagogue, cemetery, Hebrew school, and poor relief in New York, as well as to Jewish organizations in London, Jerusalem, and Newport.[32] Several witnesses to wills insisted on being "Sworn upon the five books of Moses" rather than the Christian Bible, and were so duly recorded.[33] Esther Benzaken dated her 1790 will by the English and Jewish calendars, and Manuel Myers listed the Hebrew and English names of his nieces and nephews in his 1799 will.[34] All of these written declarations were outside the normal Christian and legal conventions, indicating conscious intentions to integrate markers of Jewish identification into the public sphere.

Other behaviors, sometimes elusive, also indicate public, and perhaps confident, signaling of Jewish identity. Jacob Franks (cat. 5) and Aaron Lopez (see cat. 30) are among several merchants who strived to observe the Jewish dietary laws of *kashrut*, which mandated eating only meat butchered according to Jewish law, and not mixing meat and milk products. They also refused to conduct business on the Jewish Sabbath,

Touro (cats. 82, 83), did not wait for a crisis. In 1816 he presented himself to Boston city officials and insisted that he be "set forth in records that he was of the Jewish faith and belonged to a synagogue."[37]

All of these material and behavioral portraits suggest that "Jewishness" was not hidden in colonial America, but that contemporary American and Christian forms were adjusted, adapted, and reinterpreted by the Jewish community to allow early American Jews to integrate into the large culture even as they protected and strengthened their Judaism and

Fig. 5 *Circumcision Set (eleven pieces) and Trunk,* various makers. Circumcision clip, second from lower left, made by Myer Myers (1723–1795), late 18th c. Trunk: wood, leather, paper, and hair, 3 ¼ × 10 ¼ × 6 in.; 8 × 26 × 15.3 cm. Clip: 2 ¼ × 1 ½ in.; 6.7 × 3.4 cm. American Jewish Historical Society, Waltham, Massachusetts, and New York, New York.

even though the closing of business on Saturday, plus the *de facto* loss of business on Sunday through the legislated closing of businesses on the Christian Sabbath, could have significant economic consequences. Aaron Lopez, who could not be naturalized as a Jew under Rhode Island law in the 1760s, chose to travel to Massachusetts and be naturalized there, where he would not have to swear "upon the true oath of a Christian."[35] Moses Michael Hays in Newport encountered similar troubles. Though an ardent patriot during the American Revolution, he refused to sign Newport's loyalty oath as written "upon the true oath of a Christian." After much public battle, he was eventually allowed to sign without the offending phrase, but not without much prior public humiliation and debate.[36] Hays's nephew and ward, Abraham

Jewish identity. The experiments were variously successful. But the efforts to make a living Judaism work in the broadly pluralistic and open society of early America are exhibited in the varieties of forms of self-representation—the varieties of portraits of colonial American Jews—produced by and for the community.   ℵ ℵ ℵ

If the portrait of the colonial American Jewish community suggests an effort to craft a Jewish-American identity generally along conservative lines and within traditional forms, a very different portrait emerges of the post-Revolutionary community. The American Revolution marked a watershed for the American Jewish community, as it did for American society as a whole.

Fig. 6 *Pair of Sauceboats* (from a set of four) commissioned by Moses Michael Hays (1739–1805), by Paul Revere II (1735–1818), c. 1790. Silver inscribed "Hays" on each front, and "REVERE" on bottom. 5 ½ × 8 in.; 14 × 20.4 cm. Wunsch Americana Foundation.

Colonial Jewish society had been characterized by small, often transient populations, usually engaged in trans-Atlantic trade, whose religious and economic security was often reinforced by marriage within the family. Although the colonial Jewish community was itself pluralistic, in every colonial city with a Jewish population, Sephardic and Ashkenazic families shared the same, single synagogue. They were modest in their innovations to traditional Judaism, usually bending existing forms rather than creating new ones. Portraits and other expressions of Jewish identity reflect that accommodation both to traditional Judaism and to the traditions of the Christian society in which it was making its home. Painted portraits, in particular, looked to European models, portraying Jews as looking very much like each other, and like everyone else.

Much of this changed with the American Revolution. Demographically, the war shifted traditional Jewish population centers, providing a new mix of people and a change of cities with concentrated Jewish populations. The war permanently dispersed the colonial Jewish population of Newport, and economically devastated Savannah and Boston, rendering them less attractive to Jewish merchants. Wartime migrations sent many Jews to Philadelphia. Baltimore, Richmond, and Charleston were also winners in the reshuffling. Simultaneously, Jewish population numbers rose, likely from higher birth rates rather than from new immigration, although the

reasons are not fully understood. Overall, the postwar American Jewish population reconfigured, relocated, and grew, adding scale and, most importantly, more diversity to the mix.

The war also changed the nature of business traditionally conducted by colonial Jewry. Severed ties with England confounded prior patterns of trans-Atlantic trade. At the beginning of the nineteenth century, Jewish economics turned more local and became more modest in scale. Despite a few merchants engaged in the newly emerging trade with the Far East, most Jewish merchants in the early Republic concentrated on domestic commerce. The young nation, engaged in establishing its own infrastructure, provided new opportunities for local manufacturing, merchandising, and trade. Jewish life incorporated this new diversity of population, space, and economic options. The era of a singular, hierarchical, East Coast Jewish merchant class was at an end.

The political theory guiding the American Revolution and the early Republic also directly affected Jewish self-understanding in the new nation. Concepts of democracy, self-determination, political power residing with the people, and written constitutions defining rights and responsibilities of the citizenry had a direct impact on the practice and structure of American Judaism. Beginning in the 1790s, synagogues began to adopt written constitutions and to structure their governance along the Federal model. "We the members of K. K.

Shearith Israel," began the nation's oldest synagogue's new 1790 constitution, which then went on to offer a wider franchise, a "bill of rights," and a "state happily constituted upon the principles of equal liberty, civil and religious."[38] Richmond's Congregation Beth Shalome's 1789 constitution translated secular, democratic purpose into religious aims. "We the subscribers of the Israelite religion resident in this place desirous of promoting divine worship," the document began, and went on to offer an expanded male franchise.[39] These trends represented a radical change from the colonial pattern, where power resided in a small board of lay leaders with powers to legislate, judge, and discipline. Synagogues instituted elections and routinely amended their constitutions and by-laws. Multiple voices, with multiple opinions, began to characterize a formerly singular synagogue structure.

Indeed, one of the hallmarks of the post-Revolutionary Jewish community was its fracturing. Whereas before the Revolution every city with Jewish populations had but one synagogue, after the Revolution, communities generated several synagogues. Some were started by break-away groups; others were founded as new organizations representing a particular point of view, age group, or taste for a specific form of worship or liturgy. By 1795, Philadelphia became the first city in America to have two synagogues. By 1850, New York City alone had fifteen.[40] Jewish communal services and organizations formerly allied with the synagogue—including education, burial societies, poor relief, and social groups—now proliferated as autonomous institutions. The single "synagogue-community" of pre-Revolutionary America gave way to a "community of synagogues" after the war.[41]

This diversity within the Jewish population, and a rising sense of individual identity and interests, pair with the population's desire to fit in with the democratic values and behaviors of the surrounding Christian and secular worlds. Their optimism is reflected in the portraits painted of American Jews after the Revolution. Based on European and American Romantic and neoclassical models, the portraits now display a broader range of poses, costumes, and individual expressions. The paintings reflect the growing differentiation and self-consciousness within the Jewish community itself, while reinforcing the community's shared attachment to the conventions, values, and visions of Federal America.

This dual trend is most immediately evident in the articulation of individual identities among the sitters for post-Revolutionary portraits. The portraits move from stylized colonial images where status, occupation, and gendered rela-

tionships are revealed through common, conventional symbols, to portraits that celebrate individuality. Postwar portraits are more literally self-referential—images that intend to reflect who each individual actually is, or at least how they wish to be seen. Occupation is no longer signaled by background codes, but by costume and title. The portraits of *Colonel Isaac Franks* (cat. 45) and *Major Mordecai Myers* (cat. 43) descended through their families with their ranks intact [42]; Uriah Phillips Levy (cat. 44), a life-long Navy man and the nation's first Jewish commodore, was painted early in his career in full dress uniform aboard his sailing ship. Gershom Mendes Seixas (cat. 37) is depicted in clerical robes and collar. The title "Reverend" and Protestant-style religious garb were common for Jewish religious leaders in the early national period, and indicate the willingness of American Jews to adapt general American religious conventions to their own situations.[43] Judges, journalists, and merchants were also depicted in more real-life settings than their colonial counterparts. While none of these constructions are uniquely Jewish images, the images are particular to each sitter, reflecting what distinguishes the subject within society as much as what makes him or her a part of it.

Costume and clothing aid the effort. In male sitters, dress most commonly signifies social or occupational standing. Among women, clothing appears even more distinctive, perhaps signaling perceived personalities and societal roles in lieu of occupational status. Whether the elaborated (actual) costume of *Shinah Solomon Etting* (cat. 50), or the more fanciful costume of *Rebecca Gratz* (Plate 7, cat. 39), many post-Revolutionary portraits of women move outside the family-centered, passive, gendered images that dominate colonial portraiture, and continue beyond.[44]

Indeed, the sheer number of portraits of early American Jewish women can surprise. They comprise a considerable proportion of the portraits in the present exhibition, and of known surviving images of early American Jews. Most were commissioned as part of a husband-wife pair—the *Moses Raphael Levys* (cats. 1, 2), *Franks* (cats. 3, 5), *Israels* (cats. 13, 14), *Samson Levys* (cats. 20, 21), *Nathans* (cats. 16, 17), *da Silva Solises* (cats. 32, 33), and *Noahs* (cats. 47, 48), for example; part of a family series—the *Levy-Franks* (cats. 1, 2, 3, 5, 7, 8, 11), *Harts* (cats. 55–57), *Ettings* (cats. 50, 64, 65, 73–75), and *Myers* (cats. 69–71); or with their children—the *Nathans* (cat. 15) and *Sarah Rivera Lopez* and *Joshua Lopez* (Plate 6, cat. 30).

But after the Revolution, a noticeable minority of portraits were commissioned of women on their own, outside a domestic context. Rebecca Gratz (Plate 7, cats. 39, 40), one of American Judaism's most significant educators and organizational founders, remained unmarried, and so had no other context. But Rachel Phillips Levy (cat. 41), one of twenty-one children and herself mother of ten, was also painted as a beautiful, lithely-costumed, free-spirited young woman. Traditional women's roles and status did not substantially change after the Revolution; women's portraits still focused on virtue, domesticity, and status. But portraits of women also signaled that aspects of opportunity and image, aspects of individual character and achievement, did open more publicly.

So did a focus on children. In the early-eighteenth-century Levy-Franks portrait series, the children assume the same poses, costumes, and expressions as their parents. In the early-nineteenth-century portraits of the Solomons children (Plate 5, cat. 27, 28), the context of the family portrait series is gone, and the individual characters of the children pop off the canvas. The miniature of *Adolphus Simeon Solomons* (cat. 28)—wearing the same costume as in the large canvas, and likely copied from it—is a calm rendition of a more generic child; but in the context of the full painting, young Adolphus fairly jumps off the canvas and out of his sister's grasp. All props attached to him indicate activity and masculinity, particularly the military hat half his size tucked under his arm. *Mary Jane Solomons* (cat. 27) exhibits bearing, and a prototypic maternal tolerance and calm, but her sheer scale gives her an authority and importance unattributed to children in earlier portrait styles. Nineteenth-century American society would become more child-focused as it progressed; the Solomons children, painted in 1828, both herald the trend, and announce that even society's youngest members were occasionally seen—and represented—as individuals slightly outside formulaic boundaries.

The desire to connect with the individual aspects of portraits is perhaps most clearly conveyed by the rising popularity of the miniature portrait. A common form for centuries, miniature portraits enjoyed a revival in popularity in post-Revolutionary America, and judging from their surviving numbers, certainly among a Jewish clientele. Miniature portraits were extremely intimate objects. If large-format canvases hung in the private spaces of domestic settings, miniatures could reside in the private recesses of one's own person. They were variously framed to hang on walls, to stand on desks, to wear as jewelry, to carry in one's pocket. They were portable, accessible, affordable, and best appreciated through close physical contact. Wear patterns to the frames indicate that they were intensely personal pieces, often handled and carried close to the heart. The beautifully detailed miniature of *Judah Eleazer Lyons* (cat. 52) contains a lock of his hair framed onto the back of the image. Such portraits not only depict unique individuals, but are packaged to allow individual relationships with the images, reinforcing particular identity—both seen and experienced.

If the image of American Jews had changed with their identity and experience, their gaze had likewise shifted. On the walls of Monticello, Thomas Jefferson's eighteenth-century estate in Virginia, hung a series of paintings owned by Monticello's nineteenth-century owner and restorer, Uriah Phillips Levy (cat. 44). Among them was the spectacular portrait of his mother, *Rachel Machado Phillips Levy* (cat. 41), painted by the Swedish artist Adolph Wertmüller about 1795. Rachel, declared a great beauty in America and England, is depicted in a late-eighteenth-century shepherdess costume. Her posture and gaze are animated; the large, flowered Marlborough-style bonnet focuses attention to her face. It is very much the portrait of an individual, and one treasured by her son.

But alongside Rachel, on Monticello's walls, hung a series of other kinds of paintings, indicative of the new kinds of visual images—historical, environmental, and religious—coming to dominate mid-nineteenth-century America. Their titles included "The Children of Israel Collecting Manna in the Desert," "Judith and the Headd of Holofernes" [sic], "Holy Family," "David with the Head of Goliath," "A Rural Scene," and "The Wreck of the Frigate Madison."[45] These, too, Uriah valued, and he drew from them, as he did from Monticello itself, in fashioning both his deep patriotism and his strong sense of Jewish identity. Jewish identity—Jewish identification—no longer resided exclusively in the faces of family members, in portraits of the tribe. Jewish-American identity now encompassed the full range of history and metaphor that were becoming the nation's own self-created identity and myth.

By the 1840s, photography, silhouettes, and other less expensive forms of image replication had supplemented portraiture as the primary form of human representation. But temperament as well as technology had moved beyond the portrait form. Where colonial Jewish portraiture had signaled experiments with imitation and belonging, and Jewish portraiture of the early Republic had explored the growing diversity and individuation of the American-Jewish community, by 1830 portraiture itself had fallen away as a prime carrier of the American-Jewish image and experience. An explosion in American-Jewish publications, institutional development, and new immigrations lay on the near horizon. Portraits would remain part of the social fabric of the nineteenth- and twentieth-century American-Jewish communities, but no longer would they be signal markers of American-Jewish identity and self-image.

Yet in the eras they had dominated, painted portraits told the tale of the early American-Jewish community. As consciously created artifacts, they reflected the Jewish community's desire to be seen as part of the broader community—to be seen as looking like everyone else. In the daily, domestic context in which they were viewed, the portraits spoke to the felt ambiguities of melding American and Jewish life. The portraits never sat placidly on the walls. They marked the changes, tensions, and the creativity exhibited by the American Jewish community in creating an evolving American-Jewish identity. And, in the words of Abigail Levy Franks, the portraits brought "raptures" and joy "not to be Expresst."

NOTES

1. Abigail Franks to Naphtali Franks, October 17, 1739, in Leo Hershkowitz and Isidore S. Meyer, eds. *Letters of the Franks Family (1733–1748)* (Waltham, Mass.: American Jewish Historical Society, 1968), p. 66.

2. Hershkowitz, *Letters of the Franks Family*. Thirty-eight known letters survive, dating between May 7, 1733, and October 30, 1748. All are addressed to Naphtali Franks in England. Thirty-four are from his mother Abigail, one is from his father Jacob, and two are written by his brother David. Thirty-one of these letters were acquired by Lee Max Friedman in 1941 and bequeathed by him to the American Jewish Historical Society in 1957. The other six letters are in private and public collections in England.

3. Ibid., Abigail Franks to Naphtali Franks, July 9, 1733, p. 8; Abigail Franks to Naphtali Franks, June 9, 1734, pp. 30, 32. There is some question whether Abigail's stepmother, Grace Mears Levy, refers to a portrait of Moses, her husband, or Moses, her step-grandson. A single portrait and at least one copy of Moses Levy survives, but no single portrait of Moses Franks is known.

4. Ibid., Abigail Franks to Naphtali Franks, June 9, 1734, p. 30; Abigail Franks to Naphtali Franks, June 21, 1741, p. 88.

5. See, for example, Jonathan L. Fairbanks, "Portrait Painting in Seventeenth-Century Boston," in Jonathan L. Fairbanks and Robert F. Trent, eds., *New England Begins: The Seventeenth Century*, 3 vols. (Boston: Museum of Fine Arts, 1982), vol. 3: 413–79; Wayne Craven, *Colonial American Portraiture: The Economic, Religious, Social, Cultural, Philosophical, Scientific, and Aesthetic Foundations* (Cambridge, England: Cambridge University Press, 1986); and Peter Benes, ed., *Painting and Portrait Making in the American Northeast* (Boston: Boston University, 1995).

6. Hannah R. London, *Portraits of Jews by Gilbert Stuart and Other Early American Artists* (New York: William Edwin Rudge, 1927) and Hannah R. London, *Miniatures of Early American Jews* (Springfield, Mass.: The Pond-Ekberg Company, 1953).

7. The whereabouts of many portraits listed by London, in private collections in 1927 and 1953, are presently unknown.

8. European Jewish portraiture does, of course, exist, but is not spread as commonly throughout the Jewish community. See, for example, Alfred Rubens, *Anglo-Jewish Portraits: A Biographical Catalogue of Engraved Anglo-Jewish and Colonial Portraits from the Earliest Times to the Accession of Queen Victoria* (London: The Jewish Museum, 1935).

9. Marcus, Jacob R., *Studies in American Jewish History* (Cincinnati: Hebrew Union College Press, 1969), p. 50.

10. The dating and artistic attribution of the Levy-Franks portrait series are extremely complex. See Erica E. Hirshler, "The Levy-Franks Family Portraits". *The Magazine Antiques* (November 1990): 1025–27; and Erica E. Hirshler, "The Levy-Franks Family Colonial Portraits," Exhibition brochure (Boston: Museum of Fine Arts, 1990). Abigail Franks often writes of the exchange and progress of portraits with Naphtali—and of her son Moses's training and talent in music, drawing, and painting on glass; see *Letters of the Franks Family*, ed. Hershkowitz and Meyer. pp. 41, 48, 49, 55. Oddly, she makes no mention of this large series of portrait commissions in her surviving letters of 1734, 1735, or 1736, possibly calling the dating of the Levy-Franks portrait series into question.

11. The portraits of Mrs. Hallett and the Countess of Ranelagh, along with two additional portraits that are also prototypes for the Levy-Franks women, are reproduced in Wayne Craven, *Colonial American Portraiture*, pp. 136–37. Interestingly, Craven does not discuss or illustrate even one early American Jewish portrait in his book. Nor do any of the earlier surveys of colonial American painting, including James Thomas Flexner, *History of American Painting*, 3 vols. (Boston: Little, Brown, and Company, 1947–62). Part of the reason may be that the American Jewish Historical Society's extensive collection of portraits has not been published in readily accessible form. Nevertheless, early American Jewish portraiture has, to this day, been considered in publications focusing specifically on Jewish American portraits, including this exhibition. See also *Early American Jewish Portraiture*, catalogue for an exhibition at The Jewish Museum, February to July 1952, published by the American Jewish Historical Society, 1952; Hannah R. London, *Portraits of Jews and Miniatures of Early American Jews*; Hannah R. London, *Shades of My Forefathers* (Springfield, Mass.: The Pond-Ekberg Company, 1941); and Norman Kleeblatt and Gerard C. Wertkin, *The Jewish Heritage in American Folk Art* (New York: Universe Books, 1984, for The Jewish Museum, New York, and the Museum of American Folk Art, New York).

12. For a discussion of the English visual sources for the Levy-Franks portrait of "David and Phila Franks" not exhibited in this exhibition, see Kleeblatt and Wertkin, *The Jewish Heritage in American Folk Art*, p. 31; and Erica Hirshler, "The Levy-Franks Family Colonial Portraits," Exhibition brochure, figs. 5, 6 and 7.

13. *Letters of the Franks Family*, ed. Hershkowitz and Meyer. p. xix. New York was the third most populous colonial city, behind Boston and Philadelphia.

14. *Letters of the Franks Family*, Abigail Franks to Naphtali Franks, October 17, 1739, p. 65; Abigail Franks to Naphtali Franks, May 7, 1733, p. 4.

15. Ibid., Abigail Franks to Naphtali Franks, July 9, 1733, pp. 7, 8.

16. Ibid., Abigail Franks to Naphtali Franks, June 21, 1741, p. 87, and Abigail Franks to Naphtali Franks, October 7, 1733, p. 13.

17. Ibid., Jacob Franks to Naphtali Franks, November 22, 1743, pp. 125, 126, xxix.

18. Ibid., Abigail Franks to Naphtali Franks, October 17, 1739, p. 66. Abigail read widely, continually supplied by Naphtali. Among her favorite authors were Pope, Joseph Andrews, Fielding, Smollet, Dryden, Montesquieu, Addison, and *Gentleman's Magazine*. She admonished Naphtali not to send her "Idle Trash"; see Abigail Franks to Naphtali Franks, November 20, 1738, p. 64.

19. *Letters of the Franks Family*, Abigail Franks to Naphtali Franks, December 20, 1741, p. 100.

20. Ibid., Abigail Franks to Naphtali Franks, December 5, 1742, p. 110.

21. Ibid., David Franks to Naphtali Franks, April 1, 1743; Abigail Franks to Naphtali Franks, June 7, 1743; Jacob Franks to Naphtali Franks, November 22, 1743; and see cat. 8 (Phila Franks) in this book.

22. Overall estimates of intermarriage among Jews before the Revolution are difficult to determine. Malcolm Stern estimates that almost 16 percent of marriages by Jews in America before 1840 were with Christians, and that most Jews (up to 87 percent) who intermarried assimilated into Christian society.

Cited in Eli Faber, *A Time for Planting: The First Migration 1654–1820* (Baltimore: The Johns Hopkins University Press, 1992). This number is lower than for many other religious groups of the era.

23. See David de Sola Pool, *Portraits Etched in Stone: Early Jewish Settlers, 1682–1831* (New York: Columbia University Press, 1952).

24. Wischnitzer, Rachel, *Synagogue Architecture in the United States: History and Interpretation* (Philadelphia: Jewish Publication Society, 1955). Only New York and Newport had colonial synagogue buildings. Post-Revolutionary synagogues proliferated, as did synagogue architectural experimentation and reform.

25. Isaac Pinto, trans., *Prayers for Shabbath, Rosh-Hashanah, and Kippur* (New York, 1765/66).

26. Leo Hershkowitz, *Wills of Early New York Jews (1704–1799)* (New York: American Jewish Historical Society, 1967), pp. 62, 86, 125, 130, 152.

27. Ibid., p. 51.

28. See, for example, the "Record Book 1776–1843" of Jacob Raphael Cohen, in the Papers of Jacob Raphael Cohen, American Jewish Historical Society.

29. *Letters of the Franks Family,* Jacob Franks to Naphtali Franks, November 22, 1743, p. 127.

30. Ellen Smith, "Strangers and Sojourners: The Jews of Colonial Boston". In *The Jews of Boston* (Boston: Combined Jewish Philanthropies, 1995), ed. Jonathan D. Sarna and Ellen Smith, p. 38.

31. See, for example, the genealogical charts of colonial Jewish families in Malcolm H. Stern, *First American Jewish Families: 600 Genealogies, 1654–1988,* 3rd ed. (Baltimore: Ottenheimer Publishers, 1991) including pp. 67, 223, 267.

32. Hershkowitz, *Wills of Early New York Jews,* pp. 161, 186, 197.

33. Ibid., specifically the following wills: Samuel Levy, 1719, p. 29; Joshua Isaacs, 1744, p. 71; Isaac Levy, 1745, p. 76; Phillip Isaacs, 1756, p. 96; Mattathias Gomez, 1784, p. 154; and Manuel Myers 1799, p. 211.

34. Ibid., pp. 193, 209.

35. Jacob R. Marcus, *The Colonial American Jew, 1492–1776,* 3 vols. (Detroit: Wayne State University Press, 1970), vol. I: 436–38.

36. Smith, "Strangers and Sojourners," *The Jews of Boston,* p. 36.

37. Ibid., p. 41. The synagogue was probably Shearith Israel in New York City, to which Touro contributed $666.43 in 1817.

38. Quoted in Jonathan Sarna, "The Impact of the American Revolution on American Jews," in Jonathan D. Sarna, Benny Kraut, and Samuel K. Joseph, eds., *Jews and the Founding of the Republic* (New York: Markus Wiener Publishing, 1985), p. 66.

39. Ibid., pp. 66–67.

40. Ibid., p. 67.

41. Ibid., p. 67.

42. Isaac Franks was a cousin of Jacob Franks, two generations younger.

43. Until the 1840s, no European-trained rabbis presided over any American synagogue. Leadership in early American synagogues remained in the hands of lay leaders and locally-trained religious authorities, who often looked to local models for title and dress.

44. For a discussion of gender and colonial portraiture, see Deborah I Prosser, "'The rising prospect or the lovely Face': Conventions of Gender in Colonial American Portraiture," in Peter Benes, ed., *Painting and Portrait Making in the American Northeast* (Boston: Boston University, 1995): 181–200.

45. Photostat copy of the "Inventory of the Personal Estate of Uriah Phillips Levy," 1862, Papers of Uriah Phillips Levy, American Jewish Historical Society. The inventory lists twenty-one separate oil paintings, but not that of Rachel Phillips Levy.

Color Plates

Plate 1 (cat. 1) *Moses Raphael Levy*, attributed to Gerardus Duyckinck, c. 1720–28. Oil on Canvas, 43 ¼ × 34 ¾ in.; 109.86 × 88.27 cm. Museum of the City of New York. Bequest of Alphonse H. Kursheedt, 36.343.1.

Plate 2 (cat. 7) *David and Phila Franks,* attributed to Gerardus Duyckinck, c. 1735. Oil on canvas, 45 ½ × 36 in; 116 × 91.5 cm. American Jewish Historical Society, Waltham, Massachusetts, and New York, New York. Gift of Captain N. Taylor Phillips.

Plate 3 (cat. 11) *Rachel Levy Seixas (Mrs. Isaac Mendes Seixas),* attributed to John Wollaston, 1750. Oil on canvas, 30 × 25 in.; 76 × 63.5 cm. American Jewish Historical Society, Waltham, Massachusetts, and New York, New York. Gift of Captain N. Taylor Phillips.

Plate 4 (cat. 12) *Benjamin. S. Judah,* by Ralph Earl, 1794. Oil on canvas, 48 ⅝ × 34 ½ in.; 123.51 × 87.63 cm.
Wadsworth Atheneum, Hartford, Connecticut. The Ella Gallup Sumner and Mary Catlin Sumner Collection Fund.

Plate 5 (cat. 27) *Adolphus Simeon Solomons and Mary Jane Solomons,* artist unknown, 1828. Oil on canvas, 57 × 43 ⅝ in.; 144.8 × 110.9 cm. American Jewish Historical Society, Waltham, Massachusetts, and New York, New York. Bequest of Irma P. Sellars.

Plate 6 (cat. 30) *Sarah Rivera Lopez (Mrs. Aaron Lopez) and Her Son Joshua Lopez,* by Gilbert Stuart, 1775. Oil on canvas. 26 × 21 ½ in.; 66 × 54.6 cm. The Detroit Institute of Arts, Gift of Dexter M. Ferry, Jr.

Plate 7 (cat. 39) *Rebecca Gratz,* by Thomas Sully, 1830. Oil on canvas mounted on masonite, 20 × 17 in.; 50.8 × 43.18 cm. Delaware Art Museum. Gift of Benjamin Shaw II.

Plate 8 (cat. 43) *Major Mordecai Myers,* by John Wesley Jarvis, c. 1813. Oil on wood panel, 33 ⅞ × 26 ⅝ in.; 86.04 × 67.63 cm. The Toledo Museum of Art. Purchased with funds from the Florence Scott Libbey Bequest in Memory of her Father, Maurice A. Scott.

Plate 9 (cat. 46) *Mordecai Manuel Noah,* by John Wesley Jarvis, date unknown.
Oil on canvas, 30 × 26 in.; 76.2 × 66. 04 cm. Courtesy of the Trustees of
Congregation Shearith Israel, New York, New York.

Plate 10 (cat. 49) *Barnard Gratz,* by Charles Peale Polk, c. 1792. Oil on canvas, 40 × 35 in.; 101.6 × 88.9 cm. Collection of E. Norman Flayderman.

Plate 11 (cat. 71) *John Myers,* by Thomas Sully, 1808. Oil on paper mounted on canvas, 21 ¼ × 24 ½ in.; 53.98 × 62.23 cm. The Chrysler Museum of Art, Norfolk, Virginia; Moses Myers House, Norfolk, Virginia. The Historic Houses are the property of the City of Norfolk and are operated by The Chrysler Museum of Art M51.1.271.

Plate 12 (cat. 74) *Solomon Etting,* by John Wesley Jarvis, c. 1810–12. Oil on panel, framed 34 ³⁄₁₆ × 26 ⅛ in.; 86.81 × 66.37 cm. The Maryland Historical Society, Baltimore. Gift of Eleanor S. Cohen.

Plate 13 (cat. 76 and cover) *Solomon Isaacs,* by John Wesley Jarvis, date unknown. Oil on canvas, 28 ¼ × 26 ⅝ in.; 71.76 × 67.64 cm.
The Jewish Museum, New York. Museum Purchase; Gift of Mr. and Mrs. Jacob D. Shulman and the J.E. and Z.B. Butler Foundation,
by exchange; with funds provided by the estate of Gabriel and Rose Katz; and gift of Kallia H. Bokser, by exchange, 1996–6.p

Plate 14 (cat. 84) *Mendes I. Cohen,* artist unknown, 1832. Oil on paperboard, framed 12 $\frac{7}{16}$ × 9 $\frac{3}{4}$ in.; 31.59 × 24.77 cm. The Maryland Historical Society, Baltimore. Bequest of Harriet Cohen Coale.

Plate 15 (cat. 87) *Hetty Sayre Judah (Mrs. Moses Judah),* by William Dunlap, 1818. Oil on canvas, 49 ½ × 41 ½ in.; 125.73 × 105.41 cm. Cincinnati Art Museum. The Edwin and Virginia Irwin Memorial, 1970.21.

Catalogue of
the Exhibition

Entries prepared by

Elizabeth Lamb Clark
Joellyn Wallen Zollman
Ellen Smith
Charlotte Emans Moore

Beginnings: Models, Manners, Modes

1

Moses Raphael Levy

(1665–1728)

Attributed to Gerardus Duyckinck (1695–1746)
New York, c. 1720–28
Oil on canvas
43 ¼ × 34 ¼ in.; 109.86 × 88.27 cm
Museum of the City of New York.
Bequest of Alphonse H. Kursheedt, 36.343.1

1   *Moses Raphael Levy*

2   *Grace Mears Levy (Mrs. Moses Raphael Levy)*

This aristocratic portrait of Moses Levy (Plate 1) is something of an icon of early American Jewish culture. It has appeared in countless exhibitions.

Literally a founding father of the early American Jewish community and the ancestor of numerous sitters in this exhibition, German-born Moses Raphael Levy immigrated to America in the late-seventeenth century and settled in New York City where he was made freeman in June 1695. Established as an independent merchant-trader, Moses owned a fleet of ships, invested in real estate, and conducted business in Europe, India, the Caribbean, and North America, primarily through his family connections in England and Germany. Like many Jews of his era, he was prominent in both New York's Jewish community and the larger society: he became president of Congregation Shearith Israel and also contributed to the Trinity Church steeple building fund. Moses married twice and fathered twelve children: five with his first wife, Richea Asher Levy, whom he married in London in 1695; and seven with his second wife, Grace Mears Levy (cat. 2), whom he married in London in 1718.

Moses's second marriage strained his relations with the children of his first, and may explain the fact that two similar portraits of Moses Levy survive. The portrait in this exhibition is the original painting, executed sometime before Moses's death; it was rendered as a pendant to the portrait of his second wife, Grace Mears Levy. The two portraits are similarly sized and interact with each other in their gestures, each sitter gracefully extending a hand toward the other. Moses Levy's portrait is part of a baroque portrait tradition. He is depicted in a domestic interior with a dog, symbolizing marital fidelity, and with a view outside a window of a large sailing vessel signifying Levy's status as a merchant-trader and ship owner. Both Mary Black and Erica Hirshler have attributed the Levy portraits to Gerardus Duyckinck.

One of the inherent problems with early American portraiture concerns the copy, the replica, and duplicate. The children of large, mercantile families understandably wanted copies of original portraits.[1] It has been suggested that Moses's eldest daughter,

Bilhah Abigail Levy Franks who has been documented in her letters as contemptuous of her stepmother, Grace Mears Levy, may have commissioned a replica of Moses Levy's original portrait; it now hangs in the American Jewish Historical Society.[2] The original portrait of Moses, in this exhibition, has descended through the family of Grace Mears Levy; the copy of the portrait, executed with fewer details, less modeling, and less overall skill with color and line, has descended through the family of Abigail Levy Franks.   ELC

Notes
1. In a small way, the two Moses Levy portraits illustrate the problem of multiple versions of the same portrait. In general, the more famous the sitter and the larger his family the more versions exist. During my travels examining paintings for this exhibition, I repeatedly found many, many versions of the same portrait.
2. Ellen Smith, a scholar of the Levy-Franks family, cites a letter of Abigail Franks to Naphtali Franks, June 9, 1734. In *Letters of the Franks Family (1733–1748)*, ed. Leo Hershkowitz and Isidore S. Meyer (Waltham, Mass.: American Jewish Historical Society, 1968), p. 28.

References
Hirshler, Erica E. "The Levy-Franks Family Portraits." *The Magazine Antiques*, (November 1990): 1020–29. Illus. p. 1020.
Early American Jewish Portraiture, Stephen S. Kayser and Isidore S. Meyer, eds. New York: American Jewish Historical Society, 1952. Exhibition catalogue, Illus., pp. 7–8, p. 16.
Kleeblatt, Norman L., and Gerard C. Wertkin. *The Jewish Heritage in American Folk Art*. Exhibition catalogue. The Jewish Museum and the Museum of American Folk Art. New York: Universe Books, 1984. Color plate p. 67.
London, Hannah R. *Portraits of Jews by Gilbert Stuart and Other Early American Artists*. Rutland, Vt.: Charles E. Tuttle Company, 1969.

3   *Bilhah Abigail Levy Franks (Mrs. Jacob Franks)*

2

Grace Mears Levy (Mrs. Moses Levy)

(1694–1740)
Attributed to Gerardus Duyckinck (1695–1746)
New York, c. 1720–28
Oil on canvas
45 × 36 in.; 114.3 × 91.44 cm
Museum of the City of New York.
Bequest of Alphonse H. Kursheedt, 36.343.2

The iconic image of Grace Mears Levy, like the portrait of her husband, Moses Raphael Levy (Plate 1, cat. 1) endures as a rare benchmark in the history of early American art. Together the pendant pair has appeared in innumerable exhibitions; the literature on the few examples of early American Jewish portraiture seldom fails to mention the Moses Levy portraits.

Grace Mears was born in Jamaica of English parents. At age twenty-four she married Moses Levy, thirty years her senior, in London; this painting may have been commissioned to celebrate their marriage. A decade after Grace Mears Levy became the second wife of Moses Levy, her husband died, leaving her not only with seven children under the age of eleven from their union, but also with five children from his first marriage. To support this large family she opened up a retail establishment, which she managed. Seven years later in 1756 she married David Hays; it proved to be an unhappy marriage.

This Baroque portrait, alternately attributed to Gerardus Duyckinck and Pieter Vanderlyn, has an English mezzotint source, the *Countess of Ranelagh* by John Smith after Sir Godfrey Kneller. Like other colonial portraits, it borrows English motifs, which, of course, have their sources specifically in the Dutch and Flemish traditions. The sitter is placed outdoors in the landscape with a view of distant trees and sky at left; she is seated within a Leonardesque brown rocky grotto.   ELC

References

Hirshler, Erica E. "The Levy-Franks Family Portraits." *The Magazine Antiques* (November 1990): 1020–29.

Kleeblatt, Norman L., and Gerard C. Wertkin, eds. *The Jewish Heritage in American Folk Art.* Exhibition catalogue. The Jewish Museum and the Museum of American Folk Art. New York: Universe Books, 1984. Color plate p. 67.

London, Hannah R. *Portraits of Jews by Gilbert Stuart and Other Early American Artists.* Rutland, Vt.: Charles E. Tuttle Company, 1969.

5   *Jacob Franks*

4   *Anna Cruger*

3

Bilhah Abigail Levy Franks (Mrs. Jacob Franks)

(1696–1756)

Attributed to Gerardus Duyckinck (1695–1746)
New York, c. 1735

Oil on canvas
44 × 35 in.; 111.76 × 88.9 cm
American Jewish Historical Society, Waltham, Massachusetts, and New York, New York.
Gift of Captain N. Taylor Phillips

No colonial woman has left a more engaging portrait of contemporary family, political, and social life than Bilhah "Abigail" Franks. Her letters to her son Naphtali in England, covering the years 1733–48, discuss the lives of his growing siblings, life in New York City, her extensive reading, and her love of good Scotch snuff. The daughter of Moses Raphael Levy (Plate 1, cat. 1) and Richea Asher Levy, Abigail married the merchant Jacob Franks (cat. 5) in 1712. They had nine children, and Abigail devoted her life to raising them as Jews and as engaged citizens of New York.

Abigail's letters also shed rare light on a colonial and Jewish woman's view of the world. "I think [the faire Charecter Our Familys has in the place by Jews & Christians] its the greatest happyness a Person Can Injoy Next to the haveing a good Conscience" she wrote Naphtali in 1733.[1] Having said farewell, one by one, to England-bound children she would never see again, she nevertheless remained close to them through letters they wrote and passed around. And while she noted the irony that children left home only after they were "grown Up and behave in Such a maner As to Give Sattisfaction,"[2] she treasured the adults she raised, as well as the portraits of them as young children that gave her company and comfort throughout her life.

The artistic attribution of the Levy-Franks family portrait series to Gerardus Duyckinck remains problematic. The poses of all of the women in the Levy-Franks series are based on English portrait and mezzotint models.[3] None of the portraits are signed, and no written records survive to confirm the attribution.[4] Nevertheless, several strong arguments for the Duyckinck attribution can be put forward. Duyckinck and the Franks family knew each other socially, and Duyckinck served in Captain Henry Schuyler's militia company with Jacob Franks and his sons Moses and David. The green undertones of the flesh and the rendering of the flowers, most clearly seen in this portrait and that of daughter Phila (cat. 8), strongly point toward an artist with Dutch training or background. The portraits also exhibit a Dutch glazing technique in which colors are built up with thin layers of translucent paint. Duyckinck's grandfather, Evert, trained in Holland and passed on the techniques of classical Dutch painting to his family. In the absence of firm evidence, the Duyckinck attribution is tentative, but one increasingly supported by scholars over the past decade.   EJS

Notes
1. Abigail Franks to Naphtali Franks, May 7, 1733. In *Letters of the Franks Family (1733–1748)*, ed. Leo Hershkowitz and Isidore S. Meyer (Waltham: Mass.: American Jewish Historical Society, 1968), 5.
2. Abigail Franks to Naphtali Franks, October 18, 1741, *Letters of the Franks Family*, p. 93.
3. See Erica E. Hirshler, "The Levy-Franks Family Portraits," *The Magazine Antiques* (November 1990): 1020–29; and Wayne Craven, *Colonial American Portraiture; The Economic, Religious, Social, Cultural, Philosophical, Scientific, and Aesthetic Foundations* (Cambridge, Eng.: Cambridge Univ. Press, 1986).
4. For a discussion of the Duyckinck attribution, see Erica E. Hirshler, "The Levy-Franks Family Portraits." *The Magazine Antiques* (November 1990): 1026–27; and Erica E. Hirshler, "The Levy-Franks Family Colonial Portraits," Exhibition brochure (Boston: Museum of Fine Arts, 1990).

References
Early American Jewish Portraiture. Stephen S. Kayser and Isidore S. Meyer, eds, New York: American Jewish Historical Society, 1952. Exhibition catalogue. Illus. 6.
Franks Family Papers, American Jewish Historical Society, Waltham, Mass., and New York, N.Y.
Hershkowitz, Leo, and Isidore S. Meyer, eds. *Letters of the Franks Family (1733–1748)*. Waltham, Mass.: American Jewish Historical Society, 1968.
Hirshler, Erica E. "The Levy-Franks Family Portraits." *The Magazine Antiques* (November 1990): 1020–29. Illus. pp. 1018 (detail); 1023.
In the Footsteps of Columbus: Jews in America, 1654–1880. Tel Aviv: Beth Hatefutsoth, 1986.

London, Hannah R. *Portraits of Jews by Gilbert Stuart and Other Early American Artists*. New York: William Edwin Rudge, 1927. Illus. p. 85.
Love, Richard H. "Gerardus Duyckinck, New York Limner: A Recent Discovery." *The Magazine Antiques* 113 (January 1978): 28–29.

4
Anna Cruger
(1704–after 1744)
Artist unknown
New York City, c. 1725–30
Oil on canvas
45 × 36 in.; 114.3 × 91.44 cm
Museum of the City of New York.
Gift of Mrs. Bernice Chrysler Garbisch, 57.230.2

Anna Cruger was the oldest of eight children born into the distinguished mercantile household of John and Maria Cuyler Cruger. Of German extraction, her father, John Cruger, Sr., probably arrived in the colonies in 1698 from Bristol, England. Five years later in 1703, he married Maria Cuyler, daughter of Hendrick and Annetje Cuyler of Albany. Residing with his family on Broad Street in New York City, Cruger maintained a lucrative shipping business with commercial ties to Bristol, England, and the West Indies. In local politics, he served the British Crown as an alderman from 1712 to 1734, and as mayor of New York from 1739 until his death. Members of the province's powerful and influential Dutch Reformed Church, the Crugers were buried in the cemetery of the Old Dutch Church in New York City. John Cruger, Jr., Anna's brother, also was active in public service as an alderman and as mayor of New York from 1756 until 1765. At the time of the American Revolution, because of business, governmental, and personal connections, he was suspected of sympathizing with the British Crown, although no retaliatory action was taken against him.

As members of New York City's affluent and influential colonial society, Anna Cruger and her family aspired to associate with the British monarchy of the second quarter of the eighteenth century. In this portrait, Anna's likeness is based directly upon a mezzotint engraving of Queen Caroline, rendered shortly after the sovereign's coronation in 1727 by the British artist John Faber, Jr., from a painting by his compatriot Joseph Highmore. In composition, pose, and gesture, Anna Cruger's portrait utilizes codes of meaning shared with engraved renderings of English monarchs distributed throughout the British Empire during this period. These images provided the basis for transmitting late Baroque portrait styles from England to the colonies, and served as the impetus for provincial adaptations of courtly portraiture.

Like her royal counterpart, Anna is depicted in a three-quarter-length format as a woman of status, standing against an imposing monumental architectural column at the left with one hand gracefully resting on the corner of a cloth-covered table.

Omitting Queen Caroline's elaborate robes decorated with jewels and ermine, the unidentified artist has depicted his subject with realistic, less idealized facial features, wearing a modest garment defined by fabrics appearing sensuous and costly in their simplicity. The swag of sumptuous fabric draped over Anna's left arm provides no specific function in her costume except to serve as a symbol of affluence, a visual attribute commonly found in portraiture of this period.   CEM

References

Belknap, Jr., Waldron Phoenix. *American Colonial Painting: Materials for a History.* Cambridge, Mass.: Harvard University Press, 1959. Illus. 28A, p. *xxix*.

Blackburn, Roderic H., and Ruth Piwonka, eds. *Remembrance of Patria: Dutch Arts and Culture in Colonial America, 1609–1776.* Albany: Albany Institute of History and Art, 1988.

Craven, Wayne. *Colonial American Portraiture: The Economic, Religious, Social, Cultural, Philosophical, Scientific, and Aesthetic Foundations.* Cambridge, Eng.: Cambridge University Press, 1986.

Hassell, Bentley D. "The Cruger Family in America—A Genealogical Chart Showing the Descendants of John Cruger and Their Alliances," 1892.

Johnson, Allen, and Dumas Malone, eds. *Dictionary of American Biography.* Vol. 2: 582. New York: Charles Scribner's Sons, 1927; rpt. 1964.

New-York Historical Society. *Catalogue of American Portraits in the New-York Historical Society.* Vol. 1: 178–79. New Haven and London: Yale University Press, 1974.

Nicoll, Maud Churchill. *The Earliest Cuylers in Holland and America and Some of their Descendants.* New York: Tobias A. Wright, 1912.

Saunders, Richard H., and Ellen G. Miles. *American Colonial Portraits, 1700–1776.* Washington, D.C.: Smithsonian Institution Press for the National Portrait Gallery, 1987.

5

Jacob Franks

(1688–1769)

Attributed to Gerardus Duyckinck (1695–1746),
New York, c. 1735

Oil on canvas
44 × 35 in.; 111.76 × 88.9 cm
American Jewish Historical Society, Waltham,
Massachusetts, and New York, New York.
Gift of Captain N. Taylor Phillips

Son of a London broker, Jacob Franks immigrated to New York City about 1708 and married Abigail Levy (cat. 3) in 1712. Deeply involved in the Jewish community, he was one of four men to lay the cornerstone of Congregation Shearith Israel's Mill Street Synagogue in 1729, and served as its *parnas*, or president, in 1730. His business letters are often peppered with Hebrew.

Jacob conducted his shipping, wholesale, and retail business in conjunction with his brother, his brothers-in-law, and his son Naphtali (all in England) and traded throughout Europe, the Caribbean, North America, and as far away as India. Although his fortunes remained steady, he never attained the ranks of the truly wealthy or powerful colonial merchants. His English relations far surpassed him, and the discrepancy caused tension within the family. Abigail complained to Naphtali: "I think your Fathers Treatment from you & your Uncle Especially from the Latter is more Like a Slave than a Freemen."[1]

The stresses of his business could also make him testy: "Your father is Very full of buissness. Its a Very great Fatigue And makes him Very Peevish to those he imploys," Abigail wrote her son and Jacob's business partner, Naphtali, in 1741. But against the pressures of business, the Jewish Sabbath offered Jacob and his family a respite. "I never knew the benifit of the Sabath before but Now I am Glad when it comes for his Sake that he may have a Little ReLaxation from t[ha]t Continuall Hurry he is in."[2]

Jacob Franks is painted in the pose and costume favored in contemporary prints and portraits of English aristocrats. A virtual mirror image of the portrait of his father-in-law Moses Raphael Levy (cat. 1), the painting intentionally defines Franks as a member of a European, trans-Atlantic mercantile culture.

Gerardus Duyckinck was one of four generations of Duyckincks who painted in the American colonies beginning in the 1630s. Trained in Dutch painting and glazing techniques, Duyckinck, like most painters in the colonies, could never support himself entirely from portrait commissions. A 1735 advertisement lists "Lookin-glasses new silvered, and the frames plain Japan'd or Flowered, also all sorts of picktures, made and Sold, all manner of painting Work done" among the services he offered.[3]

EJS

Notes

1. Abigail Franks to Naphtali Franks, November 25, 1745, in *Letters of the Franks Family (1733–1748)*, ed. Leo Hershkowitz and Isidore S. Meyer (Waltham, Mass.: American Jewish Historical Society, 1968), p. 130.

2. Abigail Franks to Naphtali Franks, June 21, 1741, *Letters of the Franks Family*, p. 87.

3. *New-York Weekly Journal*, January 6, 1735.

References

Early American Jewish Portraiture, Stephen S. Kayser and Isidore S. Meyer, eds. New York: American Jewish Historical Society, 1952. Exhibition catalogue. Illus. 5.

Franks Family Papers, American Jewish Historical Society, Waltham, Mass., and New York, N.Y.

Hershkowitz, Leo, and Isidore S. Meyer, eds. *Letters of the Franks Family (1733–1748)*. Waltham, Mass.: American Jewish Historical Society, 1968.

Hirshler, Erica E. "The Levy-Franks Family Colonial Portraits." Exhibition brochure. Boston: Museum of Fine Arts, 1990. Illus.

Hirshler, Erica E. "The Levy-Franks Family Portraits." *The Magazine Antiques* (November 1990): 1020–29. Illus. pp. 1018 (detail); 1023.

London, Hannah R. *Portraits of Jews by Gilbert Stuart and Other Early American Artists.* New York: William Edwin Rudge, 1927. Illus. p. 85.

6

Mary (Polly) Warner

(c. 1750–c. 1770)
Joseph Blackburn (active 1753–1763)
Portsmouth, New Hampshire, c. 1761
Oil on canvas
50 × 40 in.; 130 × 101.6 cm
The Warner House Association,
Portsmouth, New Hampshire 1937.6

6 *Mary (Polly) Warner*

Polly was born in Portsmouth, the daughter of Jonathan Warner and Mary Nelson. In 1769, when she was nineteen, she married Colonel Samuel Sherburne from a prominent Portsmouth family; she died the following year, possibly during childbirth. The portrait is signed and dated, "I. Blackburn Pinxit 1761."

ELC

References
Morgan, John H., and Henry Wilder Foote. "An Extension of Lawrence Park's Descriptive List of the Work of Joseph Blackburn." *Proceedings of the American Antiquarian Society*, 1936.
Park, Lawrence. "Joseph Blackburn, Portrait Painter with a Descriptive List of His Work." *Proceedings of the American Antiquarian Society*, 1923.

7

David (1720–1794) *and Phila Franks* (1722–1811)
Attributed to Gerardus Duyckinck (1695–1746)
New York, c. 1735
Oil on canvas
45 ¹/₂ × 36 in.; 116 × 91.5 cm
American Jewish Historical Society, Waltham, Massachusetts and New York, New York.
Gift of Captain N. Taylor Phillips

Three of the paintings in the Levy-Franks family portrait series depict the children of Abigail Levy Franks (cat. 3) and Jacob Franks (cat. 5), but it is difficult to provide a definitive identification of the children. Phila Franks would have been thirteen years old in 1735. Because her sister Richa's birth date is not known, it remains an open question whether Phila or Richa is actually represented in the single portrait (cat. 8). A portrait of two Franks children not exhibited likely portrays Moses (age seventeen in 1735) or David (age fifteen), and possibly Richa; its usual title as "David and Phila" is certainly incorrect.

The double portrait illustrated here also bears the traditional title *David and Phila*, but if a 1735 date is used, the children are more likely David (age fifteen) and Aaron (not quite three), or possibly Abigail ("Poyer," birthdate unknown). The Franks's daughter Sara died at twenty-two months of age in November of 1733, and the loss of that child may have motivated the commissioning of portraits of the rest of the family. On the other hand, Abigail makes no mention of these portraits in her letters of the 1730s, possibly arguing for a later date. If the traditional 1735 date is used, and the portraits are identified as Phila; Moses and Richa; David and Aaron; then all the living Franks children are accounted for, except for "Poyer," and oldest son Naphtali who was in England. All the children are portrayed against the same stylized backgrounds and, as was the fashion during the eighteenth century, in the same modeled costumes as the adults.[1] The children's portraits were directly modeled on English print and portrait sources, including those by John Smith and Sir Godfrey

Joseph Blackburn traveled from Bermuda through New England during his decade in America. He was a master of the lighthearted, English Rococo portrait that appealed to the elite colonial merchant class. His portraits, frequently three-quarter length, featured stylish clothing in rich fabrics of luscious colors; these costumes were placed upon slender, elegant figures posed to suggest graceful movement. His deft handling of draperies, especially satin and lace, profoundly influenced young John Singleton Copley during Blackburn's residence in Boston.

In 1761 the competition from Copley in Boston forced Joseph Blackburn to seek opportunities elsewhere. In Portsmouth, New Hampshire, he painted six members of the Warner family in their Georgian brick house; five of those portraits remain on view there today. The portrait of Polly Warner exemplifies Blackburn's delightful rococo style; the young girl, only eleven or twelve years old, is placed in a rose morning landscape; she is posed like a graceful dancer with her pet bird, which symbolizes a patient and nurturing nature. Her hair is dressed with flowers and pearls; and the lace on the sleeves of her golden-brown satin gown is a tour de force. The mood of this charming portrait is blithe; it makes no pretense toward a character study.

7 *David and Phila Franks*

8 *Phila Franks*

Kneller.[2] Abigail Levy doted on her children. Her lifelong fears for all her children concerning intermarriage were ultimately realized. Among Abigail and Jacob Franks's nine children, six are known to have reached adulthood. Naphtali and Moses married Jewish women while David and Phila took Christian spouses. It is not known if the other children wed. Among Abigail and Jacob's more than two dozen grandchildren, not one of them passed on Judaism to their descendants.   EJS

Notes
1. As an adult in England, Moses Franks had his portrait painted by Joshua Reynolds in 1761. Reynolds painted Phila in 1766; Gainsborough also did her portrait. See Alfred Rubens, *Anglo-Jewish Portraiture* (London: The Jewish Museum, 1935).
2. Erica E. Hirshler, "The Levy-Franks Family Colonial Portraits," Exhibition brochure (Boston: Museum of Fine Arts, 1990), figs. 4, 5, 7.

References
Franks Family Papers, American Jewish Historical Society, Waltham, Mass. and New York, N. Y.
Hirshler, Erica E. "The Levy-Franks Family Colonial Portraits." Exhibition brochure. Boston: Museum of Fine Arts, 1990. Illustration.
Hirshler, Erica E. "The Levy-Franks Family Portraits." *The Magazine Antiques* (November 1990): 1020–1029. Illus. p. 1027.
London, Hannah R. *Portraits of Jews by Gilbert Stuart and Other Early American Artists.* New York: William Edwin Rudge, 1927. Illus. 87.
Stern, Malcolm H. *First American Jewish Families: 600 Genealogies, 1654–1988.* 3rd edition. Baltimore: Ottenheimer Publishers, 1991.

8
Phila Franks
(1722–1811)
Attributed to Gerardus Duyckinck (1695–1746)
New York, c. 1735
Oil on canvas
46 × 36 in.; 115 × 91.5 cm
American Jewish Historical Society, Waltham, Massachusetts and New York, New York.
Gift of Captain N. Taylor Phillips

Phila Franks was the fourth child and oldest daughter of Abigail Levy Franks (cat. 3) and Jacob Franks (cat. 5), routinely described by her mother as a good and devoted daughter. But Abigail fretted about her daughter's marriage prospects in New York. She dismissed local Jewish suitors as unfit while instructing her daughters to marry within the faith, even as she encouraged their active social life in the broader New York community. Abigail summed up her dilemma and frustration in a 1742 letter to their brother Naphtali. "Now pray Tell me doe you Expect Your Sisters to be Nuns."[1]

Phila, however, took matters into her own hands. On September 8, 1742, in a secret ceremony, Phila wed Oliver

9 *Joseph Reade*

Notes
1. Abigail Franks to Naphtali Franks, December 5, 1742. In *Letters of the Franks Family* (*1733–1748*), ed. Leo Hershkowitz and Isidore S. Meyer (Waltham, Mass.: American Jewish Historical Society, 1968), 109–10.
2. David Franks to Naphtali Franks, April 1, 1743, *Letters of the Franks Family*, p. 114.
3. Abigail Franks to Naphtali Franks, June 7, 1743, *Letters of the Franks Family*, pp. 116, 118.

References
Early American Jewish Portraiture. Stephen S. Kayser and Isidore S. Meyer, eds. New York: American Jewish Historical Society, 1952. Exhibition catalogue. Illus. 7.
Hershkowitz, Leo, and Isidore S. Meyer, eds. *Letters of the Franks Family (1733–1748)*. Waltham Mass.: American Jewish Historical Society, 1968.
Hirshler, Erica E. "The Levy-Franks Family Colonial Portraits." Exhibition brochure. Boston: Museum of Fine Arts, 1990. Illustration.
Hirshler, Erica E. "The Levy-Franks Family Portraits." *The Magazine Antiques* (November 1990): 1020–29. Illus. p. 1018 (detail), 1025.
In the Footsteps of Columbus: Jews in America, 1654–1880. Tel Aviv: Beth Hatefutsoth, 1986.
London, Hannah R. *Portraits of Jews by Gilbert Stuart and Other Early American Artists*. New York: William Edwin Rudge, 1927. Illus. p. 89.

9

Joseph Reade

(1694–1771)

John Wollaston (active c. 1733–1775)
New York City, c. 1749–52
Oil on canvas
30 × 25 in.; 76.2 × 63.5 cm
The Metropolitan Museum of Art Purchase.
Gift of Mrs. Russell Sage, by exchange, 1948

Delancey (1718–1785), son of a prominent Huguenot New York merchant family. She remained with the Franks family over the winter, but in the spring of 1743 she announced the deed and went to live with her husband. The Franks family went from shock to mourning to stony silence, and Abigail never reconciled with her daughter. David wrote the news to Naphtali in the spring of 1743: "In very great uneasiness & great Concern of Acc[oun]t of Philla's being Marry'd to Oliver D Lancy."[2] Abigail declared her pain and fury more openly: "I am now retired from Town ... from the Severe Affliction I am Under on the Conduct of that Unhappy Girle Good God Wath a Shock.... I wish it was in my Power to Leave this part of the world."[3]

Pleadings from Oliver, Abigail's Christian friends, and eventually from Jacob, Naphtali, and Richa were to no avail. Although the remainder of the Franks family quietly saw and wrote to Phila, Abigail never did. Phila and Oliver Delancey prospered in New York among its social elite. (Delancey Street in New York City is named after the family.) Ardent Loyalists during the American Revolution, they moved permanently to England after Britain's defeat.

The portrait of Phila Franks adds support to a Gerardus Duyckinck attribution as the artist of the portrait series. In addition to the Dutch thin-glazing technique, and the use of green undertones in the flesh—clearly seen under her chin—the flowers in her basket are rendered in a decidedly Dutch-trained style. EJS

John Wollaston, possibly the son of a British artist, worked in America for about twenty years in New York City, Philadelphia, and in the environs of the port cities of Maryland, Virginia, and South Carolina. A prolific painter, he completed nearly three hundred portraits of upper-class colonials. He arrived in America with his English Rococo style already in place; in general, he used formulaic arrangements and featured lustrous satins in handsome colors, emphasizing his early training as a drapery painter. The posture of his almond-eyed sitters appears somewhat stiff though elegant.

A successful man of affairs, Joseph Reade was prominent politically and socially in New York City. He was a member of the governor's council, a vestryman of Trinity Church for fifty years, and lent his support to important community efforts. Reade Street in Lower Manhattan is named after him.

Wollaston stayed in New York from 1749 to 1752 and probably executed the Reade portraits during his visit. The artist has carefully rendered the sitter's rich brown coat, elegant long wig, and stock while managing to convey something of his self-confidence and self-knowledge, rather an exception to Wollaston's œuvre. ELC

The magnificent original frames of both Reade portraits are exceptionally handsome examples of Rococo frames that have been carved and gilded; certainly they rank among the finest examples extant.

ELC

Reference
Caldwell, John, and Oswaldo Rodriguez Roque et al. *American Paintings in the Metropolitan Museum of Art*. Vol. I. New York: Princeton University Press and The Metropolitan Museum of Art, 1994.

10 *Anna French Reade (Mrs. Joseph Reade)*

Reference
Caldwell, John, and Oswaldo Rodriguez Roque et al. *American Paintings in the Metropolitan Museum of Art*. Vol. I. New York: Princeton University Press and The Metropolitan Museum of Art, 1994.

10

Anna French Reade (Mrs. Joseph Reade)

(1701–1778)
John Wollaston (active c. 1733–75)
New York City, c. 1749–52
Oil on canvas
30 × 25 in.; 76.2 × 63.5 cm
The Metropolitan Museum of Art Purchase.
Gift of Mrs. Russell Sage, by exchange, 1948

Anna French and Joseph Reade (cat. 9) were married in 1720, and their union produced seven children. Unlike her husband's unique portrait, Mrs. Reade's pose and costume are quite typical of Wollaston's portraits during this period. Although the artist's American oeuvre consists of several hundred portraits of the cultured mercantile class, Wollaston repeats the sitter's costume and posture, which creates an identifiable sameness to his portraits. Despite the repetitious and formulaic nature of his works, however, they are sensitively executed and representative of the light and airy Rococo style then in fashion in England.

11

Rachel Levy Seixas (Mrs. Isaac Mendes Seixas)

(1719–1797)
Attributed to John Wollaston (active c. 1733–1775),
New York, 1750
Oil on canvas
30 × 25 in.; 76 × 63.5 cm
American Jewish Historical Society, Waltham,
Massachusetts, and New York, New York.
Gift of Captain N. Taylor Phillips

Rachel Levy (Plate 3) was the oldest of the seven children of Grace Mears Levy (cat. 2) and Moses Raphael Levy (cat. 1), making Rachel Levy the half-sister of Abigail Levy Franks. Although Grace was widely disliked, Rachel Levy was well-loved

11 *Rachel Levy Seixas (Mrs. Isaac Mendes Seixas)*

throughout the entire Levy-Franks circle: "A Very good Girle," Abigail wrote of her in 1740.[1]

Nevertheless, good Rachel caused her own uproar with her 1740 marriage to London merchant Isaac Mendes Seixas (1708–1780). Son of a noted Sephardic Portuguese family, Isaac made a decidedly "mixed" marriage in taking Rachel Levy, descended from "Tudesco" (Ashkenazic Central European) Jewish stock, as his bride. The union crossed contemporary social, status, and Jewish ethnic lines. "The Portugueze here where in A Violent Uproar abouth it," Abigail Franks recorded, "for he Did not invite any of them to ye Wedding."[2]

There were other objections as well. Isaac's "Untractable Dispossision" gave the Franks family pause, as did the young Seixas couple's move to New Jersey where Isaac opened a "Small Contry Store." Nonetheless, Abigail Franks changed her assessment of the match after a weeklong stay with them, decreeing Isaac "A person of his Temper Soe much Mended. … they Seem to be Very happy in each other."[3] The happy union eventually produced eight children, including Gershom Mendes Seixas (cat. 37).

English artist John Wollaston arrived in America in 1749 and over the next eighteen years changed the focus and look of American portrait painting. The son of London portrait painter John Wollaston "the elder" (c. 1672–1740), Wollaston "the younger" trained with London's famed drapery painter Joseph van Aken in the 1740s before venturing to the colonies at mid-century. His aims were commercial and his American career took him from New York City to Philadelphia, Maryland, Virginia, Charleston, and several Caribbean islands. Overall, Wollaston executed almost three hundred known portraits during his time in the colonies from 1749 to about 1767. Wollaston's first work in America was painted for New York City clients between 1749 and 1752. At least fifty portraits are known from that period. Among the earliest of them is the portrait of Rachel Levy Mendes Seixas painted in 1750.

The Seixas portrait is an excellent example of Wollaston's early American work, which would influence succeeding American painters in characteristic ways. The portrait exhibits the slightly slanting, almond-shaped eyes typical of many of his works. The sitter's pose is informal. The painting emphasizes the rich textures and highlights in the fabric, and there is also an emphasis on a smiling, well-colored, animated face. Each of these slightly rococo approaches establishes a trend away from the more formal, detailed style of earlier colonial portraiture. The Seixas portrait stands as a beacon of what was to follow in American painting. Clearly, practitioners and sitters liked what they saw, for Wollaston's success was virtually unmatched during his time.   EJS

Notes
1. Abigail Franks to Naphtali Franks, August 3, 1740. In *Letters of the Franks Family (1733–1748)*, ed. Leo Hershkowitz and Isidore S. Meyer (Waltham, Mass.: American Jewish Historical Society, 1968), 75–76.
2. Abigail Franks to Naphtali Franks, August 3, 1740, *Letters of the Franks Family*, p. 76.
3. Abigail Franks to Naphtali Franks, November 9, 1750, *Letters of the Franks Family*, p. 81.

References
Craven, Wayne. "John Wollaston: His Career in England and New York City." *American Art Journal* 7, no. 2 (1975): 19–31.
Hershkowitz, Leo, and Isidore S. Meyer, eds. *Letters of the Franks Family (1733–1748)*. Waltham, Mass.: American Jewish Historical Society, 1968.
Early American Jewish Portraiture. Kayser, Stephen S., and Isidore S. Meyer, eds. Exhibition catalogue. New York: The Jewish Museum, 1952. Illus. 35.
Franks Family Papers, American Jewish Historical Society, Waltham, Mass., and New York, N.Y.
London, Hannah R. *Portraits of Jews by Gilbert Stuart and Other Early American Artists*. New York: William Edwin Rudge, 1927. Illus. p. 93.
Saunders, Richard H., and Ellen G. Miles. *American Colonial Portraits, 1700–1776*. Washington D.C.: Smithsonian Institution Press for the National Portrait Gallery, 1987. Illustration.

12

Benjamin S. Judah

(1760–1831)
Ralph Earl (1751–1801),
New York, 1794
Oil on canvas
48 ⅝ × 34 ½ in.; 123.51 × 87.63 cm
Wadsworth Atheneum, Hartford, Connecticut.
The Ella Gallup Sumner and
Mary Catlin Sumner Collection Fund

In this urbane portrait, Ralph Earl appears to have left his Connecticut country style behind and returned to his more sophisticated British manner. Indeed, Benjamin Judah, from a prominent Jewish family, was painted by Earl in New York City. The landscape scene outside the window is not Earl's ubiquitous and site-specific view of the Connecticut countryside common to his portraits from this date, but rather a non-specific vista.

Seated in a side chair that has been placed diagonally to the picture plane and richly upholstered in red damask, the sitter is portrayed as a man of fashion and an image of urbane affluence. The prosperous thirty-four-year-old is attired in silks and satins and has chosen a powdered wig that seems not incongruous with his opulent floral-embroidered ivory waistcoat. He also boasts an azure blue undervest, black satin breeches, and light blue-gray frock coat with narrow unbuttoned coat sleeves. He holds a leather-bound volume on his lap, his hand resting upon one of his business papers that indicate he is not only an international merchant but an educated gentleman.

Born into a prominent New York family, Benjamin Judah was the son of Samuel Judah, patriot and merchant-trader, and Jessie

12   *Benjamin S. Judah*

13
Israel Israel

(1744–1822)

Artist unknown, 1775

Oil on canvas
30 × 26 in.; 76.2 × 66.04 cm
Abby Aldrich Rockefeller Folk
Art Center, Williamsburg, Virginia

Israel Israel was the son of Midrach Israel, a Jew, and Mary J. Paxton, an Episcopalian; he was baptized on June 13, 1746, in Pennsylvania. At age twenty-one, Israel Israel left for Barbados where he remained for ten years. He returned with a fortune and married Hannah Erwin (cat. 14), a Quaker, in the Holy Trinity Church (Old Swede's Church), in Wilmington, Delaware, on September 7, 1775. The couple lived on a farm near Wilmington in the first few years following their wedding. The pendant portraits celebrate their marriage.

During the Revolution, Israel was captured as a spy by the British while transporting provisions to his elderly parents; he was imprisoned on a British frigate on the Delaware River. Before his trial, a compassionate sailor informed him that the ship's officers had a Masonic lodge aboard and that it would help if he were a mason. During the trial, Israel made the secret sign of the Masonic brotherhood, the judge dismissed the charges, and all prisoners were released. In later years a Grand Master of the Masonic order in Pennsylvania, Israel Israel has been depicted here making the secret Masonic sign with his right hand.   ELC

Jonas; his grandfather, Baruch Judah, was one of the founders of Shearith Israel, the oldest synagogue in New York City. Benjamin's extensive enterprises in marine trade suffered greatly during the War of 1812. At the time of this portrait, Benjamin is still a bachelor; in eight years he would marry Elizah Israel and become the father of ten children.

The portrait remained in the Judah family until 1984 when it was purchased by the Wadsworth Atheneum in Hartford, Connecticut, from Benjamin Judah's great-great-granddaughter, Hildegard Whitehead Reed.   ELC

References
Kornhauser, Elizabeth. *Ralph Earl: The Face of the Young Republic.* New Haven: Yale University Press, 1991. Illus. p. 196.
London, Hannah R.. *Portraits of Jews by Gilbert Stuart and Other Early American Artists.* Rutland, Vt.: Charles E. Tuttle Company, 1969.
Stern, Malcolm H., *First American Jewish Families: 600 Genealogies, 1654–1988.* Baltimore: Ottenheimer Publishers, 1978.

References
Abby Aldrich Rockefeller Folk Art Center, Williamsburg, Va., archival folder.
London, Hannah R. *Portraits of Jews by Gilbert Stuart and Other Early American Artists.* Rutland, Vt.: Charles E. Tuttle Company, 1969.
Martin, Sheila W. "The Secret Sign: Israel Israel's adventures as an American Patriot in Delaware." *Delaware Today,* 14, no.7, July 1776: 15.
Stern, Malcolm H.. *First American Jewish Families: 600 Genealogies, 1654–1988.* Baltimore: Ottenheimer Publishers, 1978.
Wolf, Edwin 2nd, and Maxwell Whiteman. *The History of the Jews of Philadelphia from Colonial Times to the Age of Jackson.* Philadelphia: Jewish Publication Society of America, 1957.

13 *Israel Israel*

14 *Hannah Erwin Israel (Mrs. Israel Israel)*

14

Hannah Erwin Israel (Mrs. Israel Israel)

(1757–1813)
Artist unknown, 1775
Oil on canvas
30 × 26 in.; 76.2 × 66.04 cm
Abby Aldrich Rockefeller Folk Art
Center, Williamsburg, Virginia

From 1942 to 1955 the unique portraits of Hannah Erwin Israel and her husband, Israel Israel (cat. 13), both American Revolutionary patriots, hung in the Rockefeller guest cottage at Williamsburg; the positive identification of the sitters was based on their later portraits; unfailingly Hannah Israel is depicted wearing a simple Quaker-style dress, and her husband has a most distinctive hairline.

Hannah Erwin was born a Quaker in Wilmington, Delaware. She married thirty-one-year-old Israel Israel in 1775 when she was only nineteen years old; these singular portraits commemorate their union.

She always presents herself, as she does in this portrait, in plain Quaker dress. An educated woman, she is seated holding a book in her right hand, a pleated muslin bonnet, without adornment, covering her brown hair; the décolletage of the simple dark dress, also a Quaker style, is covered modestly by a scarf. The forthright expression in her clear blue eyes gives credence to her heroic defiance of British gunfire.   ELC

References
Abby Aldrich Rockefeller Folk Art Center, Williamsburg, Va., archival folder.
London, Hannah R. *Portraits of Jews By Gilbert Stuart and Other Early American Artists*. Rutland, Vt.: Charles E. Tuttle Company, 1969.
Martin, Sheila W. "The Secret Sign: Israel Israel's adventures as an American Patriot in Delaware." *Delaware Today*, 14, no.7, (July 1776): p. 15.
Stern, Malcolm H. *First American Jewish Families: 600 Genealogies, 1654–1988*. Baltimore: Ottenheimer Publishers, 1978.
Wolf, Edwin 2nd, and Maxwell Whiteman. *The History of the Jews of Philadelphia from Colonial Times to the Age of Jackson*. Philadelphia: Jewish Publication Society of America, 1957.

Families: Private and Public, Resemblances and Relationships, Physiognomical and Nominal

15

Grace Mendes Seixas Nathan (Mrs. Simon Nathan)

(1752–1831) *and Her Son Seixas Nathan* (1785–1852)

New York, c. 1824

Silhouette; cut at the Hubard Gallery

9 ½ × 7 ½ in.; 23.7 × 18.7 cm

Collection of Henry Hendricks Schulson

15 *Grace Mendes Seixas Nathan (Mrs. Simon Nathan) and her son Seixas Nathan*

who count among their descendants Supreme Court Justice Benjamin Nathan Cardozo and Emma Lazarus, whose poem "The New Colossus" is inscribed on the base of the Statue of Liberty.   JWZ

Notes
1. Alice Van Leer Carrick. *A History of American Silhouettes: A Collector's Guide, 1790–1840* (Rutland, Vt.: Tuttle Publishing, 1968) p. 86.
2. Grace Mendes Nathan to Seixas Nathan, November 1827, Nathan Family Papers, American Jewish Historical Society, Waltham, Mass.

References
Pool, David de Sola. *Portraits Etched in Stone: Early Jewish Settlers, 1682–1831*. New York: Columbia University Press, 1952, pp. 438–41.
Wolff, Frances Nathan. *My Life and Memoirs of New York For Over Eighty Years*. New York: Colonial Press, 1939.

16

Grace Mendes Seixas Nathan (Mrs. Simon Nathan)

(1752–1831)

Henry Inman (1801–1846)

c. 1820

Miniature; pen and ink on paper

3 × 2 ½ in.; 7.5 × 6.25 cm

American Jewish Historical Society, Waltham, Massachusetts, and New York, New York.

Bequest of Sarah Lyons

Master Hubard prided himself on his skilled, scissored approach to the silhouette.[1] Here Hubard, or an artist under his employ, captures a seated Grace Mendes Seixas Nathan (cat. 16) with her son, Seixas, standing before her. Seixas was the only child born to his parents, Grace and Simon Nathan (cat. 17). However, Seixas's own offspring would never lack for siblings, since he and his wife, Sarah Seixas, had sixteen children. In a farewell letter to Seixas, his mother encourages him to continue the moral and religious education of her "endearing" grandchildren.[2] Indeed, morality and religion endured in the family of Grace and Seixas,

"I have read the whole of Lord Byron's work very lately indeed, and I recommend them *to you*," wrote Grace Mendes Nathan to her niece Sarah Kursheedt.[1] Poet and patriot, wife and mother, Nathan dedicated her mind and heart to her family, her religion, and her country. Born the seventh child of Isaac and Rachel Levy Mendes in New York City on November 24, 1752, she fled with her family to settle in Philadelphia in the wake of the Revolution. There she met and married her husband, Simon Nathan (cat. 17), in 1780.

16   *Grace Mendes Seixas Nathan (Mrs. Simon Nathan)*

17   *Simon Nathan*

Her life with Simon in both New York and Philadelphia is reflected in her creative, intelligent family letters and a book of unpublished poems. In a letter to her son Seixas near the end of her life, she wrote, "I die in the full faith of my Religion. Need I exhort you to the cultivation of your endearing children and give them a just idea of their religious and moral principles, these being the corner stones of all good."[2] Grace's counsel, as well as her literary talent, filtered through her descendants, emerging in, among others, her great-granddaughter, Emma Lazarus.

Inman portrays Nathan as a mature woman "in the full faith of her religion," with her head and neck both modestly covered. Though modest, the ruffles of her bonnet and collar lend a festive air to her image.   JWZ

Notes
1. Grace Mendes Nathan to Sarah Kursheedt, undated, Nathan Family Papers, American Jewish Historical Society, Waltham, Mass.
2. Grace Mendes Nathan to Seixas Nathan, November 1827, Nathan Family Papers, American Jewish Historical Society, Waltham, Mass.

References
Early American Jewish Portraiture. Kayser, Stephen S., and Isadore S. Meyer, eds. Exhibition catalogue. New York: The Jewish Museum, 1952, p. 17. Illus. 24.
London, Hannah. *Miniatures of Early American Jews.* Springfield, Mass.: The Pond-Ekberg Company, 1953, Illus. 131.
Pool, David de Sola. *Portraits Etched in Stone: Early Jewish Settlers, 1682–1831.* New York: Columbia University Press, 1952, pp. 438–441.
Wolff, Frances Nathan. *My Life and Memoirs of New York For Over Eighty Years.* New York: Colonial Press, 1939.

17

Simon Nathan

(1746–1822)
Henry Inman (1801–1846)
c. 1820
Miniature; pen and ink on paper
3 × 2 ½ in.; 7.5 × 6.25 cm
American Jewish Historical Society, Waltham,
Massachusetts and New York, New York.
Bequest of Sarah Lyons

English-born merchant Simon Nathan had the occasion to establish himself as a patriot shortly after his 1773 arrival in America. In response to a plea by Governor Thomas Jefferson of Virginia, Nathan provided an interest-free loan of 300,000 continental dollars to clothe five hundred men at Fort Pitt.[1] However, the depreciation of continental currency, along with other generous loans of supplies and currency on Nathan's part, resulted in a significant financial loss from which he never recovered. Despite financial difficulties, however, Nathan prospered as a public figure. He moved to Philadelphia in about 1780, where he met and married Grace Mendes Seixas (cats. 15, 16). Through the prominent Seixas family, he became involved in public life, serving two terms as president of Philadelphia's Congregation Mikveh Israel (in 1782 and 1783). After the Revolution, Simon and Grace Nathan moved to New York where Simon established an auction business and continued to play an active role in the Jewish community, serving as *parnas*, or president, of Shearith Israel in 1785, 1786, 1794, and 1796.

While this portrait depicts Nathan near the end of his life, it was executed by Henry Inman at the beginning of his career. Completed just one year after Inman finished an apprenticeship with John Wesley Jarvis, this portrait of Simon Nathan demonstrates Inman's skill with paper sketches—a skill that would establish him as one of the highest paid painters in America.

JWZ

Note

1. David de Sola Pool, *Portraits Etched in Stone: Early Jewish Settlers, 1682–1831* (New York: Columbia University Press, 1952), p. 415.

References

Early American Jewish Portraiture. Kayser, Stephen S., and Isadore S. Meyer, eds. Exhibition catalogue. New York: The Jewish Museum, 1952, p. 17. Illus. 23.
London, Hannah R.. *Miniatures of Early American Jews.* Springfield, Mass.: The Pond-Ekberg Company, 1953. Illus. 131.
Wolff, Frances Nathan. *My Life and Memoirs of New York For Over Eighty Years.* New York: Colonial Press, 1939.

18

Samson Levy, Jr.

(1761–1831)
Charles Balthazar Julien Févret de Saint-Mémin (1770–1852)
1802
black crayon with white chalk on paper
prepared with pink wash
18 × 11 in.; 45.72 × 27.94 cm
The Jewish Museum, New York
Museum purchase with funds provided by
the Joshua Lowenfish and Rictavia Schiff
Bequests, 1993–104

Charles Balthazar Julien Févret de Saint-Mémin, destined for a military career, fled his native Dijon because of the French Revolution; he arrived in America via Switzerland in 1793, only twenty-three years old. To support his family he turned to his artistic avocation, landscape painting, but he soon learned that there was a demand only for portraiture in America.

Growing up in neoclassical France, the young aristocrat was certainly aware of the history of the classical profile portrait. By using a physiognotrace, an invention of Gilles-Louis Chrétien in 1786, he was able to draw extraordinary profile portraits very efficiently. He charged thirty-five dollars for women and twenty-five dollars for men; this included a drawing (about 20 × 15 inches), a small round engraved plate (about 2.5 inches in diameter), and twelve engravings. The original drawing was done in black chalk, later stumped, with graphite and white chalk additions; he used

18   Samson Levy, Jr.

19   Martha Lampley Levy (Mrs. Samson Levy, Sr.)

buff drawing paper that had been brushed and coated with a chalk-like liquid, tinted pink. Frequently he placed his finished drawings in a unique gilded frame of his design; the glass was decorated with a "verre églomisé" technique of black with gold. When the drawing was complete, a pantograph would transfer a reduced image from the drawing onto a copper plate. Saint-Mémin himself would etch and engrave the plate that somewhat resembled an enlarged Roman imperial coin when finished. The engravings would then be printed from the plate, the number depending upon the sitter. A public figure might order hundreds of engravings, whereas a private individual like Samson Levy, Jr., would order the usual twelve.

Samson Levy, Jr. (see also cat. 20), probably ordered Saint-Mémin drawings of himself, his wife, Sarah Coates Levy (cat. 21), and his mother, Martha Lampley Levy (cat. 19). Unfortunately the drawing of Sarah Coates Levy is unlocated; only small engravings exist. The drawings of mother and son have descended in the family directly from the sitters to Eleanor Carroll Bancroft of New York and The Jewish Museum.   ELC

References

London, Hannah R.. *Miniatures and Silhouettes of Early Jews.* Rutland, Vt.: Charles E. Tuttle Company, 1970.

London, Hannah R. *Portraits of Jews by Gilbert Stuart and Other Early American Artists.* Rutland, Vt.: Charles E. Tuttle Company, 1969.

Miles, Ellen G. *Charles Balthazar Julien Févret de Saint-Mémin and the Neoclassical Profile Portrait.* Washington, D.C.: National Portrait Gallery and the Smithsonian Institution, 1994.

Stern, Malcolm H. *First American Jewish Families: 600 Genealogies, 1654–1988.* Baltimore: Ottenheimer Publishers, 1978.

19

Martha Lampley Levy (Mrs. Samson Levy, Sr.)

(1731–1807)

Charles Balthazar Julien Févret de Saint-Mémin (1770–1852)

1802

Black crayon with white chalk on paper

prepared with pink wash

18 × 11 in.; 45.72 × 27.94 cm

The Jewish Museum,

New York Museum purchase

with funds provided by the Joshua Lowenfish and Rictavia Schiff.

Bequests, 1993–103

Martha Lampley Levy, widow of James Steel Thompson, married Samson Levy, Sr., on November 3, 1752. Martha was a gentile, but Samson, Sr., was a son of Moses Raphael Levy (Plate 1, cat. 1) and his second wife, Grace Mears Levy (cat. 2). After their marriage, the couple attended St. Peter's Church in Philadelphia. Their first child, Nathan, was circumcised according to Jewish law; however their other children, including Samson Levy, Jr.

(cats. 18, 20) and Judge Moses Levy (cat. 23), were raised as Episcopalians. The Levy family was prominent in Philadelphia's social circles and belonged to the Dancing Assembly.

Mrs. Levy wears conservative Philadelphia clothes. She is dressed appropriately for an older woman, and wears a simple Quaker-like bonnet concealing her hair and a crisp white fichu over her plain dark dress.   ELC

References

London, Hannah R. *Miniatures and Silhouettes of Early Jews.* Rutland, Vt.: Charles E. Tuttle Company, 1970.

London, Hannah R. *Portraits of Jews by Gilbert Stuart and Other Early American Artists.* Rutland, Vt.: Charles E. Tuttle Company, 1969.

Miles, Ellen G. *Charles Balthazar Julien Févret de Saint-Mémin.* National Portrait Gallery 1994.

Stern, Malcolm H. *First American Jewish Families: 600 Genealogies, 1654–1988.* Baltimore: Ottenheimer Publishers, 1978.

20

Samson Levy, Jr.

(1761–1831)

Thomas Sully (1783–1872)

1808

Oil on canvas

29 × 24 in.; 73.66 × 60.96 cm

The Montclair Art Museum.

Gift of Mr. Howard A. Van Vleck, 62.14

Samson Levy, Jr. (see also cat. 18), was born in Philadelphia, the son of Samson Levy, Sr., and Martha Lampley Levy (cat. 19); he was also the grandson of the New York notable Moses Raphael Levy (Plate 1, cat. 1) and his second wife, Grace Mears Levy (cat. 2). Samson, Jr., married a gentile, Sarah Coates (cat. 21), as did his father and his brother Judge Moses Levy (cat. 23). Both brothers were lawyers; additionally they belonged to the Dancing Assembly and participated in Philadelphia's social circles. A practicing Christian, Samson did not participate in Jewish communal life.

Thomas Sully has outdone himself in Samson Levy's Romantic portrait. He wears a very high-collared dark coat and high white stock with ruffled front. The sitter appears to have been interrupted while reading; his long slender fingers are delicately placed within a leather-bound volume edged with green. He is seated within a domestic interior; his cardinal upholstered chair perfectly compliments the red shawl in his wife's companion portrait (cat. 21) done by Sully in the same year. The sitter's prominent slender nose and full lips are offset by his sensitive eyes, long luxuriant sideburns and the requisite tousled coiffure. Sully's register states that he began the work on March 1, 1808, and completed it on May 24, 1808—price thirty dollars.

20 *Samson Levy, Jr.*

21 *Sarah Coates Levy (Mrs. Samson Levy, Jr.)*

From this portrait alone it appears that Samson inclined more toward the arts than jurisprudence. But he is remembered for both the intelligence and wit that he brought to the bar.[1] Hannah London refers to him as "an eccentric," conspicuous for his mellifluous speech and brilliance of argument.[2] That said, it is hardly surprising that he was also one of the incorporators of the Pennsylvania Academy of the Fine Arts.   ELC

Notes
1. Henry R. Morais. *The Jews of Philadelphia* (Philadelphia: Levy Type Co., 1894), 39–41.
2. Hannah R. London. *Portraits of Jews by Gilbert Stuart and Other Early American Artists.* Rutland, Vt.: Charles E. Tuttle Company, 1969.

References
Biddle, Edward, and Mantle Fielding. *Life and Works of Thomas Sully,* 1921.
London, Hannah R. *Portraits of Jews by Gilbert Stuart and Other Early American Artists.* Rutland, Vt.: Charles E. Tuttle Company, 1969.
Stern, Malcolm H. *First American Jewish Families: 600 Genealogies, 1654–1988.* Baltimore: Ottenheimer Publishers, 1978.
Wolf, Edwin 2nd, and Maxwell Whiteman. *The History of the Jews of Philadelphia from Colonial Times to the Age of Jackson.* Philadelphia: Jewish Publication Society of America, 1957.

21

Sarah Coates Levy (Mrs. Samson Levy, Jr.)

(1776–1854)
Thomas Sully (1783–1872)
1808
Oil on canvas
29 × 24 in.; 73.66 × 60.96 cm
The Montclair Art Museum.
Gift of Mr. Howard A. Van Vleck, 62.15

Sarah Coates married Samson Levy, Jr. (cats. 18, 20) in Philadelphia on September 5, 1793; their children included Margaret Maria and Sophia, who married Major Dixon Stanbury.

Sully's register specifies that he began Sarah Levy's portrait on May 31, 1803, and completed it on July 10, 1808; the portrait cost thirty dollars. The young Thomas Sully has depicted her in a neoclassical white dress with a scarlet shawl thrown over her left shoulder and cascading down over her arm; as always, Sully has excelled in rendering the white lace mantilla that covers her dark hair.

The thirty-two-year-old woman is seated on a terrace reading a green leather-bound book: behind her, at left, a large classical urn is placed on an architectural plinth; at right, an early-morning landscape is rendered in a sketchy manner. The graceful sitter in a modest and contemplative mood does not gaze outwardly at the viewer, but, rather, her eyes appear directed beyond our world. Thomas Sully's classical references, magnificent painterly landscape setting, as well as the sitter's contemplative pose are characteristics that he will develop as he matures and that will be present in many of his masterworks.   ELC

References
Biddle, Edward, and Mantle Fielding. *Life and Works of Thomas Sully*, 1921.
London, Hannah R. *Portraits of Jews by Gilbert Stuart and Other Early American Artists.* Rutland, Vt.: Charles E. Tuttle Company, 1969.
Stern, Malcolm H. *First American Jewish Families: 600 Genealogies, 1654–1988.* Baltimore: Ottenheimer Publishers, 1978.
Wolf, Edwin 2nd, and Maxwell Whiteman. *The History of the Jews of Philadelphia from Colonial Times to the Age of Jackson.* Philadelphia: Jewish Publication Society of America, 1957.

22

Mary Pearce Levy (Mrs. Moses Levy)

(1756–1826)
Charles Willson Peale (1741–1827)
Philadelphia, 1808
Oil on paper, mounted on canvas
28 × 23 ½ in.; 71.12 × 59.69 cm
The Montclair Art Museum
Museum purchase, 65.43

Mary Pearce, a gentile, was born at "Poplar Neck" in Cecil County, Maryland. She married Judge Moses Levy (cat. 23), a son of Samson Levy, Sr., and descendant of Moses Raphael Levy of New York (cat. 1), on June 26, 1791; their children included Henrietta (cat. 24) and Martha Mary Ann (cat. 25), who married John Jones Milligan. Many of the Levy portraits in the exhibition have descended from Martha Levy Milligan down to her granddaughter Elise Milligan Bancroft.

For many years this problematic portrait was attributed to Rembrandt Peale. After he completed Judge Levy's portrait, the thirty-year-old son of Charles Willson Peale embarked upon two additional portraits—one of Mrs. Moses Levy and the other of Elizabeth Bordley—while awaiting a ship to take him to France. Presently from Baltimore came news of a ship soon to set sail for Europe; the young man promptly departed, leaving his sixty-seven-year-old father to complete his unfinished works. The Bordley was almost completed and presented no difficulty; however, Mrs. Levy's portrait was barely started and Charles Willson Peale adamantly insisted upon a new beginning. After delicate negotiations, Judge and Mrs. Levy agreed. Charles Coleman Sellers, the Charles Willson Peale scholar, confirms this attribution in a letter to the Montclair Art Museum on September 26, 1971.[1]

In her portrait, Mrs. Levy is seated in a red chair gazing directly at the viewer. She is dressed in black satin, her décolletage modestly covered and secured with a tiny jeweled pin. She also wears a lace covering on her head and long white gloves; she holds a fan in her right hand.

The Levys' pendant portraits offer a rare but not unique opportunity to compare the styles of the father and son: the son soon to assume a colorist style in France, and the father trying to paint like the son while ameliorating the situation with the Levys. Upon completion the father wrote to the son in France, reporting that "the family are highly pleased with it."[2] The negotiated price was one hundred dollars.   ELC

Notes
1. Montclair Art Museum, Montclair, New Jersey, archival records.
2. Charles Willson Peale to Rembrandt Peale, *In Pursuit of Fame: Rembrandt Peale, 1778–1860* (Seattle and Washington, D.C.: University of Washington Press for the National Portrait Gallery, 1992).

References
London, Hannah R. *Portraits of Jews by Gilbert Stuart and Other Early American Artists.* Rutland, Vt.: Charles E. Tuttle Company, 1969.
Miller, Lillian B. *In Pursuit of Fame: Rembrandt Peale, 1778–1860.* Seattle and Washington, D.C.: University of Washington Press for the National Portrait Gallery, 1992.
Stern, Malcolm H. *First American Jewish Families: 600 Genealogies, 1654–1988.* Baltimore: Ottenheimer Publishers, 1960, 1978.

23

Judge Moses Levy

(1756–1826)
Rembrandt Peale (1778–1860)
Philadelphia, 1820
Oil on canvas
29 × 24 ½ in.; 73.66 × 62.23 cm
The Montclair Art Museum
Museum purchase, 60.20

Both Judge Moses Levy and his brother, Samson Levy, Jr. (cats. 18, 20) were born in Philadelphia, the sons of Samson Levy, Sr., and Martha Lampley Levy (cat. 19); similarly they were the grandsons of Moses Levy (Plate 1, cat. 1) and his second wife, Grace Mears (cat. 2), founders of a branch of the Levy dynasty in America. Like his father and brother, he married a gentile, Mary Pearce (cat. 22). Both brothers were prominent members of the legal, social, and cultural circles in Philadelphia.

In this portrait the Judge sits with his arm casually draped over the back of his chair and holds a solitary glove in his gloved hand; he wears the ubiquitous dark suit with white stock and has a draped red curtain in the background. Unfortunately the lower section of his body is not successful but it is of no consequence because Rembrandt Peale has made a remarkable character

22 *Mary Pearce Levy (Mrs. Moses Levy)*

23 *Judge Moses Levy*

study of the noble white-haired Judge with his careworn face set with intense gray eyes; herein lies his biography.

At the time of this portrait Judge Levy was a prominent magistrate in Philadelphia and a trustee of the University of Pennsylvania; later he would become a member of the Pennsylvania Legislature. He had matriculated at the fledgling University of Pennsylvania when it was still the Academy and College of Philadelphia, and was admitted to the bar in 1778. In his youth an ardent Jeffersonian Democrat, he later became a conservative Federalist. Judge Levy was a practicing Episcopalian; but he was not immune to being attacked as a Jew by his political enemies. For example, after Moses Levy successfully defended Dr. Benjamin Rush in a libel suit against the English journalist William Cobbett at the turn of the century, Cobbett's New York journal, *The Rush-Light,* continued to revile Moses Levy as "Levi the Jew."[1]

Active in the cultural life of Philadelphia, Judge Levy was one of the first twelve directors of the Pennsylvania Academy of Fine Arts, which was the first school in the country founded, in 1805, to train American artists. No doubt the selection of Rembrandt Peale for his portrait in 1808, the same year that Samson Levy, Jr., commissioned his portraits (see cats. 20, 21) from Thomas Sully,

would have been enthusiastically endorsed by the Peale patriarch, Charles Willson Peale.   ELC

Note
1 Edwin Wolf 2nd, and Maxwell Whiteman. *The History of the Jews of Philadelphia from Colonial Times to the Age of Jackson* (Philadelphia: Jewish Publication Society of America, 1957), 208–9, 442.

References
London, Hannah R. *Portraits of Jews by Gilbert Stuart and Other Early American Artists.* Rutland, Vt.: Charles E. Tuttle Company, 1969. Illus. p. 109.
Miller, Lillian B. *In Pursuit of Fame: Rembrandt Peale, 1778–1860.* Seattle and Washington, D.C.: University of Washington Press for the National Portrait Gallery, 1992.
Stern, Malcolm H. *First American Jewish Families: 600 Genealogies 1654–1988.* Baltimore: Ottenheimer Publishers, 1978.

24 *Henrietta Levy*

painted by Ralph Earl during his years in England. *Sophia Drake* (Ralph Earl, 1784, Count de Salis, Switzerland) is also dressed in a simple gown with youthful décolletage and long sleeves. Both educated young women (aged eighteen and nineteen), Henrietta Levy and Sophia Drake are seated in the landscape under a spreading tree, each holding a book in her hand. Unlike Sophia, Henrietta does not gaze directly at the viewer but rather seems lost in her own thoughts.

Lovely young women are often portrayed in nature's nurturing landscape for a host of attributive reasons. The age-old source of this convention of portraiture can be traced back to antiquity and images of the beautiful Roman Goddess, Flora; similarly, the mature woman is frequently portrayed as a Roman Goddess who represents Mother Earth and her fecundity.

ELC

Note
1. Edward Biddle, and Mantle Fielding. Life and Works of Thomas Sully, 1921, p. 209.

References
Biddle, Edward, and Mantle Fielding. *Life and Works of Thomas Sully,* 1921.
London, Hannah R. *Portraits of Jews by Gilbert Stuart and Other Early American Artists.* Rutland, Vt.: Charles E. Tuttle Company, 1969.

24
Henrietta Levy
(1793–1889)
Thomas Sully (1783–1872)
1810
Oil on panel
22 ¾ × 18 ¼ in.; 57.79 × 46.36 cm
Indiana University Art Museum.
The Morton and Marie Bradley Memorial Collection

25
Martha Levy at the Spinet
(1798–1889)
Thomas Sully (1783–1872)
1810
Oil on panel
23 ¹⁄₁₆ × 18 ¼ in.; 58.58 × 46.36 cm
Indiana University Art Museum.
The Morton and Marie Bradley
Memorial Collection

The birth of Henrietta Levy is not registered in Malcolm H. Stern's impressive genealogy; his record of Christian births is not infallible. Nonetheless the provenance of this work is secure because it has descended, along with the pendant of her sister, Martha Levy (cat. 25), in the Levy, Milligan, and Bancroft families. Although a great-granddaughter of Moses Raphael Levy (Plate 1, cat. 1), she was born a Christian, the granddaughter of Martha Lampley Levy (cat. 19) and the daughter of Judge Moses Levy (cat. 23) and Mary Pearce Levy (cat. 22); she was also the niece of Samson Levy, Jr. (cats. 18, 20).

Thomas Sully painted the sisters' portraits, still in their original frames, in 1810; according to Edward Biddle and Mantle Fielding, Henrietta is "sitting under a spreading tree and holds a book in her hand,… dressed in pale apricot."[1] The likely sources for the portraits of the Levy sisters are the pendant portraits of two British sisters, Sophia Drake and Mary Ann Drake, that are typical of the traditions of British portraiture; the works were

Martha Levy was born in Philadelphia and married John Jones Milligan there in 1820. Her granddaughter Elise Milligan Bancroft (Mrs. Robert Hale Bancroft) inherited many Levy portraits that entered the art market from her estate. Martha was born Episcopalian, the granddaughter of Martha Lampley Levy (cat. 19), and the daughter of Judge Moses Levy (cat. 23) and Mary Pearce Levy (cat. 22); she was also the sister of Henrietta Levy (cat. 24), the niece of Samson Levy, Jr. (cats. 18, 20), and the great-granddaughter of the Levy patriarch, Moses Raphael Levy (Plate 1, cat. 1), and his wife Grace Mears Levy (cat. 2).

According to Thomas Sully's register, the painting was begun on November 11, 1810, and was finished on December 16, 1810; the price was sixty dollars. The most probable source for this sibling pendant portrait was Ralph Earl's pendants of two British sisters: one is depicted in a simple gown in a landscape (cat. 24); the other is more formally attired and placed within a domestic

25   *Martha Levy at the Spinet*

interior near a keyboard instrument. *Mary Ann Drake* (Ralph Earl, 1783, Count de Salis, Switzerland), is indeed elegantly attired and seated near an elaborate harpsichord and a pembroke table. According to Edward Biddle and Mantle Fielding, Martha Levy is "standing by a spinet turning leaves of a music book."[1] Both paintings convey the image of a cultivated and elegant young woman dressed in the fashion of the day. Like Mary Ann Drake, twelve-year-old Martha Levy is formally dressed in a long gown; both talented young women wear eye-catching rose-pink sashes at the waist that terminate in a deep elaborate fringe.   ELC

Note
1. Edward Biddle and Mantle Fielding. *Life and Works of Thomas Sully,* 1921, p. 209.

References
Biddle, Edward, and Mantle Fielding. *Life and Works of Thomas Sully,* 1921.
London, Hannah R. *Portraits of Jews by Gilbert Stuart and Other Early American Artists.* Rutland, Vt.: Charles E. Tuttle Company, 1969.
Stern, Malcolm H. *First American Jewish Families: 600 Genealogies, 1654–1988.* Baltimore: Ottenheimer Publishers, 1978.

26

Rebecca Myring Everette (Mrs. Thomas Everette) (1787–1833) *and Her Children* (*Mary Augusta, Rebecca, John, Thomas, Jr., and Joseph Myring Everette*)

Joshua Johnson (active c. 1796–c. 1824)
Baltimore, Maryland, 1818
Oil on canvas
Framed: 38 ⅞ × 55 ³⁄₁₆ in.; 98.74 × 140.18 cm
The Maryland Historical Society.
Bequest of Miss Mary Augusta Clarke

Joshua Johnson, the artist of this ambitious composition, is recorded as a portrait painter and "Free Householder of Colour" in the 1816/1817 Baltimore city directory. Probably from the West Indies, he is believed to have been a slave or a servant before pursuing portrait painting as a profession. On December 10, 1798, Johnson placed the first known advertisement for his services in the Baltimore *Intelligencer*, identifying himself as a "self-taught genius, deriving from nature and industry his knowledge of the Art." Although he claimed to be self-educated, Johnson has been linked historically and stylistically to the Peale family of artists who were active in Baltimore and Philadelphia during this period, including Charles Willson Peale (1741–1827), his son Rembrandt (1778–1860), and his nephew Charles Peale Polk (1767–1822).

One of only five recorded complex group portraits Johnson executed during his known period of painting activity in Baltimore—between the years 1796 and 1825—this composition is ambitious in its representation of six family members on one canvas. Rebecca Myring Everette is depicted as a proud mother surrounded by her five children. A high-style, neoclassically inspired sofa of the Federal era, decorated with gleaming brass upholstery tacks, defines the family's domestic environment. Residents of Baltimore, Mrs. Everette, her husband, and family lived at 179 and 224 Baltimore Street during the years between the couple's marriage in 1802 and 1818. Mr. Everette worked as a prosperous hardware retailer and umbrella manufacturer until his death in about 1818, just before this painting was rendered. In Johnson's other single-canvas portraits documenting the familial relationships of parents and offspring, the father is depicted seated on a sofa with his sons while his wife is depicted in her gender-determined position with the couple's daughters. However, Mrs. Everette's new status as a widow is suggested silently in this work by her husband's absence from the sofa that terminates at some point outside the composition on the right.

While their siblings hold objects commonly found in Johnson's portraits of children, such as the rose and strawberries, Thomas, Jr., and his brother Joseph Myring are shown with books, attributes of middle-class respectability, suggesting that

26 *Rebecca Myring Everette (Mrs. Thomas Everette) and Her Children*

they are literate and thus probably schooled in religion. Upon her death in 1833, Mrs. Everette provided for the disposal of a number of family likenesses, including this group portrait. In her will, she recorded that her daughter Mary Augusta would receive "the large Family painting of my self [sic] and 5 children painted by J Johnson in 1818 ... and a Pocket Bible with a pale yellow cover." In fact, Mrs. Everette bequeathed a painting and a Bible to each of her five children, ensuring that even after her death they would be mindful of their family heritage and of the religious obligations that presumably she had taught them in her domestic role as moral arbiter of the home.   CEM

References
Caldwell, John, and Oswaldo Rodriguez Roque et al. *American Paintings in the Metropolitan Museum of Art,* Vol. 1: 197–98. New York: Princeton University Press and The Metropolitan Museum of Art, 1994.
Chotner, Deborah. *American Naive Paintings: The Collections of the National Gallery of Art Systematic Catalogue.* Washington, D.C.: Cambridge University Press for The National Gallery of Art, 1992.
Object file for Joshua Johnson. *Portrait of Mrs. Thomas Everette and Her Children.* Courtesy Jeannine A. Disviscour, Maryland Historical Society, Baltimore.
Rumford, Beatrix T., ed. *American Folk Portraits: Paintings and Drawings from the Abby Aldrich Rockefeller Folk Art Center.* Boston: New York Graphic Society for the Colonial Williamsburg Foundation, 1981.
Weekley, Carolyn J., and Stiles Tuttle Colwill et al. *Joshua Johnson: Freeman and Early American Portrait Painter.* Williamsburg, Va., and Baltimore, Md.: The Colonial Williamsburg Foundation and The Maryland Historical Society, 1987. Illus. 77, p. 161.

27

Adolphus Simeon Solomons (1826–1910) *and Mary Jane Solomons* (1818–1905)

Artist unknown
New York, 1828
Oil on canvas
57 × 43 ⅛ in.; 144.8 × 110.9 cm
American Jewish Historical Society, Waltham,
Massachusetts and New York, New York.
Bequest of Irma P. Sellars

In an 1851 letter to Adolphus Solomons, his fiancée, Rachel Seixas Phillips, wrote of a Sabbath evening dinner that she spent with his family: "I took your picture with me on Friday evening. I told them that I would not bring it again, for as soon as they looked at it, they all began to cry as if it had been some dreadful looking object, and you are not, for to me you are the best looking man that I know: ahem, pull up your shirt collar after that compliment."[1] Adolphus's shirt collar would need constant adjustments in the years to come, as he assumed a leading role as a politician, businessman, and social activist in Washington D.C.

The son of journalist John Solomons and Julia Levy Solomons and a great-grandson of Moses Raphael Levy (Plate 1, cat. 1), Adolphus spent the first thirty-three years of his life in New York, where he met and married Rachel Seixas Phillips. Adolphus and Rachel moved their family of four daughters to Washington, D.C., in 1859, where he would make significant contributions to his country, his religion, and his family (four more daughters!). He helped Clara Barton found the American Red Cross, served as general agent of the Baron de Hirsch fund, act-ed as a special agent for the census office that compiled statistics regarding Jewish citizens, and he promoted fine arts in the Washington community through the gallery and photography studio at his firm, Philips and Solomons, Stationer.[2]

Adolphus (see also cat. 28) is pictured here at nineteen months of age, with his older sister Mary Jane, aged nine. This image of Mary Jane is one of the only pieces of evidence that exists regarding her life. At the center of the composition, she appears calm and poised, with a countenance older than her years. With her

27 *Adolphus Simeon Solomons and Mary Jane Solomons*

left hand, she gestures toward the light, the river, and the mountains that form the dramatic dark landscape of this portrait. Her right hand is entwined with her brother's. Adolphus is a vision of bouncing youth beside his sister's statuesque composure. The children both wear a double strand of coral beads, which was a common children's amulet meant for protection against the evil eye.   JWZ

Notes

1. Rachel Seixas Phillips to Adolphus Simeon Solomons, 1851, Adolphus Simeon Solomon Papers, American Jewish Historical Society, Waltham, Mass.

2. The firm of Philips and Solomons took the last photograph of President Lincoln before his assassination. For a discussion of the activities of the firm, see Robert Shosteck and Samuel H. Holland. "Adolphus Simeon Solomons: His Washington Years." *The Record: Publications of the Jewish Historical Society of Greater Washington* 5, 1 (May 1970): 13.

References

Kleeblatt, Norman L., and Gerard C. Wertkin, eds. *The Jewish Heritage in American Folk Art.* Exhibition catalogue. The Jewish Museum and the Museum of American Folk Art. New York: Universe Books, 1984. Illus., p. 46.

Marcus. Jacob Rader, ed. *Memoirs of American Jews: 1775–1865.* Vol. 3. Philadelphia: The Jewish Publication Society, 1956, 349–56.

Marshall, Louis. "Adolphus Simeon Solomons: Necrology." *Publications of the American Jewish Historical Society* 20 (1911): 166–70.

28 *Adolphus Simeon Solomons*

28

Adolphus Simeon Solomons

(1826–1910)
Artist unknown
New York, c. 1828
Miniature; watercolor
2 ¾ × 2 in.; 6.99 × 5.08 cm
American Jewish Historical Society, Waltham, Massachusetts, and New York, New York.
Bequest of Captain N. Taylor Phillips

Adolphus Simeon Solomons helped, literally, to define what it meant to be a Jew in America. In 1872, Solomons initiated correspondence with both Webster's Dictionary and Worcester's Dictionary regarding the definition of the word "Jew." He expressed his dissatisfaction with the word's negative connotation

published by both firms in their dictionaries: both publications associated the word with cheating. In response to Adolphus's objections, both dictionaries altered their definitions to reflect the literal religious and ethnic meaning of the term rather than its pejorative usage.[1]

Solomons continued to define Judaism on his own terms while a resident in Washington, D.C. Troubled by the fact that there was no Sephardic synagogue in the nation's capital, Solomons borrowed an eternal light from New York's Congregation Shearith Israel, where he was a member for thirty-three years. The eternal light illuminated Sabbath services at the Solomons' home on K Street for as many years as they lived in Washington.[2]

Solomons is portrayed here as a young boy, one of four children born to John and Julia Levy Solomons. His older sister, Mary Jane, appears with him in a full-size portrait (cat. 27).[3] Adolphus Simeon is pictured here in the same attire that he is wearing in that full-size portrait, although his pose in this miniature is more static and conventional than in the painting, where the energetic Adolphus appears ready to jump off the canvas.　　JWZ

Notes

1. Adolphus Simeon Solomons to Worcester's Dictionary of Boston, 1872, and to Webster's Dictionary, 1872. Adolphus Simeon Solomons Papers, American Jewish Historical Society, Waltham, Mass.

2. Robert Shosteck and Samuel H. Holland, "Adolphus Simeon Solomons: His Washington Years." *The Record: Publications of the Jewish Historical Society of Greater Washington* 5, no. 1 (May 1970): 30. After the death of Adolphus's youngest daughter, the eternal light was returned to Shearith Israel, where it now hangs in a chapel dedicated to Judaica from the original Mill Street synagogue.

3. The first-born Solomons son died in infancy; no images of his younger brother Wellington are known to exist.

References

London, Hannah R. *Miniatures of Early American Jews,* Springfield, Mass.: The Pond-Ekberg Company, 1953. Illus. p. 109.

Marcus, Jacob Rader, ed. *Memoirs of American Jews: 1775–1865,* Vol. 3. Philadelphia: Jewish Publication Society of America, 1956, 349–56.

Marshall, Louis. "Adolphus Simeon Solomons: Necrology." *Publications of the American Jewish Historical Society* 20 (1911): 166–70.

29

Jacob Rodriguez Rivera

(1717–1789)
Attributed to Gilbert Stuart (1754–1828)
Newport, 1774
Oil on canvas
34 ½ × 27 ¼ in.; 87.63 × 69.22 cm
Redwood Library and Athenaeum

Jacob Rodriguez Rivera arrived in Newport in about 1745, probably as a refugee from the Portuguese Inquisition. A prominent leader among the handful of Sephardic families in Newport, he

29   *Jacob Rodriguez Rivera*

if one looks closely, Jacob's right hand appears to be holding a dark hat. This is an exception in the exhibition; very few Jewish gentlemen are depicted with hats in interior settings.

The portrait was given to Redwood Library, where Jacob Rivera was made a member on September 27, 1758. It was commissioned by the wealthy merchant Samuel Rodman, who had begun his career in Rivera's counting-house noted for its innovative methods. The canvas was presented to the Redwood Library by Rodman's great-granddaughters.   ELC

Note
1. Morris A. Gutstein. "The Jews of Newport in Pre-Revolutionary Days." *Touro Synagogue of Congregation Shearith Israel*. (Newport, Rhode Island: The Friends of Touro Synagogue, 1948), p. 20.

Reference
London, Hannah R. *Portraits of Jews by Gilbert Stuart and Other American Artists*. Rutland, Vt.: Charles E. Tuttle Company, 1969.

30
Sarah Rivera Lopez (Mrs. Aaron Lopez) (1747–1840)
and Her Son Joshua Lopez (1768–1845)
Gilbert Stuart (1754–1828)
1775
Oil on canvas
26 × 21 ½ × 21 ½ in.; 66.04 × 54.61 cm
The Detroit Institute of Arts.
Gift of Dexter M. Ferry, Jr.

was one of three congregation members who owned the land upon which the Touro Synagogue was built; he and Aaron Lopez had the honor of laying the first stones.[1] He also prospered in Newport's two primary businesses—the triangular trade and whaling. From the whale's oil a waxy white substance known as spermaceti was extracted for candle making, a thriving industry that Jacob Rivera introduced to Newport. One of his business associates, the renowned "merchant prince" Aaron Lopez, married his daughter Sarah Rivera (cat. 30).

The Rivera portrait, earlier attributed to Edward Savage, is a very rare, early work by the Rhode Island-born Gilbert Stuart. The twenty-one-year-old artist had difficulty with the crudely rendered sitter's body; the left arm is oddly foreshortened and one shoulder appears larger than the other. As Hannah London has remarked, Jacob has a "prominent nose and protruding lower lip"; his splendid face with its dark, somewhat florid complexion is clean-shaven. The head is turned so that he gazes out at the viewer with piercing brown eyes. The sitter wears a dark suit, gray wig, white stock, and cuffs; no waistcoat is visible. His body is turned three-quarters to the picture plane in the chair with his left arm inserted into his coat. Upon minute inspection, his right arm appears to rest upon a plinth that holds a classical vase; and,

Sarah Rivera Lopez, daughter of Jacob Rodriguez Rivera (cat. 29) and Hannah Pimental Sasportas, lived among the twenty wealthy Sephardic families of Newport, Rhode Island. She married one of her father's employees, Aaron Lopez (1731–1782), who became a renowned and wealthy international trader, known as the "merchant prince" of Newport. Lopez owned thirty ships and transported rum, molasses, and African slaves as well as spermaceti candles, hardware, furniture, and assorted provisions. Aaron shared his good fortune among the Newport community, contributing to the founding of the Touro Synagogue and the Redwood Library. Aaron Lopez had nine children by each of his two wives; Aaron's son Joshua, pictured here, would marry the only daughter of Isaac Touro, the first spiritual leader of the congregation

This delightful portrait of a youthful mother and son was first attributed to the Scottish artist Cosmo Alexander (1724–1772), who was one of Gilbert Stuart's first teachers in Newport. After some instruction, Cosmo took the fifteen-year-old Stuart—born in Rhode Island of a Scottish mill operator—abroad for further instruction. But Cosmo died in Edinburgh, leaving the young man destitute and forced to work his way back to Newport as a sailor.

30 *Sarah Rivera Lopez and Her Son Joshua Lopez*

The rare double portrait was painted after Stuart's return to Newport.

Few examples of Stuart's early works exist; at the Redwood Library in Newport, *Mrs. John Bannister and Her Son* bears a strong resemblance to this work; both young women have identical faces except for their distinctive complexions. Both double portraits portray seated mothers with their young sons standing beside them in a manner approximating an English mezzotint. Mrs. Lopez wears her hair tightly pulled back with Portuguese lace prominently displayed at the neckline and in her small mantilla. Both boys, dressed as miniature adults—which was the custom at the time—wear waistcoats and shirts; young Lopez has a prominent dark neck scarf tied in a bow. Although the Lopez double portrait, most probably done before Stuart reached twenty years of age, bears little resemblance to Gilbert Stuart's great mature works, it provides an exciting, rare glimpse of the artist's early style.   ELC

References
London, Hannah R. *Portraits of Jews by Gilbert Stuart and Other Early American Artists.* Rutland, Vt.: Charles E. Tuttle Company, 1969.
McLanathan, Richard. *Gilbert Stuart.* New York: Harry N. Abrams, for The National Museum of American Art, Smithsonian Institution, 1986.
Stern, Malcolm H. *First American Jewish Families; 600 Genealogies, 1654–1988.* Baltimore: Ottenheimer Publishers, 1978.

31
Jacob da Silva Solis

(1780–1829)
Artist unknown
Date unknown
Oil on canvas
Framed: 31 × 26 in.; 78.74 × 66.04 cm
Collection of Emily da Silva Solis Nathan

In 1760 the House of Turin and Villa Real was threatened by extinction; according to family tradition, the grandfather of Jacob da Silva Solis was offered the succession to the line with the understanding that he must embrace the Catholic faith. When he declined, the Portuguese ambassador, himself descended from Conversos, exclaimed, "You fool! It is one of the greatest dignities of Europe." Whereupon Jacob da Silva Solis replied, "Not for the whole of Europe would I forsake my faith and neither would my son Solomon."[1]

Jacob da Silva Solis was born into this distinguished Sephardic family in London in 1780 and died in New York City in 1829. He was the son of Solomon da Silva Solis and Benvenida da Isaac Henriques Valentine, and a descendant of Solomon da Silva Solis

31 *Jacob da Silva Solis*

32 *Charity Hays Solis (Mrs. Jacob da Silva Solis)*　　　33 *Jacob da Silva Solis*

and Donna Isabel da Fonseca (a daughter of the Marquis of Turin and Count of Villa Real and Monterey). Both his parents were refugees of the Inquisition who were married as Jews in Amsterdam. Jacob arrived in America in 1803 and eight years later married Charity, daughter of David Hays and granddaughter of Jacob Hays, who had arrived in America from Holland. The Hays family—of Ashkenazic origin, probably from Central Europe and Yiddish-speaking—were one of the oldest and most prominent families in colonial Westchester.

Despite Jacob da Silva Solis's aristocratic lineage, after his marriage to Charity Hays in 1811 he lived and worked within the Jewish community of rural Westchester, and was certified as a ritual slaughterer, or *shochet*; he also traveled to Wilmington, Delaware, and New Orleans, where he lived and worked for a time. A visionary philanthropist, Jacob da Silva Solis is remembered for his plan to set up a vocational school to educate Jewish orphans. While the plan essentially failed in his lifetime, it laid the foundations for future Jewish educational and philanthropic organizations that would flourish to the present time.

Today Jacob da Silva Solis's portrait still remains within his family; one of Jacob da Silva Solis's seven children married a Nathan, and the portrait has descended in that family. Little is known about the artist and the portrait itself; but the Frick Art Reference Library has stated that it might be of the American School and dated 1801 to 1850.　　　　　　　　　　　ELC

Note
1. Nathan Family Papers, Collection of Emily da Silva Solis Nathan.

References
Shargel, Baila R., and Harold L. Drimmer. *The Jews of Westchester: A Social History.* New York: Purple Mountain Press, 1994.
Stern, Malcolm H. *First American Jewish Families: 600 Genealogies, 1654–1988.* Baltimore: Ottenheimer Publishers, 1978.

32
Charity Hays Solis (Mrs. Jacob da Silva Solis)
(1782–1839)
Artist unknown
c. 1811
Miniature; oil on paper
5 × 4 in.; 12.5 × 10 cm
Collection of Joan Sturhahn

Charity Hays belonged to "Westchester's most durable family."[1] Of Ashkenazic origin and probably Yiddish-speaking, her grandfather, Jacob Hays, settled in the village of Rye upon his arrival in America from Holland in 1721, and counted Moses Raphael Levy (Plate 1, cat. 1), who owned a summer property nearby, among his neighbors. The Hays family prospered as year-round residents in rural Westchester county. Charity grew up on a farm in Bedford, New York, where her father, David, ran a store, and contributed to the family business, an inn and tavern. During the Revolutionary War, the village of Bedford was burned by the Tories; and after the war, in 1796, David Hays settled on a homestead in nearby Mt. Pleasant and became a farmer.[2] The family depended on Shearith Israel for religious community, "commuting" to New York City for life-cycle events and festivals, although after the War—during which Shearith Israel was abandoned—the family were no longer members.

On April 24, 1811, Charity married Jacob da Silva Solis (cats. 31, 33). Together the couple had seven children before Jacob's untimely death in 1829. Although her husband regularly traveled in search of economic opportunity, Charity and the children remained in Westchester, except for a brief stint in Wilmington, Delaware, where Jacob managed a store from 1814 to 1821.

Charity Hays Solis is distinguished here by her elaborate hat, the ribbons of which cascade down the front of her collar and dress. Her costume demonstrates that although Charity was removed from urban life, she was not removed from fashion.

JWZ

Notes
1. Harold R. Drimmer and Baila R. Shargel. *The Jews of Westchester: A Social History* (New York: Purple Mountain Press, 1994), pp. 13, 14, 50.
2. Ibid., p. 49.

References
Shargel, Baila R., and Harold R. Drimmer. *The Jews of Westchester: A Social History.* New York: Purple Mountain Press, 1994. Illus. p. 53.
Sturhahn, Joan. *Carvalho: Portrait of a Forgotten American.* Merrick. New York: Richwood Publishing Company, 1976. Illus. p. 38.

33

Jacob da Silva Solis

(1780–1829)

Artist unknown

c. 1811

Miniature; oil on paper

5 × 4 in.; 12.5 × 10 cm

Collection of Joan Sturhahn

Jacob da Silva Solis promoted the establishment of Jewish institutions in the outpost communities of the early Federal Republic. A native of London's Sephardic Jewish community, Solis sailed for America in 1803. He established himself first in New York, where he joined Shearith Israel and met his future bride, Charity Hays (cat. 32). Jacob and Charity were married in April of 1811 in Mt. Pleasant, New York, site of the Hays homestead.

Living in rural Westchester County with his bride made the procurement of kosher meat a challenge. Therefore Solis obtained training as a ritual slaughterer, or *shochet*, so as to provide kosher meat for his family. Fifteen years later, in 1826, when Solis journeyed to New Orleans in search of economic opportunity, a similar culinary dilemma occurred. He found himself in New Orleans during Passover, with no source of matzah. Family lore attests that Solis ground his own meal for matzah, and that this conundrum inspired him to organize a Jewish community in New Orleans. The synagogue that resulted from Solis's efforts, Shanarai-Chasset (Gates of Mercy), recalled him with fondness, even though he did not remain in the New Orleans community beyond 1827. Upon his death, the congregation wrote a letter of condolence to his widow stating that the officers of the congregation would wear crepe on their left arm for thirty days in memory of their founder.[1]

In addition to his activities in New Orleans, Solis contributed to the organization of Cincinnati congregation Bene Israel, and proposed the establishment of a Jewish vocational school in Westchester County. The vocational school was among the first proposals in America for establishing a Jewish institution independent of a synagogue. Although the plan was not realized in Jacob's lifetime, his son, Solomon, would implement his father's plan by establishing a Hebrew Education Society in Philadelphia in 1848.

Like his wife, Jacob is fashionably attired in this portrait, in which his high-collared shirt meets his stylishly long sideburns.

JWZ

Note
1 A. Solomons, Secretary Pro Temp. of the congregation, to Charity Hays Solis, February 17, 1830, Hays Family Papers, Collection of the American Jewish Historical Society, Waltham, Mass.

References
Korn, Bertram Wallace. *The Early Jews of New Orleans.* Waltham, Mass.: The American Jewish Historical Society, 1969.
Shargel, Baila R., and Drimmer, Harold R. *The Jews of Westchester: A Social History.* New York: Purple Mountain Press, 1994. Illus. p. 53.
Solis-Cohen, Jacob Jr. "Jacob S. Solis: Traveling Advocate of American Judaism." *American Jewish Historical Quarterly* 52: 310–19.
Sturhahn, Joan. *Carvalho: Portrait of a Forgotten American.* Merrick. New York: Richwood Publishing Company, 1976. Illus. p. 38.

34

Samuel Hays

(1764–1838)

James Sharples (c. 1751–1811)

1802

Pastel on paper

9 × 7 in.; 22.86 × 17.78 cm

Courtesy of the Kenneth and Sandra Malamed Trust, Los Angeles, and Bernard and S. Dean Levy, Inc.

For many years the extraordinary portraits of James Sharples could be viewed in Philadelphia's Old State House collection. The British artist, an exhibitor at the Royal Academy, posed the elite of America's Federalist period either in profile or in three-quarter view; he usually rendered the portraits in pastel on thick gray paper. His drawing supports were carefully prepared and smoothed to a faultless finish that raised the pastel drawings to the quality of paintings. The artist favored the cabinet-sized piece. Sharples and his family arrived in America in 1793 and remained here for eight years; primarily he worked as an itinerant artist in the New York and Philadelphia areas.

Samuel Hays, grandson of Jechiel Hays who had arrived in America from Holland, lived in Philadelphia, traveled in prominent circles there, and was involved in the East India trade. He had served as an apprentice to the noted Revolutionary financier Haym Salomon before entering business himself. In 1805 Samuel became the first Jewish member of the Philadelphia Chamber of Commerce trade claims committee, which met monthly to settle trade disputes by arbitration.[1] He was also a founding member of Congregation Mikveh Israel in 1782 and later a trustee.

In Philadelphia on December 10, 1793, Samuel married into the prominent Gratz family. His bride, Richea Gratz, was the daughter of Michael Gratz (cat. 54) and Miriam Simon Gratz; she was also the sister of Rebecca Gratz (Plate 7, cats. 39 and 40) and Rachel Gratz Etting (cat. 73). The couple produced ten surviving children.

Dr. Isaac Minis Hays, one of their many grandchildren, maintained an important collection of Gratz family portraits including this unique Sharples pastel which was exhibited at the Tenth Annual Exhibition of Miniatures at the Pennsylvania Academy of the Fine Arts in 1911.   ELC

Note
1. Edwin Wolf 2nd, and Maxwell Whiteman. *The History of the Jews of Philadelphia from Colonial Times to the Age of Jackson* (Philadelphia: Jewish Publication Society of America, 1957), p. 340.

References
London, Hannah R. *Portraits of Jews by Gilbert Stuart and Other Early American Artists* Rutland, Vt.: Charles E. Tuttle Company, 1969.
Stern, Malcolm H. *First American Jewish Families: 600 Genealogies, 1654–1988* Baltimore: Ottenheimer Publishers, 1978.

35
Leonard Bleecker
(1753–1844)
James Sharples (c. 1751–1811)
New York, 1795
Pastel drawing on paper
9 ¼ × 7 ⅜ in.; 23.50 × 18.73 cm
The New-York Historical Society.
Bequest of Mrs. Elizabeth B. Knight

Major Leonard Bleecker was an original member at the founding in 1783 of the Society of the Cincinnati, an elite organization of General George Washington's officers. Part of Lafayette's forces, he was witness to the surrender of Cornwallis at the battle of Yorktown and fought in the battles of Trenton, Princeton, and Long Island. After his military service was completed, he spent the rest of his life serving his fellow man as a philanthropist devoted to organizations of a religious and benevolent nature.

Leonard Bleecker's worldliness, yet gentle kindness, is convincingly depicted in this outstanding pastel profile by James Sharples. Smaller than life-size, it is of cabinet size, a specialty of Sharples, one of the finest pastel artists in America.   ELC

Reference
Portraits in the New-York Historical Society. New Haven: Yale University Press, 1974.

34   *Samuel Hays*

35   *Leonard Bleecker*

36
Aaron Rodriguez Rivera
(1793–1838)
Artist unknown
1825/30
Miniature; watercolor on parchment
3 ½ × 2 ½ in.; 8.89 × 6.35 cm
The Jewish Museum, New York, 8–79

36   Aaron Rodriguez Rivera

In this singular situation an important portrait, owned by The Jewish Museum, speaks eloquently for itself. According to the genealogist Malcolm Stern, little is known about Aaron Rodriguez Rivera except that he lived in Wilmington, North Carolina, for most of his adult life. However, his miniature portrait informs the viewer of his illustrious heritage when compared to the familial portraits of his great-grandfather, Jacob Rodriguez Rivera (cat. 29) and his grandmother, Sarah Rivera Lopez (Plate 6, cat. 30) in the exhibition.

One of four sons, Aaron Rodriguez Rivera was named by his father, Abraham Rodriguez Rivera, and his mother, Hannah Lopez, for his famous maternal grandfather, the wealthy Newport merchant and trader, Aaron Lopez, husband of Sarah Rivera Lopez (cat. 30). The sitter was a descendant of Abraham Rodrigues de Rivera, a refugee from the Portuguese Inquisition who had outwardly practiced Catholicism; upon his arrival in America he resumed his Jewish practices and took a Hebrew name. Abraham Rodrigues de Rivera was the founder of old New York and Newport families. He died in Newport on July 7, 1765.

Aaron Rodriguez Rivera's magnificently rendered miniature portrait depicts the traditionally dressed sitter at age thirty-five.

His classical profile reflects his dramatic high coloring and connects him to the most prominent Sephardic families in Newport, the main repository for the Aaron Lopez papers.

ELC

References
London, Hannah R. *Miniatures and Silhouettes of Early Jews.* Rutland, Vt.: Charles E. Tuttle Company, 1970.
Pool, David de Sola. *Portraits Etched in Stone: Early Jewish Settlers, 1682–1831.* New York: Columbia University Press, 1952.
Stern, Malcolm H. *First American Jewish Families: 600 Genealogies, 1654–1988.* Baltimore: Ottenheimer Publishers, 1978.

37
Gershom Mendes Seixas
(1745–1816)
Artist unknown
c. 1770
Miniature; oil on ivory
3 ½ × 2 ¾ in.; 8.89 × 6.99 cm
Collection of E. Norman Flayderman

George Washington invited thirteen religious leaders to his inauguration in 1789; Gershom Mendes Seixas, the first American-born leader of a Jewish congregation, was among the chosen group. At the ceremony Seixas was invited to pronounce the blessing upon America's first president.

Gershom Mendes Seixas was the son of Isaac Mendes Seixas and Rachel Levy Seixas (cat. 11), the daughter of Moses Raphael

37   Gershom Mendes Seixas

Levy (cat. 1) and Grace Mears Levy (cat. 2). Reverend Seixas, as he was known, fathered sixteen children by his two wives, Elkalah Myers-Cohen and Hannah Manuel. Gershom's brother Benjamin had twenty-two children, and their descendants are legion.

Seixas, although never ordained as a rabbi, was the first *hazzan*, or leader of public worship, to preach in English in a synagogue; he became minister of Congregation Shearith Israel in 1768. An ardent Revolutionary patriot, he refused to offer prayers for King George III or to fly the British flag over Shearith Israel when the British defeated Washington in New York in August 1776. Instead he chose to close the synagogue and flee the city. In 1780, he served as minister to Congregation Mikveh Israel in Philadelphia, returning to Shearith Israel in 1784 following the British occupation. Gershom Mendes Seixas expanded the role of the *hazzan*-reader as he delivered sermons and participated in national events such as President Washington's inauguration. This miniature portrays Gershom Mendes Seixas in the typical clerical garbworn by Protestant ministers.

In New York City, Seixas was not only a strong advocate of Judaism but a Trustee of Columbia College from 1787 to 1815. Among his many descendants are Benjamin N. Cardozo, a former Associate Justice of the U.S. Supreme Court, and Annie Nathan Meyer, who was a trustee of Barnard College.

ELC

References
London, Hannah R. *Miniatures of Early American Jews.* Springfield, Mass.: The Pond-Ekberg Company, 1953.
Pool, David de Sola. *Portraits Etched in Stone: Early Jewish Settlers 1682–1831.* New York: Columbia University Press, 1952.

Role Playing: Beauties, Handsome Officers, Worthy Burghers

38
Miriam Etting Myers (Mrs. Jacob Myers)
(1787–1808)
Benjamin Trott (1770–1843)
1804
Miniature; watercolor on ivory
3 × 2 ½ in.; 7.62 × 6.35 cm
The Maryland Historical Society
Eleanor C. Cohen Collection

38   *Miriam Etting Myers (Mrs. Jacob Myers)*

Miriam Etting Myers was a daughter of the distinguished business and civic leader Solomon Etting (Plate 12, cat. 74) and his first wife, Reyna (Rachel) Simon. After Reyna's death, Solomon Etting married Barnard Gratz's (cat. 49) daughter Rachel (cat. 73). Nineteen-year-old Miriam Etting married Jacob Myers on July 31, 1806, in Baltimore; she gave birth to sons in succeeding years and died prematurely in Germantown, Pennsylvania, in 1808.

Benjamin Trott's miniatures are known for their clarity, lively hatch-marks, and incredibly thin wash of watercolor on ivory. Frequently the ground is left bare, thereby creating another hue of luminous ivory. His female sitters were often rendered with beautiful attenuated necks, displaying a certain directness in their gaze toward the viewer. Trott studied with the masters: first with Gilbert Stuart in Boston, and then with Thomas Sully in Philadelphia from 1806 to 1819.

This miniature portrait of Miriam Etting depicts the young woman fashionably attired in a low-cut neoclassical, dress with curls spilling over her forehead above her huge dark eyes. It was painted in 1804, before her marriage to Jacob Myers, when she was only seventeen years old. Benjamin Trott also painted a miniature portrait of her father, Solomon Etting.   ELC

References
London, Hannah R.. *Miniatures of Early American Jews*. Springfield, Mass.: The Pond-Ekberg Company, 1953. Illus. p. 145
London, Hannah R. *Portraits of Jews by Gilbert Stuart and Other Early American Artists*. Rutland, Vt.: Charles E. Tuttle Company, 1969.
Stern, Malcolm H. *First American Jewish Families: 600 Genealogies, 1654–1988*. Baltimore: Ottenheimer Publishers, 1978.

39
Rebecca Gratz
(1781–1869)
Thomas Sully (1783–1872)
Philadelphia, 1830
Oil on canvas mounted on masonite
20 × 17 in.; 50.8 × 43.18 cm
Delaware Art Museum.
Gift of Benjamin Shaw II

An image of this painting appeared as a United States postage stamp on May 20, 1980, the first day of issue. The occasion was the B'nai B'rith Philatelic Service's recognition of Rebecca Gratz (Plate 7, cat. 40) as an educator and philanthropist.[1]

The enigmatic Rebecca Gratz remains today the best-known Jewish woman in nineteenth-century America, although some mystery still swirls about this painting and her personal life. Thomas Sully's register states categorically that it was erased; family tradition proffers the suggestion that her relatives were disturbed by a depiction of Rebecca in exotic apparel. Yet it remains a Romantic nineteenth-century portrayal of Rebecca as on Old Testament heroine; her ivory turban is tied under her chin with a handsome French blue-gray and green ribbon. A

39 *Rebecca Gratz*   40 *Rebecca Gratz*

shawl is wrapped around her camel-colored garment and is decorated with soft rose, grayed-green, and blue ribbons. Thomas Sully has chosen a soft blue and gray-green background to set off Rebecca's brown eyes and hair. An image of this Romantic portrait also appeared as the frontispiece for Sir Walter Scott's *Ivanhoe* in 1882.

On Monday, March 2, 1936, the *Washington Post* featured an article entitled "Half-Forgotten Romances of American History: Samuel Ewing—Rebecca Gratz."[2] Because of religious differences, Rebecca Gratz gently rejected the marriage proposal of Samuel Ewing, a young Philadelphia lawyer and son of the provost of the University if Pennsylvania; but she remained intimate friends with Samuel, his bride, Elizabeth Rodman of Philadelphia, and their family. A Ewing grandchild reminisced about Rebecca's last visit: "When my grandfather, Samuel Ewing, died, my cousin was 10 and her sister 14, and they stood at the door when the dear loyal woman (Rebecca Gratz) passed in, and remained for an hour. When she came out, she left three white roses on his breast and her miniature on his heart."[3]   ELC

Notes
1. "B'nai B'rith Philatelic Service honors Rebecca Gratz, Philadelphia educator and philanthropist. Miss Gratz, daughter of Michael and Miriam Simon Gratz, was the founder of the first Hebrew Sunday School in the United States (1838). Miss Gratz, a woman of considerable beauty, charm, and culture, is considered to be the model for Rebecca in Sir Walter Scott's *Ivanhoe*."
2. Delaware Art Museum, archival folder.
3. "Half-Forgotten Romances of American History: Samuel Ewing—Rebecca Gratz," *The Washington Post*, March 2, 1936. See also Edwin Wolf 2nd, and Maxwell Whiteman, *The History of the Jews of Philadelphia from Colonial Times to the Age of Jackson*. (Philadelphia: Jewish Publication Society of America, 1957), p. 239.

References
Biddle, Edward, and Mantle Fielding. *Life and Works of Thomas Sully*, 1921.
London, Hannah R. *Portraits of Jews by Gilbert Stuart and Other Early American Artists*. Rutland, Vt.: Charles E. Tuttle Company, 1969.
Stern, Malcolm H. *First American Jewish Families: 600 Genealogies, 1654–1988*. Baltimore: Ottenheimer Publishers, 1978.
Wolf, Edwin 2nd, and Maxwell Whiteman. *The History of the Jews of Philadelphia from Colonial Times to the Age of Jackson*. Philadelphia: Jewish Publication Society of America, 1957.

Stern, Malcolm H. *First American Jewish Families: 600 Genealogies, 1654–1988*. Baltimore: Ottenheimer Publishers, *1978*.

40

Rebecca Gratz
(1781–1869)
Thomas Sully (1783–1872)
Philadelphia, 1831
Oil on panel
20 × 17 in; 50.8 × 43.18 cm
Rosenbach Museum and Library

Rebecca Gratz is the best-known woman in our exhibition and one of the most illustrious in nineteenth-century America. Washington Irving is supposed to have described her remarkable character to Sir Walter Scott who then immortalized her as the Jewish heroine Rebecca in his novel *Ivanhoe*. Irving, who had been the fiancé of Rebecca's late friend Matilda Hoffman, provided a letter of introduction to Thomas Sully. The artist would depict Rebecca in three separate portraits (Plate 7, cats. 39, 40), all described in his register; earlier he had copied an 1804 miniature of her by Edward Malbone.

Rebecca Gratz was born in Philadelphia, the daughter of Michael Gratz (cat. 54), the German-Jewish pioneer who had arrived in America from Langendorf, Silesia, in 1759, and Miriam Simon, the daughter of a leading citizen of Lancaster, Pennsylvania. They married in 1769 and had twelve children. The Gratz brothers, Michael and Barnard (Plate 10, cat. 49), were very successful Philadelphia merchant-traders with enterprises that stretched from the Eastern seaboard to the Frontier.

Rebecca never married; it was rumored that she had fallen in love with a gentile (see cat. 39) and chose to remain a spinster. Instead she devoted her life to good works and was a founder of several Philadelphia charitable organizations—the Hebrew Sunday School Society, the first of its kind, the Jewish Foster Home, and the Philadelphia Orphan Society. Rebecca was also devoted to raising the nine children left by her beloved younger sister, Rachel Gratz Moses, who died in 1823 at age forty.

This small signed portrait owned by the Rosenbach Museum and Library was a commission from Rebecca's sister-in-law and confidante, Maria Gist Gratz (Mrs. Benjamin Gratz). The beautiful fifty-year-old Rebecca wears a pleated Dutch-style ruff around her neck; her brown curly hair and pale olive complexion is enhanced by pensive brown eyes and a thoughtful expression. Some have questioned her age here but the date is a firm one; Rebecca was an acknowledged beauty, and no artist could better Sully at rendering the handsome female.   ELC

References
Letters of Rebecca Gratz, ed. David Philipson. Philadelphia: The Jewish Publication Society of America, 1929.
London, Hannah R. *Portraits of Jews by Gilbert Stuart and Other Early American Artists*. Rutland, Vt.: Charles E. Tuttle Company, 1969.

41

Rachel Machado Phillips Levy
(1769–1839)
Attributed to Adolph Ulrich Wertmüller (1751–1811)
c. 1795
Oil on canvas
25 ½ in. diameter; 64.77 cm, diameter
American Jewish Historical Society, Waltham, Massachusetts, and New York, New York.
Museum Purchase, 1996

Born to a prominent Philadelphia Jewish family, Rachel Machado Phillips Levy became the mother, grandmother, and great-grandmother of some of nineteenth-century America's most influential Jewish men and women. Daughter of Jonas Phillips and Rebecca Machado, Rachel was the sixth of their twenty-one children. Her twin sister died as a toddler. In 1787 she married Philadelphia merchant Michael Levy; their ten children included naval hero Uriah Phillips Levy (cat. 44).

Rachel was considered a "great beauty" in her lifetime, a beauty clearly captured in the portrait of her attributed to the Swedish painter Adolph Wertmüller. Wertmüller's first American tour (1794–96) brought him both to Philadelphia and Annapolis, and Rachel could have sat for him in either location. Rachel would then have been in her mid-twenties, already the mother of five children. But Wertmüller has captured a decidedly non-maternal, neoclassical beauty: vivacious, unsentimental, very much the portrait of an independent, autonomous personality.

Rachel spent her last years at Thomas Jefferson's estate, Monticello, with her son Uriah, who had purchased the property in 1836 and restored it. Her portrait hung in Monticello, and she is buried on Monticello's grounds, a Star of David on her headstone. The portrait remained in Monticello until 1923, when Monticello was acquired by the Thomas Jefferson Memorial Foundation. Rachel's portrait was then privately purchased, and eventually made its way to Sweden. In 1996, the American Jewish Historical Society bought the portrait from its owners, reuniting the paintings of Rachel Levy and her son Uriah. The Society also owns a miniature copy of the Wertmüller portrait.

Adolph Ulrich Wertmüller was born in Stockholm in 1751. He trained in sculpture and painting at the Stockholm Academy, and privately in Paris (1772–75) and Rome (1775–79). In 1781 Wertmüller moved to Paris where he specialized in neoclassical paintings, becoming a member of the French Academy in 1784 and First Painter to Gustavus III of Sweden. A dearth of portrait

41   *Rachel Machado Phillips Levy*

commissions prompted his relocation to Madrid in 1792 and to Cadiz in early 1794. By May 1794 he was in Philadelphia.

Wertmüller had a successful stay in America, continuing with his Neoclassical paintings, and specializing in portraits, including a rare life-portrait of George Washington. His travels took him from Philadelphia to Annapolis to New York. From 1797 to 1799 Wertmüller lived again in Sweden, but returned permanently to the United States in January 1800 to marry Betsy Henderson, granddaughter of the American painter Gustav Heselius. By 1802, failing eyesight virtually ended Wertmüller's career as a painter, although he kept a list of commissions he hoped to execute until his death on his Chester, Pennsylvania, farm in 1811.   EJS

References

Benisovich, Michel N. "Further Notes on A. U. Wertmüller in the United States and France." *The Art Quarterly*, 26 (1963): 7–30.

Uriah Phillips Levy Papers, American Jewish Historical Society, Waltham, Mass., and New York, N.Y.

Scott, F. D. *Wertmüller: Artist and Immigrant Farmer.* Chicago, 1963.

Turner, Jane, ed. *The Dictionary of American Art.* Vol 33: 86. New York: Macmillan, 1996.

42

Stephen Decatur

(1779–1820)

Rembrandt Peale (1778–1860)

c. 1815–20

Oil on canvas

29 × 23 ⅝ in.; 73.66 × 60 cm

The New-York Historical Society.

Gift of Thomas J. Bryan

Born on the eastern shore of Maryland, Stephen Decatur spent his youth in Philadelphia. After attending the city's Episcopal Academy and studying for a year at the University of Pennsylvania, Decatur worked briefly for Gurney and Smith, a local shipping firm. At the outbreak of war with France, in 1789 he entered the U. S. Navy as a midshipman and quickly gained recognition for his courage and leadership skills. He rose to national prominence as a naval hero through his exploits as commander of his own ship during the war with Tripoli in 1803–4, in which he led a number of successful tactical raids. Admiral Horatio Nelson characterized Decatur's destruction of the vessel *Philadelphia* in 1804, then in Tripolitan hands, as "the most bold and daring act of the age." During the War of 1812, Decatur achieved perhaps his most celebrated victory when he captured the British frigate Macedonian, incurring only twelve casualities to England's 104. Following subsequent successful and acclaimed naval assignments after the war, Decatur served on the Board of Navy Commissioners until his death in 1820, the result of injuries suffered during a duel.

Between the years 1810 and 1820, the artist Rembrandt Peale painted likenesses of illustrious Americans for the picture gallery of his museum located in Baltimore. Ultimately Peale executed well over one hundred such canvases, including this portrait. The War of 1812 had provided him with a new generation of war heroes to commemorate, in particular those naval officers who had defended the city of Baltimore, including Decatur, Commodore William Bainbridge, and Commodore Oliver Hazard Perry. Set against a dramatic background of turbulent clouds, Stephen Decatur is depicted as a public figure of national prominence, wearing the formal military uniform of a Commodore. This portrait is an example of the many paintings produced during this period—including the portrait of Commodore Uriah

42 *Stephen Decatur*

P. Levy (cat. 44)—that served to define virtue for the newly enfranchised American populace through the representation of acclaimed military and civic leaders.   CEM

References

Caldwell, John, and Oswaldo Rodriguez Roque et al. *American Paintings in the Metropolitan Museum of Art.* Vol. 1: 197–98. New York: The Metropolitan Museum of Art and Princeton University Press, 1994.

Johnson, Allen, and Dumas Malone, eds. *Dictionary of American Biography.* Vol. 3: 187–90. New York: Charles Scribner's Sons., 1927; rpt. 1964.

Miller, Lillian B. *In Pursuit of Fame: Rembrandt Peale, 1778–1860.* Seattle: University of Washington Press, 1992.

New-York Historical Society. *Catalogue of American Portraits in the New-York Historical Society.* Vol. 1: 36–37, 194; Vol. 2: 615–16. New Haven: Yale University Press, 1974.

43 *Major Mordecai Myers*

groom was thirty-eight and his bride was seventeen years old. Their union produced ten surviving children.

After his discharge in 1815, Mordecai and Charlotte moved to New York City, where he became active in politics. A popular gentleman, he counted among his friends President Van Buren. DeWitt Clinton, Aaron Burr, and Alexander Hamilton. Later mayor of Schenectady and a Freemason, Myers was also elected to the New York State Assembly for six terms, representing a ward in New York City. Although his wife was not Jewish, he sustained a lifelong interest in Jewish affairs.

John Wesley Jarvis, who also painted General Andrew Jackson in uniform, clearly excels in the heroic male portrait. He chose to depict the dashing Major Myers in his uniform standing proudly in a traditional military pose with hand on sword, probably around 1813. In this portrait the artist has successfully captured the major's noble spirit and steadfast nature, yet has also managed to convey the sitter's well-known affability. Jarvis is known for the commission he received from the Corporation of the City of New York to paint a series of portraits of the military heroes of the War of 1812, still on view at City Hall in New York City.   ELC

References

Dickson, Harold. *John Wesley Jarvis*. New York, 1949.

London, Hannah R. *Portraits of Jews by Gilbert Stuart and Other Early American Artists*. Rutland, Vt.: Charles E. Tuttle Company, 1969.

Stern, Malcolm H. *First American Jewish Families: 600 Genealogies, 1654–1988*. Baltimore: Ottenheimer Publishers, 1978.

The Toledo Museum of Art. *American Paintings*. Catalogue by Susan E. Strickler, ed. William Hutton. Toledo, 1979.

43

Major Mordecai Myers

(1776–1871)

John Wesley Jarvis (1780–1840)

c. 1813

Oil on wood panel

33 ⅞ × 26 ⅛ in.; 86.04 × 67.63 cm

The Toledo Museum of Art.
Purchased with funds from the Florence
Scott Libbey Bequest in Memory of her
Father, Maurice A. Scott

Major Mordecai Myers (Plate 8), son of Benjamin Myers who had arrived in America from Hungary, had a lengthy, honorable, and successful life. Born in Newport, Rhode Island, of Loyalist parents, he grew up in New York City and was a long-standing member (1791–1814) of Congregation Shearith Israel. As a young man he studied military tactics under one of Napoleon's French officers. He distinguished himself at the Battle of Chrysler's Farm near Niagara, New York, where he was wounded. While recuperating nearby he met his future wife, Charlotte Bailey, the daughter of the prominent Judge William Bailey, one of the founders of Plattsburg, New York. They were married at Plattsburg on January 24, 1814, after Mordecai's recovery; the bride-

44

Commodore Uriah Phillips Levy

(1792–1862)

Artist unknown

c. 1816

Oil on canvas

32 ¼ × 27 in.; 83.2 × 68.8 cm

American Jewish Historical Society, Waltham,
Massachusetts, and New York, New York.
Gift of Amelia Levy Mayhoff

In 1802, a ten-year-old boy ran away from home, and against his parents' firmest wishes, went to sea. Across the next six decades, Uriah Phillips Levy rose from cabin boy to Commodore of the Mediterranean fleet of the United States Navy.

Levy was born to a distinguished Philadelphia family, fourth of ten children of Michael Levy and Rachel Phillips Levy (cat. 41). As a sailing master during the War of 1812, he captured more than twenty ships before himself being sunk. In 1816, recognizing his "extraordinary service and extraordinary merit," the Navy

44 *Commodore Uriah Phillips Levy*

rank in the U.S. Navy. Levy married his young niece Virginia Lopez in 1853. They lived at Thomas Jefferson's Virginia estate, Monticello, which Levy had purchased in 1836, and spent great time and effort restoring. When Levy died in 1862, his will instructed that the estate be converted to a school for orphan children of naval officers. But after twenty-five years of legal challenges to the will, Levy's nephew, Jefferson Monroe Levy (1852–1924), acquired the property. J. M. Levy continued the restoration of Monticello, and in 1923 Monticello was sold to the Thomas Jefferson Memorial Foundation, which maintains it for the American people.

The Levy Chapel at the Norfolk Naval Station is named in memory of Uriah P. Levy, and a plaque at the Monticello gravesite of Uriah's mother, Rachel Phillips Levy, honors U. P. Levy as well: "At two crucial periods in the history of Monticello, the preservation efforts and stewardship of Uriah P. and Jefferson M. Levy successfully maintained the property for future generations." EJS

References
Hosmer, Charles P., Jr. "Monticello—the Second Mount Vernon." *Presence of the Pasts: A History of the Preservation Movement in the United States Before Williamsburg.* New York: G. P. Putnam's Sons, 1965, 153–92.
Kanof, Abram. "Uriah Phillips Levy: The Story of a Pugnacious Commodore." *Publications of the American Jewish Historical Society,* 39 (1949): 1–66.
Uriah Phillips Levy Papers and Jefferson Monroe Levy Papers. American Jewish Historical Society, Waltham, Mass., and New York, N.Y.

commissioned Levy as a lieutenant, a rare event for an ex-cabin boy and sailing master. This portrait of Levy is believed to have been painted for the occasion. Against the dark colors and thick paint of the background, Levy stands forth as a commanding, singular, but isolated figure. Such was his role throughout his lifetime.

In 1837, Levy was promoted to Commander and, in 1838, he received his first command as captain of the *Vandalia.* There he virtually abolished flogging as a naval discipline, and likely co-authored the anti-flogging tract, *An Essay of Flogging in the Navy* (1849).

Ironically, Levy himself faced repeated discipline from his commanders. Described as an excellent sailor and brave patriot, Levy has also been described as pugnacious, difficult to work with, and quick to anger. The combination of anti-Semitism and Levy's own difficult personality brought six courts-martial and one disciplinary proceeding against him between 1827 and 1857. Four findings were returned against him, and two others were overturned by the President of the United States. Assigned to the Mediterranean in 1858, Levy was named Commodore of the Mediterranean Fleet, 1859–60, the first Jew to hold such high

45

Colonel Isaac Franks

(1759–1822)
Gilbert Stuart (1754–1828)
Philadelphia, 1802
Oil on canvas
29 ⅛ × 24 ¹⁄₁₆ in.; 73.98 × 61.12 cm
Courtesy of the Museum of American Art
of the Pennsylvania Academy of the Fine Arts,
Philadelphia.
Bequest of Henry C. Gibson

George Washington faced multitudinous political and military challenges in his lifetime, but none appeared more insurmountable and dangerous than the Yellow Fever epidemic that descended upon Philadelphia during the summers of 1793 and 1794, killing over five thousand. The President turned to Isaac Franks, a great patriot and Revolutionary Army officer, for assistance. The colonel proffered his house in Germantown, Pennsylvania, which kept the presidential family safely away from the beleaguered city. During the Washingtons' residence in Germantown, many cabinet meetings were held in the mansion with Thomas Jefferson and Alexander Hamilton in attendance.

Davidson and fathered two surviving children, Judge Samuel Davidson Franks and Sarah Franks Huffnagle. In 1806, he moved to Ephrata, Pennsylvania; he collected a pension for military service and served in a variety of minor government posts. The Colonel's biography is marked by stunning achievements, but also insolvencies and illness.

Isaac Franks willed this portrait by Gilbert Stuart jointly to both of his children, Samuel and Sarah. In a novel arrangement, they were to share the portrait, each keeping it in his or her home during alternating years; they acted according to Colonel Franks's wishes.[2]   ELC

45   *Colonel Isaac Franks*

Notes
1. In 1949, Elliston P. Morris donated the Deshler-Morris House to the National Park Service for preservation as the oldest presidential residence in existence.
2. Morris Jastrow. "Documents Relating to the Career of Isaac Franks." *Publications of the American Jewish Historical Society* 5: 7–34.

References
Fanelli, Doris Devine. *Deshler-Morris House.* Independence National Historical Park, December 1976.
London, Hannah R. *Portraits of Jews by Gilbert Stuart and Other Early American Artists.* Rutland, Vt.: Charles E. Tuttle Company, 1969. Illus. 167.
Stern, Malcolm H. *First American Jewish Families: 600 Genealogies, 1654–1988.* Baltimore: Ottenheimer Publishers, 1978.

Known as the Deshler-Morris House, the Franks House was built in Germantown, Pennsylvania, now in Philadelphia, by David Deshler in 1752; twenty years later he added a nine-room Georgian house to the front of the existing building.[1] Isaac Franks purchased the property in 1792 after Deshler's death. In 1997, the Franks House still features the luxurious side garden with its lofty shade trees; one can imagine the presidential meetings and entertainments easily accommodated within the spacious high-ceilinged rooms. In Germantown, Gilbert Stuart painted one of Washington's portraits as well as the portrait of Isaac Franks that hangs above the mantel in the main parlor today. The portrait has been loaned to the National Park Service by the Pennsylvania Academy of the Fine Arts.

Isaac Franks was born in New York, the son of Moses and Sarah Franks; he was the great-grandson of Benjamin Franks, who served with Captain Kidd in Barbados. Isaac began his military career in 1776, and fought in the Battle of Long Island under the direct command of George Washington. In the course of the battle he was taken prisoner for three months and is said to have managed to escape in a leaky boat. When his military service ended in 1782, he moved to Philadelphia, where he married Mary

46
Mordecai Manuel Noah
(1785–1851)
John Wesley Jarvis (1780–1840)
Date unknown
Oil on canvas
30 × 26 in.; 76.2 × 66. 04 cm
Courtesy of the Trustees of Congregation
Shearith Israel, New York, New York

Mordecai Manuel Noah (Plate 9, cat. 47) was the son of German-born Manuel Noah and Zipporah Phillips, the daughter of Jonas Phillips, also German-born and a leader of the post-Revolutionary Jewish community in Philadelphia. Noah's maternal grandmother, Rebecca Mendez Machado Phillips, the daughter of a *hazzan* of Shearith Israel, and Jonas Phillips are also the parents of Rachel Machado Phillips Levy (cat. 41) and the grandparents of Commodore Uriah P. Levy (cat. 44). Born into this important early Jewish Philadelphia family with Ashkenazic and Sephardic roots, Mordecai was raised in Charleston, New York City, and later in Philadelphia by his maternal grandparents, the Phillipses, after his mother's death; his father, Manuel Noah, had earlier abandoned the family. In 1827 Mordecai married Rebecca Esther Jackson (cat. 48), from Portsmouth, England; they had seven children.

46 *Mordecai Manuel Noah*

Noah was a multifaceted man—a major in the Pennsylvania militia, newspaper publisher, playwright, politician, and diplomat; in 1813 he was appointed consul to Tunis in the Madison administration but forced to resign by Secretary of State James Monroe in a diplomatic imbroglio involving hostage negotiations for Berber captives. On his return to the States, Noah enhanced his role as an unofficial spokesman for Jewish causes. He is perhaps best known for his grandiose scheme to establish a Jewish autonomous homeland—to be called Ararat—on Grand Island in a remote region of upstate New York. No Jews settled in Ararat, and the plan was eventually abandoned.

Shearith Israel, the synagogue founded by the original Sephardic Jewish immigrants to New York, owns this handsome oval romantic portrait with a glorious sky in the background that captures Noah's public image as a Jewish leader and visionary.

ELC

References
London, Hannah R. *Portraits of Jews by Gilbert Stuart and Other Early American Artists.* Rutland, Vt.: Charles E. Tuttle Company, 1969.
Sachar, Howard M. *A History of the Jews in America.* New York: Knopf, 1992.
Sarna, Jonathan. *Jacksonian Jew: The Two Worlds of Mordecai Noah.* New York: Holmes & Meier, 1981.
Stern, Malcolm H. *First American Jewish Families: 600 Genealogies, 1654–1988.* Baltimore: Ottenheimer Publishers, 1960, 1978.
Wolf, Edwin 2nd, and Maxwell Whiteman. *The History of the Jews of Philadelphia from Colonial Times to the Age of Jackson.* Philadelphia: Jewish Publication Society of America, 1957.

47
Mordecai Manuel Noah
(1785–1851)
George A. Weeden
Newport, Rhode Island, c. 1828
Pen and ink drawing
8 × 6 ½ in.; 20.32 × 16.51 cm
Private Collection

According to the notes of a former owner found on the verso of the drawings, the *Rhode Island American and General Advertiser* published an article, on June 14, 1822, stating that the Jewish community was fast dwindling away in Newport and that the last member had already left for New York City. As a result, the article continued, the Jewish community had to assemble during the summer to worship in Newport in order to retain possession of the Touro Synagogue. M. M. Noah, Esquire, a member of the Jewish Society from New York, was designated to deliver an address to those assembled on that occasion.

As a prominent member of Shearith Israel, which controlled the Touro Synagogue, Mordecai Noah must have made more than one summer trip to the Touro Synagogue. These unfinished sketches of Mr. and Mrs. Mordecai M. Noah were done by a local Newport artist in about 1828, one year after Rebecca (cat. 48) and Mordecai were married, and the year that Peter Harrison's magnificent colonial synagogue was restored. The local artist, George Weeden, drew Mordecai Noah (see also Plate 9, cat. 46) in the pose of a Roman orator, along with the following caption, "Yes, Gentlemen, I am speaking of mechanical powers and say with a distinguished individual of certain days Arcimedas give me a plan to stand upon, and I will raise the world."

The caption has been interpreted by some as satirizing Noah's oratory and grand projects. The caricature has also been viewed as stereotypically anti-Semitic.

ELC

References
London, Hannah R. *Portraits of Jews by Gilbert Stuart and Other Early American Artists.* Rutland, Vt.: Charles E. Tuttle Company, 1969.
Stern, Malcolm H. *First American Jewish Families: 600 Genealogies, 1654–1988.* Baltimore: Ottenheimer Publishers, 1978.

47 *Mordecai Manuel Noah*

48 *Rebecca Jackson Noah (Mrs. Mordecai Manuel Noah)*

48

Rebecca Jackson Noah (Mrs. Mordecai Manuel Noah)

(1810–1866)
George A. Weeden
Newport, Rhode Island, c. 1828
Pen and ink drawing
8 × 6 ½ in.; 20.32 × 16.52 cm
Private Collection

Rebecca Esther Jackson, from Portsmouth, England, and Mordecai Manuel Noah (Plate 8, cats. 46, 47) from New York City were married in 1827. As prominent members of Shearith Israel, which oversaw the Touro Synagogue in Newport, Rhode Island, they frequently visited Newport during the summer when Mordecai Noah would address the assembled congregation.

These unfinished sketches of Rebecca and Mordecai Noah were done in Newport about 1828, one year after their marriage and the year that Peter Harrison's magnificent colonial synagogue was restored.

Little is known about George Weeden, the artist who worked up these sketches, except that he was probably a local Newport man commenting on the fashionable summer visitors from New York in a style not unlike Daumier. The sketch of Rebecca Noah is more reportial, lacking the biting satire of her husband's pose and commentary.   ELC

References
London, Hannah R. *Portraits of Jews by Gilbert Stuart and Other Early American Artists.* Rutland, Vt.: Charles E. Tuttle Company, 1969.
Stern, Malcolm H. *First American Jewish Families: 600 Genealogies, 1654–1988.* Baltimore: Ottenheimer Publishers, 1978.

49

Barnard Gratz

(1738–1801)
Charles Peale Polk (1767–1822)
c. 1792
Oil on canvas
40 × 35 in.; 101.6 × 88.9 cm
Collection of E. Norman Flayderman

Barnard Gratz (Plate 10) exemplifies the German-Jewish trader who arrived in America two decades before the Revolution. A dynamic, enterprising, yet religiously learned man, he helped open up our Western frontier along with his brother, Michael (cat. 54), father of Rebecca Gratz (Plate 7, cats. 39, 40), while simultaneously fighting for the rights of Jews to participate fully in the American political process.

Charles Peale Polk has celebrated Barnard's reputation as an erudite man by posing him with spectacles in hand, resting his elbow on a table holding the Third Book of Moses, Leviticus. Behind the conservatively dressed gentleman, a bookcase holds four additional volumes of the Torah; Thomas Stackhouse's *New History of the Bible from the Beginning of the World to the Establishment of Christianity;* Thomas Salmon's *A New Geographical and Historical Grammar;* and possibly *The History of England* by Rapin de Thoyras.

Barnard Gratz arrived in Philadelphia from Langendorf, Silesia, when he was seventeen years old. He married Richea Myers-Cohen Gratz on December 10, 1760. Their daughter Rachel Gratz (cat. 73) married Solomon Etting (Plate 12, cat. 74), which connects Barnard by marriage to Shinah Solomon Etting (cat. 50), the subject of the other portrait by Charles Peale Polk in this exhibition. Barnard served Congregation Mikveh Israel in

Philadelphia as a founding member and its first president; however, when his daughter Rachel married, he moved with her to Baltimore in 1791. Both Barnard and his son-in-law Solomon Etting fought determinedly for Jewish civil rights, such as the prerogative to hold public office, in Philadelphia and in Baltimore.

But the real story of Barnard Gratz does not appear in this somber folk portrait of an older gentleman surrounded by books in his library. The enterprising and adventurous Gratz brothers who shipped goods to Europe and the West Indies fought the non-importation laws imposed upon the American colonists by courageously running the British blockades and seeking less stringently enforced Southern ports for their overseas trade. After the American Revolution, which Barnard strongly supported, the entrepreneurial Gratz brothers continued to deal with fur traders from the Western Frontier. But they also speculated successfully in land bordering the Mississippi, Ohio, and Illinois rivers, helping to open up the Western states of Indiana, Kentucky, Illinois, and Ohio.

ELC

References
Kleeblatt, Norman L., and Gerard C. Wertkin. *The Jewish Heritage in American Folk Art.* Exhibition catalogue. The Jewish Museum and the Museum of American Folk Art. New York: Universe Books, 1984. Illus. p. 36.
London, Hannah R. *Portraits of Jews by Gilbert Stuart and Other Early American Artists.* Rutland, Vt.: Charles E. Tuttle Company, 1969.
Stern, Malcolm H. *First American Jewish Families: 600 Genealogies, 1654–1988.* Baltimore: Ottenheimer Publishers, 1978.

50   *Shinah Solomon Etting (Mrs. Elijah Etting)*

49   *Barnard Gratz*

50

Shinah Solomon Etting (Mrs. Elijah Etting)
(1744–1822)
Charles Peale Polk (1767–1822)
1792
Oil on canvas
35 ⅝ × 27 ⅝ in.; 98.11 × 70.17 cm
The Baltimore Museum of Art.
Gift of Mr. and Mrs. William C. Whitridge,
Stevenson, Maryland (BMA 1968.14)

The son of Charles Wilson Peale's sister, Elizabeth Digby Peale, and a sea captain, Charles Peale Polk was raised by his uncle after he was orphaned at age ten. He trained under his uncle to become a painter although his provincial or folk style never seemed to improve over the years and he was forced to travel in search of commissions. Nevertheless, his early works have a folk quality about them that has a certain charm.

Charles Peale Polk painted this delightful portrait of Shinah Solomon Etting when he was only twenty-five years old. Her pose comes from Charles Willson Peale's oeuvre; she is seated in a Chippendale side chair with her elbow resting on a table. Like her daughter Sally Etting (cat. 75), she is portrayed as a lady of fashion dressed à la mode. She wears a russet gown with a white fichu caught in a large bow with a verbena sprig, another of Charles Willson Peale's favorite pictorial devices. Her handsome shawl is embroidered with flowers and leaves, terminating in a fringe. She holds another sprig of verbena in one hand and a fan in the other. An elaborate coal-scuttle hat edged with a deep band of lace and decorated with a huge bow at the front crowns her dark hair. Polk's colorful palette combined with her forthright gaze gives a liveliness to the work.

Shinah was born on December 24, 1744, to a merchant from London, Joseph Solomon and his wife, Bilah. She grew up in Lancaster and later moved to York, Pennsylvania, at age fifteen when she married Elijah Etting, a recent immigrant from Frankfurt-am-Main in Germany. After her husband's death, she moved in 1780 to Baltimore for the last forty years of her life. Two of her sons, Reuben Etting (cat. 65) and Solomon Etting (Plate 10, cat. 74), were successful in business and also involved in civic affairs in Philadelphia and Baltimore. Solomon was an incorporator of the Baltimore and Ohio Railroad and one of the first Jews to hold public office in Maryland.

At her death the newspapers noted her cheerful demeanor and the affection that many held for her. In his memoirs, Captain Alexander Grayson referred to Shinah as "the sprightly and engaging Mrs. E. … always in spirits, full of frolic and glee, and possessing the talent of singing agreeably."[1] There is another portrait of Shinah Etting at the Maryland Historical Society; it possesses a darker, more somber palette and depicts her with glasses and holding a book, Thomson's *Seasons*.　　　　ELC

Note
1. Philip Sherman. "The Engaging Mrs. E." *Maryland Historical Society's 3rd Annual Maryland Antiquities Show and Sale,* ed. Lester S. Levy et al. (Baltimore: Schneidereith and Sons, 1981).

References
Kleeblatt, Norman L., and Gerard C. Wertkin, eds. *The Jewish Heritage in American Folk Art.* Exhibition catalogue. The Jewish Museum and Museum of American Folk Art. New York: Universe Books, 1984. Illus. p. 35.
London, Hannah R. *Portraits of Jews by Gilbert Stuart and Other Early American Artists.* Rutland, Vt.: Charles E. Tuttle Company, 1969.
Stern, Malcolm H. *First American Families: 600 Genealogies, 1654–1988.* Baltimore: Ottenheimer Publishers, 1978.

51　*Sally Sanford Perit (Mrs. Job Perit)*

51
Sally Sanford Perit (Mrs. Job Perit)
(1760–1829)
Reuben Moulthrop (1763–1814)
New Haven, 1790
Oil on canvas
36 1/4 × 29 3/4 in.; 92.08 × 75.57 cm
The Metropolitan Museum of Art.
Gift of Edgar William and Bernice
Chrysler Garbisch, 1965

Sally Sanford Perit married Job Perit (cat. 53), her first husband, in 1782. They lived in New Haven, Connecticut, although little is known of their lives there. In this painting Sally displays a miniature portrait of one of their children, a five-year-old girl, possibly Elizabeth.

The miniature, never a public portrait, was an intimate and personal object, often a love token. Frequently it served as a reminder or a momento of an absent loved one and was tucked away in a private place. However, it was also displayed in public and worn as jewelry, either in bracelet form or suspended as a pendant on a pin or necklace, as seen here.

The tradition of the painting within a painting is a rich and varied one that can be traced back to antiquity. The Italian Renaissance often employed the device to open up the pictorial space. The early American artists, as inheritors of the traditions of Western art, continued the technique for diverse reasons.

Mrs. Perit's dress, elaborate coiffure, and enormous hat appear as naive renderings springing from Ralph Earl's knowledge of fashionable contemporary English portraiture. The portrait, important in Moulthrop's oeuvre, is signed "Sally Perit. Aetat. 29/A.D.1790.Ruben Molthrop.Pinxit."   ELC

Reference
Caldwell, John, and Oswald Rodriguez Roque et al. *American Paintings in the Metropolitan Museum of Art*. Vol. I. New York: Princeton University Press and the Metropolitan Museum of Art, 1994.

52
Judah Eleazer Lyons
(1779–1849)
Artist unknown
c. 1820–30
Miniature; oil on ivory
2 ¼ × 2 ⅛ in.; 5.6 × 5.3 cm
American Jewish Historical Society, Waltham,
Massachusetts, and New York, New York.
Bequest of Sarah Lyons

Travel was a defining characteristic in the life of Judah Eleazer Lyons. Born in Philadelphia, the son of Dutch immigrant Eleazer Lyons and Hannah Levy Lyons, Judah Eleazer began traveling south before the age of two, as his parents relocated to Baltimore in about 1781 and then to Surinam in about 1792. The voyage between the States and the West Indies became a familiar one for

53 *Job Perit*

52 *Judah Eleazer Lyons*

Lyons, as he married in New York, raised his children with wife Mary Asser Levy in Surinam, and spent the last years of his life living in Philadelphia, and, finally, in New York. In his 1805 journal, Lyons recounts a voyage that he made with his family from New York to Surinam, painting a vivid picture of sea travel at the dawn of the nineteenth century. Along with stories of high tea with the ship's captain, Lyons's journal of the forty-five-day journey records a violent, anti-Semitic confrontation with one of the ship's mates as well as a passenger panic brought on by the depletion of both bread and sugar before the sighting of land.[1]

This miniature portrait of Lyons has been preserved in a gold locket—a case well suited for travel and a fitting symbol of the intimate, private nature of the portrait miniature. A plait of hair, meant to serve as an additional momento for the wearer, is framed on the back of the locket. Thus, wherever Judah Lyons might be in the world, the owner of the locket could remember him.

JWZ

Note
1 Journal of Judah E. Lyons, August 9th–September 24th, 1805, Judah Lyons Papers, American Jewish Historical Society, Waltham, Mass.

Reference
London, Hannah R. *Miniatures of Early American Jews*. Springfield, Mass.: The Pond-Ekberg Company, 1953, p. 33. Illus. 115.

53

Job Perit

(1751–1794)

Reuben Moulthrop (1763–1814)
New Haven, 1790
Oil on canvas
36 ⅛ × 29 ¼ in.; 91.76 × 75.57 cm
The Metropolitan Museum of Art.
Gift of Edgar William and Bernice Chrysler Garbisch, 1965

Reuben Moulthrop, a self-taught primitive artist of the Connecticut School, has been credited with about forty-five attributed works beginning in 1788. He never strayed far from New Haven, Connecticut, which means that he was influenced either by English prints or artists who painted in Connecticut. Clearly he had knowledge of the local painter Ralph Earl; his somewhat stiff forms with heavy, tight outlines set close to the picture plane might also suggest the influence of a local painter such as Winthrop Chandler.

Job Perit, son of Peter Perit and Abigail Shepard, was born in Milford, Connecticut, in 1751. Little is known about his life except that he lived in New Haven. This work is significant in the Moulthrop oeuvre because it has been signed and dated "Job Perit. Aetat. 38/A.D. 1790. Reuben Moulthrop Pinxit." Certainly Moulthrop knew the conventions of portraiture, placing his sitter's hand within his waistcoat. He sits in a Connecticut Windsor chair, with book, pen, and inkwell on a nearby table, motifs that suggest Perit was a man of affairs. ELC

Reference

Caldwell, John, and Oswald Rodriguez Roque et al. *American Paintings in the Metropolitan Museum of Art*. Vol. I. New York: Princeton University Press and the Metropolitan Museum of Art, 1994.

54

Michael Gratz

(1740–1811)

Attributed to Thomas Sully (1783–1872)
Philadelphia, c. 1805–8
Pastel on paper
28 ½ × 24 ¼ in.; 72.4 × 63 cm
American Jewish Historical Society, Waltham,
Massachusetts, and New York, New York.
Gift of an anonymous donor

Hyman Gratz accused his ambitious younger brother, Michael, of fashioning himself an "English nabob." He urged Michael to give up his rambling ways, return to their native Silesia, and marry a local woman.[1] But the "nabob" could not be dissuaded from seeking his fortune in America. From his arrival in Philadelphia in 1758, the pioneering Michael Gratz demonstrated

54   *Michael Gratz*

a zeal for the potential of the frontier. His firm, B. and M. Gratz, formed in partnership with his brother, Barnard (cat. 49), redefined boundaries in American business. B. and M. Gratz counted among their activities land speculation in the West, fur trade based in the Ohio River Valley, and a kosher-meat contract in Curaçao.

Domestic adventures in Michael Gratz's life included a marriage to Miriam Simon of Lancaster, Pennsylvania, in June of 1769. Miriam and Michael had twelve children, among them the noted "beauty" and leader of the Jewish Sunday School movement, Rebecca Gratz (Plate 7, cats. 39, 40).

This portrait is attributed to Thomas Sully, whose portraits of Rebecca Gratz and the patronage of the Gratz family helped to launch his career. The painting captures Michael Gratz's pioneering spirit even at age sixty-eight. Although his hair has grayed with age, Gratz's bright blue eyes and ruddy complexion remain as signals of a vigorous man with a penchant for adventure.

JWZ

Note

1. Letter from Hyman Gratz to Michael Gratz, 21 Sh'bat 5519, in *B. and M. Gratz, Merchants in Philadelphia 1754–1798: Papers of Interest to their Posterity and the Posterity of their Associates*, ed. William Vincent Byars (Jefferson City, Mo.: Hugh Stevens Printing Company, 1916), p. 37.

55 *Leah Nathan Hart (Mrs. Jacob Hart, Sr.)*   56 *Jacob Hart, Sr.*

Reference
London, Hannah R. *Portraits of Jews by Gilbert Stuart and Other Early American Artists.* Rutland, Vt.: Charles E. Tuttle Company, 1927. Illus. p. 179.

55

Leah Nathan Hart (Mrs. Jacob Hart, Sr.)

(1760–1854)
Philip Parisen (d. 1822)
New York, 1818
Oil on canvas
32 × 25 ¼ in.; 81.3 × 64.2 cm
American Jewish Historical Society, Waltham, Massachusetts, and New York, New York.
Gift of Misses Zillah and Rebecca Jacobs

Artist Philip Parisen painted Leah Nathan Hart's portrait when she was fifty-eight years of age. A bride at age nineteen, Leah had thirteen children and dozens of grandchildren by the time Parisen captured her image in 1818. She had lived in two other cities before sitting for this portrait in New York.

Leah Nathan and her twin sister, Rachel, were the oldest children in a family of five daughters born to Caroline Webb and Lyon Nathan, the first Jewish sexton in Philadelphia. After marriage to Jacob Hart (cat. 56) in 1777, Leah moved with him first to Baltimore and then to New York. A lifetime of experiences preceded Parisen's rendering of the paired portraits of Leah and Jacob Hart. Although Jacob died three years after sitting for his portrait, Leah would live for another thirty-five years, dying at the age of ninety-three.[1]

Leah appears the image of modesty in this portrait: her hands are folded properly on her lap; a white lace-trimmed bonnet covers her hair; and a finely wrought lace collar veils her neck.   JWZ

Note
1. Malcolm H. Stern. *First American Jewish Families: 600 Genealogies, 1654–1978* (Cincinnati: American Jewish Archives, and Waltham Mass.: American Jewish Historical Society, 1978), p. 98.

References
"Early American Jewish Portraits and Silver." Publications of the American Jewish Historical Society 42 (June 1953): 416–18.
Early American Jewish Portraiture. Kayser, Stephen S., and Isadore S. Meyer, eds. Exhibition catalogue. New York: The Jewish Museum, 1952. Illus. 11.

56

Jacob Hart, Sr.

(1746–1822)

Philip Parisen (d. 1822)
New York, 1818
Oil on canvas
31 × 25 in.; 77.5 × 62.5 cm
American Jewish Historical Society, Waltham,
Massachusetts, and New York, New York.
Gift of Misses Zillah and Rebecca Jacobs

Philip Parisen was a painter, silhouettist, hair worker, and silver-
smith who made his residence in New York during the first part
of the nineteenth century. Although American-born himself,
Parisen's father hailed from Prussia. Perhaps their common
German roots served as a topic of conversation between Parisen
and his patron, Jacob Hart, Sr.

Born in Furth, Bavaria, in 1746, Hart immigrated to America,
settling in Baltimore at age twenty-nine. A merchant and a
patriot, he supplied General Lafayette's troops with clothing and
shoes to aid in their 1781 campaign against the British.[1] Hart married Leah Nathan of Philadelphia in 1771 (cat. 55). The couple settled in New York with their family of thirteen children (including
Nathan, cat. 57), where Hart played an active role in the leadership of Shearith Israel, serving as its parnas in 1800.

Parisen portrays Hart sitting in a chair, holding several pieces of
paper in one hand, and reaching into his jacket, as if to find a pen,
with his other hand. These props—the paper and the gesture—
symbolize the important role that Hart played in his community
and his family. While other Hart family members are motionless
in their portraits, Jacob Hart is engaged in activity, an energetic
man of affairs as well as the center of family transactions.

Note
1. Ira Rosenswaike, "The Jews of Baltimore to 1810," *American Jewish Historical
Quarterly* 64, no. 4 (June 1975): 300.

References
"Early American Jewish Portraits and Silver," *Publications of the American Jewish
Historical Society* 42 (June 1953): 416–18.
Early American Jewish Portraiture. Kayser, Stephen S., and Isadore S. Meyer, eds.
Exhibition catalogue. New York: The Jewish Museum, 1952. Illus. 10.

57

Nathan Hart

(1797–1857)

Philip Parisen (d. 1822)
New York, 1817
Oil on canvas
30 ½ × 24 in.; 76.7 × 60 cm
American Jewish Historical Society, Waltham,
Massachusetts, and New York, New York.
Gift of Misses Zillah and Rebecca Jacobs

57 *Nathan Hart*

Nathan Hart was one of a set of twins born in New York to Leah
and Jacob Hart (cats. 55, 56) in December of 1797. Neither Nathan
nor his twin brother, Leon, ever married. The records of Nathan's
estate reveal that he lived a modest life in his home on Elm Street
in New York and counted various Jewish books among his possessions. At the time of his death, Hart owned a copy of Isaac Leeser's English translation of the Bible, a set of the Five Books of
Moses, five Jewish calendars, and several books of "Jewish tales."[1]

As Richard Brilliant points out in his essay in this book, the
Hart portrait trio serves as an example of the transition from
images of colonial success to those of federalist possibility. While
the portraits of Nathan's parents, Leah and Jacob Hart, convey
them as established persons, the image of their son is romanti-
cized. Nathan is portrayed here as a brooding youth, his fluid
features fixed on a Byronic notion.   JWZ

Note
1. "Estate of Nathan Hart as Assessed by Benjamin Salomon." September 21, 1857,
Nathan Hart Papers, American Jewish Historical Society, Waltham, Mass.

References
"Early American Jewish Portraits and Silver," *Publications of the American Jewish
Historical Society* 42 (June 1953) 416–18.
Early American Jewish Portraiture. Kayser, Stephen S. and Isadore S. Meyer, eds.
Exhibition catalogue. New York: The Jewish Museum, 1952, 13.

Generations: Continuity and Change

58
Joshua Isaacs
(1744–1810)
Artist unknown
New York, c. 1781
Oil on canvas
30 × 24 in.; 76.2 × 60.96 cm
Museum of the City of New York.
Bequest of Alma H. Harwood, 63.115.1

58   *Joshua Isaacs*

59   *Justina Brandly Lazarus Isaacs (Mrs. Joshua Isaacs)*

The beneficent Joshua Isaacs, president of Shearith Israel, was deemed by the congregation an "honored elder," and his name was included among the perpetual benefactors of the synagogue. Known for his munificence, he contributed regularly to various relief funds around New York and even forgave his modest one-percent interest on the mortgage of the African-American Elm Street Church. His will directed that fifty pounds should be given to Shearith Israel's Hebrew School to teach the Hebrew language to poor children. This tradition of altruism has been continued through the years by his progeny.

Joshua Isaacs was born in Grenada, British West Indies; named for his deceased father, he was born to Hannah Levy Isaacs, a daughter of the New York patriarch Moses Raphael Levy (Plate 1, cat. 1) and his second wife, Grace Mears Levy (cat. 2). In 1780 he took the American oath of loyalty and served in the Third Company, Eighth Battalion, of the Lancaster County, Pennsylvania, militia. The following year he married Justina Brandly Lazarus (cat. 59) in Lancaster, moved to New York, and eventually became the father of six children, among them Frances Isaacs (cat. 60) and Solomon Isaacs (Plate 13, cat. 76).

The uncanny resemblance between father and son can be observed in The Jewish Museum's magnificent portrait of Solomon Isaacs. Both of the handsome Sephardic men are somewhat heavy-set with dark eyes; the son, painted at a younger age, appears the dashing Romantic dandy whereas the father appears more conservative in his demeanor, suggesting a middle-aged Federal gentleman, a man of affairs, who had been a Revolutionary soldier in his youth. This stylistic difference could be accounted for by the changing times of the burgeoning nation as well as by a shifting aesthetic. However, despite the differences in pictorial style, their kindly dispositions and spiritual generosity, as well as the forthright character evident in their personal histories, have been caught by both artists.

Like his father before him, Joshua Isaacs is buried in the old cemetery of Shearith Israel on Chatham Square in New York City; his will directed that he wished "to be buried in our Jews' burying ground in New York among my relatives and friends."[1]

ELC

60   *Frances Isaacs*

Note

1. David De Sola Pool. *Portraits Etched in Stone: Early Jewish Settlers 1682–1831* (New York: Columbia University Press, 1952), p. 317.

References

Faber, Eli. *The Jewish People in America.* Vol. 1: *A Time for Planting: The First Migration, 1654–1820.* Baltimore: The Johns Hopkins Press, 1992.

Pool, David De Sola. *Portraits Etched in Stone: Early Jewish Settlers, 1682–1831.* New York: Columbia University Press, 1952.

Stern, Malcolm H. *First American Jewish Families: 600 Genealogies, 1654–1988.* Baltimore: Ottenheimer Publishers, 1978.

59

Justina Brandly Lazarus Isaacs (Mrs. Joshua Isaacs)

(1752–1825)

Artist unknown

c. 1781

Oil on canvas

30 × 24 in.; 76.2 × 60.96 cm

Museum of the City of New York.

Bequest of Alma H. Harwood, 63.115.2

Justina Brandly Lazarus was born on October 16, 1752, probably in Fredericktown, Maryland, to Sampson Lazarus and Frumet (Fanny) Cohen. Both grandfathers, paternal uncle, and father were leading citizens of Fredericktown as well as merchants and traders. Following the death of his childless brother and business partner in Fredericktown, in 1780 Sampson Lazarus moved back to Lancaster, Pennsylvania—then a vibrant frontier community with many Jewish residents—because his daughter had become of marriageable age and the elderly Jewish community of Fredericktown offered few prospects.

On March 28, 1781, Justina Brandly Lazarus married Joshua Isaacs (cat. 58) in Lancaster, Pennsylvania. Subsequently they moved to New York and had six children, among them Solomon Isaacs (Plate 13, cat. 76) and Frances Isaacs (cat. 60), who became the wife of the copper magnate Harmon Hendricks (cats. 79, 80). Frances and Harmon Hendricks had thirteen children. Brandly's descendants are among the most distinguished Jewish families in New York. Justina Brandly Lazarus died on the fifteenth anniversary of her husband's death, and, like him, is buried in the old Jewish burial ground on Chatham Square in New York.   ELC

References

Goldstein, Eric L. *Traders and Transports: The Jews of Colonial Maryland.* Baltimore: The Jewish Historical Society of Maryland, 1993.

Pool, David De Sola. *Portraits Etched in Stone: Early Jewish Settlers, 1682–1831.* New York: Columbia University Press, 1952.

Stern, Malcolm H. *First American Jewish Families: 600 Genealogies, 1654–1988.* Baltimore: Ottenheimer Publishers, 1978.

60

Frances Isaacs

(1783–1854)

Artist unknown
New York, c. 1800–05
Oil on canvas
30 ¼ × 25 in.; 76.84 × 63.5 cm
Museum of the City of New York.
Bequest of Alma H. Harwood, 63.115.3

Young Frances Isaacs was born in Lancaster, Pennsylvania, in 1783, the daughter of Justina Brandly Lazarus Isaacs (cat. 59) and Joshua Isaacs (cat. 58), and the sister of Solomon Isaacs (Plate 13, cat. 76). In a few years, on June 4, 1800, she would marry Harmon Hendricks (cats. 79, 80), founder of the first copper industry in America, and become the mother of thirteen surviving children.

In this portrait Frances Isaacs is depicted as a cultivated young woman who holds an open book in her hand; in the background the artist has depicted a sketchy landscape. These conventions of portraiture are employed frequently with the young female sitters in this exhibition of colonial and Federal portraits.

However, Frances Isaacs rests her forearm on the frame of an oval window-sill and leans her open book forward into the picture plane. This bifurcated position places her partially in the viewer's space and partially in her own space. The artist has chosen to place the innocent young girl in limbo because, at this moment in her life, she is suspended between the world of the adult and of the child. Her erect posture and large, innocent, childlike eyes, accompanied by her modestly averted glance, thereby properly avoiding any bold direct eye contact with the viewer, symbolize and confirm this dichotomy.   ELC

References
Stern, Malcolm H. *First American Jewish Families: 600 Genealogies, 1654–1988*. Baltimore: Ottenheimer Publishers, 1978.
Whiteman, Maxwell. *Copper for America: The Hendricks Family and a National Industry, 1755–1939*. New Brunswick, N.J.: Rutgers University Press, 1971.

61

Jacob I. Cohen

(1789–1869)

Artist unknown
Baltimore, c. 1780
Miniature; watercolor on ivory
Framed: 3 × 2 in.; 7.62 × 5.08 cm
The Maryland Historical Society.
Bequest of Harriet Cohen Coale

A brother of the adventurous Mendes I. Cohen (plate 14, cat. 84), Jacob Cohen was one of the unmarried sons of Judith Solomon

61   *Jacob I. Cohen*

Cohen (Mrs. Israel I. Cohen) (cat. 85). Only four years after the family's arrival in Baltimore, the young man served honorably with his brother Mendes and other Jewish men such as Solomon Etting (Plate 12, cat. 74) in Nicholson's Artillery Fencibles at Fort McHenry.

Although twenty-five years younger than Solomon Etting, Jacob Cohen followed his lead in many ways. First, they fought for Jewish political equality, which they won; subsequently both were elected to the Baltimore City Council in 1826. The pair owned private family cemeteries and belonged to Congregation Mikveh Israel in Philadelphia. They also assisted the immigrants of the German Society of Maryland and were directors of the Baltimore and Ohio Railroad, the first American railroad.

The Cohens' first family venture was a lottery business that evolved into a bank, Jacob I. Cohen and Brothers. The bank served the private and public sector and represented the Rothschild interests in the United States. Remarkably, in the panic and depression of 1837 the Cohens continued to pay dividends to the public when other banks failed. The Cohens' bank was one of the most enterprising and fiscally secure in the country.

Unlike many of Jacob Cohen's later, more dour portraits, this romantic miniature portrait framed in blue and white cloisonné crowned with arches, shield, and loop, shows a younger, yet conservative gentleman whose facial features leap out from the soft gray and buff background. It is not difficult to imagine Judith Solomon Cohen wearing her eldest son's miniature.   ELC

References

Fein, Isaac M. *The Making of an American Jewish Community: The History of Baltimore Jewry from 1773 to 1920.* Baltimore: The Jewish Historical Society of Maryland, 1985.

London, Hannah R. *Portraits of Jews by Gilbert Stuart and Other Early American Artists.* Rutland, Vt.: Charles E. Tuttle Company, 1969.

Stern, Malcolm H. *First American Jewish Families: 600 Genealogies, 1654–1988.* Baltimore: Ottenheimer Publishers, 1978.

62

Jacob De Leon

(1764–1828)

John Ramage (1748–1802)
1789
Miniature; oil on ivory
2 × 1 ¾ in.; 5 × 4.3 cm
American Jewish Historical Society, Waltham, Massachusetts, and New York, New York.
Bequest of Emma Samuel

A merchant, military man, and mason, Jacob De Leon lived in his birthplace, Jamaica, as well as in various South Carolina communities during his lifetime. De Leon first arrived in the colonies

62   *Jacob De Leon*

before 1780, for it is in that year that he is attributed the heroic rolef carrying the mortally wounded General DeKalb from the field at the battle of Camden, South Carolina.[1] In 1789, he married Hannah Hendricks in New York. Community records indicate that Hannah and Jacob returned to Jamaica for a short time in about 1790. However, all eight of their children made their homes in South Carolina. Jacob De Leon is himself buried in Columbia, South Carolina.

Jacob De Leon's miniature portrait is rendered in a style typical of artist John Ramage. Described as sporting consistently "beauish" attire himself, Ramage favored equally fine dress for his portrait sitters. Jacob De Leon, outfitted in a claret-colored coat decorated with gilt buttons, and a coordinating jabot, achieves a definitively "beauish" appearance in this portrait. Ramage's signature blue background also finds a place in the De Leon miniature. A native of Ireland, Ramage came to America sometime before 1772. He lived and worked as an artist in New York, Halifax, and Montreal.   JWZ

Note

1. Historian Barnett Elzas disputes the historicity of this claim, while simultaneously noting its important place in South Carolina Jewish folklore. See Barnett Elzas, *The Jews of South Carolina* (Philadelphia: J.B. Lippincott, 1905), pp. 95–96.

Reference

London, Hannah R. *Miniatures of Early American Jews.* Springfield, Mass.: The Pond-Ekberg Company, 1953, 12–13. Illus. 79.

63

Benjamin Gomez

(1769–1828)

Artist unknown
Early 19th c.
Miniature; watercolor
2 ½ × 2 in.; 6.25 × 5.08 cm
Collection of Ruth Hendricks Schulson

Fleshing out history of the sitters in colonial and Federal portraits can be a fascinating adventure that presents many pitfalls. It is an accepted fact that at age twenty-eight Benjamin Gomez, from an illustrious Sephardic family, married one of the sisters of copper magnate Harmon Hendricks (cats. 79, 80) on September 13, 1797. The genealogist Malcolm Stern gives her name as Catherine, although David de Sola Pool, who has recorded the history of Shearith Israel, gives it as Charlotte. De Sola Pool also traces the Gomez family to the Iberian crypto-Jew Isaac Gomez who held favor at the Spanish court. Family lore holds that the Spanish king himself warned Isaac of the impending Inquisition.[1]

Moving to New York at the beginning of the eighteenth century, the Gomezes became known as the largest, most wealthy

63 Benjamin Gomez

it has descended in the Hendricks and Nathan families, distinguished early Jewish families that settled in New York.   ELC

Note
1. See David de Sola Pool. *Portraits Etched in Stone: Early Jewish Settlers, 1682–1831* (New York: Columbia University Press, 1952), pp. 218, 432–34.

References
London, Hannah R. *Portraits of Jews by Gilbert Stuart and Other Early American Artists.* Rutland, Vt.: Charles E. Tuttle Company, 1969.
Pool, David de Sola. *Portraits Etched in Stone: Early Jewish Settlers, 1682–1831.* New York: Columbia University Press, 1952.
Stern, Malcolm H. *First American Jewish Families: 600 Genealogies, 1654–1988.* Baltimore: Ottenheimer Publishers, 1978.

64

Frances Gratz Etting (Mrs. Reuben Etting)

(1771–1852)
James Peale (1749–1831)
Philadelphia, 1794
Miniature; watercolor on ivory
2 ⅜ × 1 ⁹⁄₁₆ in.; 6.03 × 3.97 cm
Courtesy of the Museum of American Art
of the Pennsylvania Academy of the Fine Arts,
Philadelphia. Gift of Frank Marx Etting

and influential family in eighteenth-century New York, with a broad range of mercantile, trade, shipping, and real-estate interests. Benjamin Gomez, named for his grandfather, was born to Matthias and Rachel Gomez on September 17, 1769; his parents died when he was still a boy. He is known as an early Jewish publisher and bookseller in New York; but his enterprise brought him neither fortune nor security, so he became a merchant. He was head of the Fortunate Lottery Office, then a grocer, and finally a tobacconist for the last four years of his life. Committed to his faith, he served Congregation Shearith Israel over the years as treasurer and *parnas* (president).

The Gomez miniature is set in gold. Unfortunately the artist, with his distinctive brushstroke, remains unknown. Benjamin wears jaunty yet typical attire for an upper-class young gentleman. He is portrayed in a closed green coat with brown and green buttons, high collar, and wide lapels; an unusual waistcoat edged in rose; and with his stock tied in a small, lacy bow. Depicted here as a lively, intelligent, young man, with dark eyes and eyebrows that dominate his narrow mouth and pointed chin, Benjamin probably presented this miniature to his bride at the time of their marriage. This would strongly suggest a date of 1797 for the work.

The provenance of this engaging miniature is secure and confirms the identification of the sitter. Along with a Spanish Bible

Frances Gratz Etting was born in Philadelphia, the daughter of Michael Gratz (cat. 54) and Miriam Simon Gratz; she was an older sister of Rebecca Gratz (Plate 7, cats. 39, 40). On September 17, 1794, she married Reuben Etting (cat. 65) in Philadelphia, uniting two distinguished colonial families; the couple had eight children. Certainly the delightful portrait miniatures of husband and wife, initialed and dated "IP 1794," were commissioned to celebrate their marriage.

The bride, aged twenty-three, is depicted at the height of fashion in a purple gown with décolletage edged in white ruffles; she has woven a strand of pearls in her dark-brown wavy hair. She was not blessed with the regular features of her younger sisters Rachel Gratz Moses and Rebecca Gratz. However, the luminous palette of light blues, white, gray, and light red that James Peale has lavished upon her ivory miniature more than makes up for the fact that Frances was not a natural "beauty."

James Peale began his career in 1782 after serving with the Continental Army. A member of the remarkable Peale family of artists, James was taught by his elder brother Charles Willson Peale, who had studied under Benjamin West in London; together they cornered the market in colonial and Federal portraits in Philadelphia. James, who became America's finest miniaturist, started out by making frames for his brother; he would create the miniatures on ivory at three guineas, while Charles would do the patron's larger portrait on canvas.   ELC

64   *Frances Gratz Etting (Mrs. Reuben Etting)*

65   *Reuben Etting*

References

London, Hannah R. *Miniatures of Early American Jews.* Springfield, Mass.: The Pond-Ekberg Company, 1953. Illus. p. 91.

Stern, Malcolm H. *First American Jewish Families: 600 Genealogies, 1654–1988.* Baltimore: Ottenheimer Publishers, 1978.

65

Reuben Etting

(1762–1848)

James Peale (1749–1831)
Philadelphia, 1794
Miniature; watercolor on ivory
2 $^{7}/_{16}$ × 1 $^{13}/_{16}$ in.; 6.2 × 4.6 cm
Courtesy of the Museum of American Art
of the Pennsylvania Academy of the Fine Arts, Philadelphia.
Gift of Frank Marx Etting

Reuben Etting was the namesake of another Reuben Etting, a colonial soldier, who was said to have died of starvation in a British prison because his captors discovered his religion and fed him only pork. Born in York, Pennsylvania, Reuben was the first child of the Indian trader Elijah Etting and Shinah Solomon Etting (cat. 50); he was also a brother of Solomon Etting (Plate 12, cat. 74) and Sally Etting (cat. 75). In 1798, Reuben served as an officer in the Baltimore Blues; later Thomas Jefferson appointed him as Maryland's United States Marshal in 1801, a significant appointment for a Jewish citizen of a state where Jews had not yet been granted equal civil and political rights.

Reuben, probably aged thirty-two at the time of the portrait, wears a short white wig, an aubergine coat with a white double-breasted waistcoat, and ruffled stock; he is a handsome man with regular features who gazes out at the viewer with captivating gray eyes.

The miniatures of Reuben Etting and his wife, Frances Gratz Etting (cat. 64), are important documents of early American life in two respects. Not only are they exceptional examples of James Peale's miniature portraits supported by an important exhibition history; but the sitters are representatives of two prominent Jewish families—the Etting and Gratz families—who played a significant role in the development of both American society and culture during the colonial and Federal periods.

The Pennsylvania Academy of the Fine Arts considers these works important enough to keep on permanent display. Their exhibition history includes, among others, the 1887 Loan Exhibition of Historical Portraits and the Tenth Annual Exhibition of Miniatures in 1911, both at the Pennsylvania Academy of the Fine Arts. As the critic Charles Henry Hart, who was Jewish, wrote in 1887, "Collections of this kind are not only entertaining but instructive. They are historically valuable in making us acquainted with the appearance and personal in-

66   *Abraham Alexander*

In this miniature, the artist has depicted Abraham Alexander, Sr., wearing a wig, dark coat, buttoned creamy waistcoat, and a white stock. The figure appears somewhat stiff and the facial modeling is minimal. The miniature portrait is signed "Sully."

Abraham Alexander, Sr., was born in London, the son of Rabbi Joseph Raphael Alexander; he married there and had two sons, Abraham, Jr., and Moses. Arriving in Charleston, he served as a *hazzan*, or leader of public worship, at Congregation Beth Elohim, and also in the South Carolina Revolutionary forces in 1781–82. Auditor at the U.S. Custom House in Charleston, Abraham Alexander was a Mason and a founder of the Scottish Rite Masonry in 1801.

Known as a Hebrew scholar, he is remembered annually by Congregation Beth Elohim in the memorial prayer for the dead on Yom Kippur. At his death, Abraham Alexander, Sr., was given a public funeral; all the flags in Charleston harbor, as well as at the U. S. Custom House, were flown at half-mast.[1] He is buried in the Coming Street Cemetery in Charleston.[2]   ELC

Notes
1. Henry Aaron Alexander. *Notes on the Alexander Family of South Carolina and Georgia and Connections.* (Charleston, 1954.)
2. Hannah R. London. *Miniatures of Early American Jews* (Springfield, Mass.: The Pond Ekberg Company, 1953), 14–15.

References
Alexander, Henry Aaron. *Notes on the Alexander Family of South Carolina and Georgia and Connections.* Charleston, 1954.
London, Hannah R. *Miniatures of Early American Jews.* Springfield, Mass.: Pond-Ekberg Company, 1953. Illus. p. 83.
Stern, Malcolm H. *First American Jewish Families: 600 Genealogies, 1654–1988.* Baltimore: Ottenheimer Publishers, 1978.

fluence of the men and women of past generations, and they are artistically valuable in showing to students in the broadest sense of the word the method of pose, composition, and technique of our foremost portrait painters."[1]   ELC

Note
1. Hannah R. London. *Miniatures of Early American Jews.* (Springfield, Mass.: The Pond-Ekberg Company, 1953) p. 19.

References
London, Hannah R. *Miniatures of Early American Jews.* Springfield, Mass.: The Pond-Ekberg Company, 1953, p. 19. Illus. p. 91.
Stern, Malcolm H. *First American Jewish Families: 600 Genealogies, 1654–1988.* Baltimore: Ottenheimer Publishers, 1978.
Wolf, Edwin 2nd, and Maxwell Whiteman. *The History of the Jews of Philadelphia from Colonial Times to the Age of Jackson.* Philadelphia: Jewish Publication Society of America, 1957.

66
Abraham Alexander, Sr.
(1743–1816)
Attributed to Lawrence Sully (1769–1804)
c. 1795
Miniature; watercolor on ivory
2 ½ × 1 ⅞ in.; 6.25 × 4.76 cm
On loan from the Gibbes Museum of Art/
Carolina Art Association

Lawrence Sully, the older brother of Thomas Sully, was born in Ireland, trained as a miniaturist in England, and arrived in America in 1792. He worked primarily in the Southern cities of Charleston, Norfolk, and Richmond.

67
Benjamin Levy
(1786–1860)
Attributed to Edmund Brewster (active 1818–1839)
New Orleans, 1822
Oil on tin
12 ½ × 10 in.; 31.25 × 25.4 cm
American Jewish Historical Society, Waltham,
Massachusetts, and New York, New York.
Bequest of Irma P. Sellars

Artist Edmund Brewster was deemed "a very young artist of unusual merit" upon his arrival in New Orleans in 1819.[1] His reputation presumably caught the attention of prominent businessman Benjamin Levy (cat. 68), who sat for this portrait in 1822. Aside from sojourns in New Orleans from 1819–21 and 1822–24, Brewster made his home in Philadelphia.

Both portraits of Benjamin Levy are similar in physical appearance; however, Brewster's rendering conveys a different

67 *Benjamin Levy*

Benjamin Levy left New York and moved to New Orleans in 1811 where he established B. Levy and Company, a firm engaged in the printing and selling of books and stationary. New Orleans' first business journal, the *Price Currant,* emanated from Levy's press weekly from 1822 to 1839. While his business boomed, Levy's family grew as well. In 1817, he married Emilie Prieur, a member of a wealthy and influential local French Catholic family.[2] Emilie and Benjamin raised their two children, a son and a daughter, in the Catholic church. There is no evidence that Benjamin himself converted to Catholicism; however, neither do the records of the nascent Jewish community of New Orleans record him as a congregant or a donor. Upon his death in 1860, he was buried in a nondenominational cemetery.

Levy appears here as a distinguished gentleman, a leader of the New Orleans business community, dressed fashionably in a dark suit and a high-collared shirt.   JWZ

Notes
1. Simeon Levy's portrait is published in Bertram Wallace Korn. *Benjamin Levy: New Orleans Printer and Publisher* (Portland, Maine: Anthorisen Press, 1961), Plate 1, p. 17.
2. Emilie's brother, Denis, served seven terms as mayor of New Orleans.

Reference
Korn, Bertram Wallace. *Benjamin Levy: New Orleans Printer and Publisher.* Portland, Maine: Anthorisen Press, 1961.

sense of the sitter's character. Whereas Levy appears relaxed and at ease in the larger portrait (see cat. 68), the smaller likeness painted by Brewster portrays him as as stiffly settled in his chair. In addition, the background looms large around the small figure of Levy in Brewster's portrait, while Levy himself fills up the viewer's frame of vision in the larger canvas. The different messages conveyed by these portraits may result from either the varying skills of the artists or, perhaps, even a change in Levy's disposition.   JWZ

Note
1. George C. Groce and David H. Wallace. *The New-York Historical Society's Dictionary of Artists in America, 1564–1800* (New Haven: Yale University Press, 1957), p. 79.

68
Benjamin Levy

(1786–1860)

Artist unknown

c. 1830–40

Oil on canvas

36 × 28 in.; 90 × 70 cm

American Jewish Historical Society, Waltham, Massachusetts, and New York, New York.

Bequest of Irma P. Sellars

The only son of Simeon and Hetty Levy of New York, Benjamin Levy grew up in the Shearith Israel congregation where his father served as a teacher. In his own portrait, Simeon Levy is depicted holding a book, a reflection of his occupation.[1] Such a prop would be a fitting addition to his son's portrait as well.

68 *Benjamin Levy*

69 *Moses Myers*

70 *Eliza Judah Myers (Mrs. Moses Myers)*

69

Moses Myers

(1752–1835)
Gilbert Stuart (1754–1828)
1803–4
Oil on poplar
33 ¼ × 26 ¼ in.; 84.46 × 66.68 cm
The Chrysler Museum of Art, Norfolk, Virginia:
Moses Myers House, Norfolk, Virginia.
The Historic Houses are the property of the City of Norfolk
and are operated by The Chrysler Museum of Art
M51.1.269.

Secretary of State James Madison and Moses Myers both ordered pendant portraits from Gilbert Stuart. In both instances,
Stuart bestowed a graciousness and warmth on the ladies
while capturing the gentlemen's almost grim seriousness of
purpose.

The Madison state portrait displays a cloth-covered table de-
void of papers as the sitter gazes off presumably at his illustrious
future. On the other hand, as a successful man of affairs, Moses
Myers's cloth-covered table is stacked with bound letters; he has
been interrupted while reading one of them to engage the vie-

wer, which transmits a sense of immediacy while also communi-
cating the sitter's kindly nature. Dressed as a gentleman from the
mercantile class, the fifty-two-year-old Moses Myers is seated in
Gilbert Stuart's ubiquitous red-and-gold chair that links the
pendants together.

From 1808, the portraits of Moses and Eliza Myers have hung
over matching card tables in the drawing room of their Norfolk,
Virginia, home; they bracket a doorway leading to the library.
Directly opposite the portraits are floor-to-ceiling windows that
light the portraits; within the niches of the windows are benches
created for the space and upholstered in the identical crimson of
the Stuart chairs, a most effective arrangement. Over the mantel
hangs a traditional landscape and on the opposite wall are portraits of family members, among them Thomas Sully's portrait
of their son, John Myers (Plate 11, cat. 71). Today the Moses
Myers house, a historic house operated by The Chrysler
Museum of Art for the City of Norfolk, is filled with their familial possessions and creates a powerful impression on the visitor;
one feels that the family might appear at any moment. Happily
four additional historic buildings also have been preserved in the
district.

Moses Myers was the son of Hyam Myers, who arrived in America from Amsterdam, and Rachel Louzada; he was born in New York in about 1752. Moses moved to Norfolk in 1786 and the next year married the widow of Chapman Abraham, Eliza Judah Abraham (cat. 70). By profession he was a merchant-trader and a banker, representing the Bank of Richmond in 1792 as well as the French Republic in Norfolk. A leading citizen, Hannah London wrote that "he possessed in an eminent degree what may be called the chivalry of the commercial character, and displayed in bearing a dignity and grace which looked infinitely beyond an ignoble rivalry and the tricks of trade."[1] Moses Myers died in Norfolk, Virginia, on July 8, 1835.   ELC

Note
1. Hannah R. London. *Portraits of Jews by Gilbert Stuart and Other Early American Artists.* (Rutland, Vt.: Charles E. Tuttle Company, 1969) pp. 52 ff.

References
London, Hannah R. *Portraits of Jews by Gilbert Stuart and Other Early American Artists.* Rutland, Vt.: Charles E. Tuttle Company, 1969. Illus. p. 163.
McLanathan, Richard. *Gilbert Stuart.* New York: Harry N. Abrams, for The National Museum of American Art, Smithsonian Institution, 1986.
Stern, Malcolm H. *First American Jewish Families: 600 Genealogies, 1654–1988.* Baltimore: Ottenheimer Publishers, 1978.

70

Eliza Judah Myers (Mrs. Moses Myers)

(1763–1823)

Gilbert Stuart (1754–1828)

1803–4

Oil on poplar

33 ¼ × 26 ½ in.; 84.46 × 67.31 cm

The Chrysler Museum of Art, Norfolk, Virginia; Moses Myers House, Norfolk, Virginia. The Historic Houses are the property of the City of Norfolk and are operated by The Chrysler Museum of Art

M51.1.270.

71   *John Myers*

Four years after the completion of this splendid portrait, forty-five-year-old Eliza Judah Myers would fill the sunny nursery on the third floor of the great brick house in Norfolk, Virginia, for the last time. Gilbert Stuart must have been quite taken with the remarkable woman, for her 1803–4 portrait bears an uncanny resemblance to the effervescent Dolley Madison's portrait painted in Washington four years earlier. Both ladies wear white, fashionable, high-waisted French Empire dresses with tiny cap sleeves and a lace shawl wrapped around the right arm. Both have tied up their dark hair and parted it at the center with curls cascading over their foreheads; only Mrs. Myers has added a broad fillet or bandeau over her hair. Both gentlewomen are seated in Stuart's ubiquitous studio prop, a gilt-frame open armchair upholstered in crimson velvet. In both portraits the artist was able to convey the charm and graciousness of these two renowned hostesses.

However, Eliza's constancy also shines out from her portrait; not only was she the pivotal center of her large family, but she had captured her husband's heart as well. She could look out at the nearby harbor and observe one of her husband's great ships, her namesake the *Eliza*, tied up at the dock. Probably the couple embarked on the *Eliza* to cruise the coast and then up the Saint Lawrence River to Montreal, Eliza Myers's childhood home. Along the way they would have disembarked in Boston, where Gilbert Stuart painted their portraits in about 1803–4. Today, a Liverpool jug, decorated with both Moses Myers's name and an image of the *Eliza*, is among the treasures in their home, the only Jewish historic house in the United States filled with the original family's original possessions. Oddly, no Jewish decorative arts are among the visible artifacts.

Hannah London and Malcolm Stern offer slightly different versions of Eliza Judah's (or Judd's) genealogy.[1] She was the granddaughter of either Judah Abraham or Abraham Judah of Montreal and the daughter of one of two brothers, either Samuel or Abraham. She married Chapman Abraham, or

Abraham Chapman, on July 18, 1781, in Montreal; he died two years later without issue. On March 22, 1787, she married Moses Myers (cat. 69), moved to Norfolk; the couple would produce twelve children. Eliza died in Montreal on October 23, 1823.   ELC

Notes

1. Hannah R. London. *Portraits of Jews by Gilbert Stuart and Other Early American Artists.* (Rutland, Vt.: Charles E. Tuttle Publishers, 1969) pp. 52 ff. Malcolm H. Stern. *First American Jewish Families: 600 Genealogies, 1654–1988.* 3rd edition (Baltimore: Ottenheimer Publishers, 1991) pp. 141 and 218.

References

London, Hannah R. *Portraits of Jews by Gilbert Stuart and Other Early American Artists.* Rutland, Vt.: Charles E. Tuttle Company, 1969. Illus. p. 165.
McLanathan, Richard. *Gilbert Stuart.* New York: Harry N. Abrams, for The National Museum of American Art, Smithsonian Institution, 1986.
Stern, Malcolm H. *First American Jewish Families: 600 Genealogies, 1654–1988.* Baltimore: Ottenheimer Publishers, 1978.

71

John Myers

(1787–1830)

Thomas Sully (1783–1872)
1808
Oil on paper mounted on canvas
21 ¼ × 24 ½ in.; 53.98 × 62.23 cm
The Chrysler Museum of Art, Norfolk, Virginia;
Moses Myers House, Norfolk, Virginia. The Historic Houses are the property of the City of Norfolk and are operated by The Chrysler Museum of Art
M51.1.271.

Thomas Sully has surpassed himself with this magnificent portrait of a young dandy (Plate 11). The sitter's right arm is casually hooked around an elegant open armchair in the classical style; his hand is placed easily on the arm rest. His extremely high-collared dark coat is the perfect foil for his monumental white stock, wrapped around his neck and tied under the chin. The artist has just sketched in the barest drapery in the background. The sitter's tousled hair with wispy curls brushed forward on his forehead and the full sideburns enframe his youthful face; his great masculine eyebrows offer a strong contrast to his soft limpid eyes. It is evident that he has inherited not only the Myers family features but the purposeful, kindly expression evident in the portraits of both parents. It is interesting to note that although the son and heir of Moses Myers cuts a grand Romantic figure in his portrait, he was only twenty-one at the time, with a young sibling upstairs in a crib in the nursery still unable to walk and wearing diapers.

John Myers was born on September 15, 1787, the first child of Moses Myers (cat. 69) and Eliza Judah Myers (cat. 70). He was raised in the family's mansion in Norfolk, Virginia. A merchant and veteran of the War of 1812, he died in 1830 a bachelor.

Thomas Sully, age twenty-five and about to depart for Europe, painted John Myers in 1808; the young artist had visited Boston in 1807 to observe Gilbert Stuart at work. It is not unlikely that when the great master painted the young man's parents in Boston the following year, he might have recommended young Sully for their son's portrait.   ELC

Reference

Stern, Malcolm H. *First American Jewish Families: 600 Genealogies, 1654–1988.* Baltimore: Ottenheimer Publishers, 1978.

72

Henrietta Overing Auchmuty (Mrs. Robert Nicholls Auchmuty) (1760–1830)
Gilbert Stuart (1754–1828)
Newport, Rhode Island, c. 1815
Oil on canvas
34 ¼ × 28 ⅛ in.; 86.99 × 71.44 cm
The Brooklyn Museum of Art.
Gift of Herbert L. Pratt 21.55

When Henrietta Overing Auchmuty selected an artist to paint her likeness in about 1815, she unsurprisingly turned to Gilbert Stuart. As well as being the premier portrait artist of the day, Stuart had both familial and religious ties to her native Newport, Rhode Island. Having grown up in the region, as a child the artist received a scholarship to attend Trinity Church's Parish School in the city. In addition to her own childhood association with this Anglican religious institution, Mrs. Auchmuty and her husband, Robert Nicholls Auchmuty, were active congregants throughout their married lives; and Mrs. Auchmuty continued to attend the church after she was widowed.

With his acclaimed ability to capture the essence of character in portraits, Stuart depicted Mrs. Auchmuty as a dignified Newport citizen of the recently established national Republic, wearing a black dress trimmed with an elaborate lace collar and fashionable lace cap suitable for a woman of her mature years. An ornate paisley shawl is draped gracefully around her shoulders, lending a decorative quality to this composition.

A resident of Newport for most of her life, Mrs. Auchmuty descended from a long line of governmental figures who were distinguished for their loyalty to the British Crown. Judge Robert Auchmuty, her maternal grandfather, was an acclaimed barrister from England who settled in Roxbury, Massachusetts, and served as Judge of Admiralty for this colony during the second quarter of the eighteenth century. John Overing, Mrs. Auchmuty's pater-

McLanathan, Richard. *Gilbert Stuart.* New York: Harry N. Abrams, for the National Museum of American Art, Smithsonian Institution, 1986.

Townsend, Annette. *The Auchmuty Family of Scotland and America.* New York: The Grafton Press, 1992.

72 *Henrietta Overing Auchmuty (Mrs. Robert Nicholls Auchmuty)*

nal grandfather, served as Attorney General for Massachusetts during this period.

On December 8, 1785, Henrietta married her second cousin, Robert Nicholls Auchmuty (1755–1813) of New York City, thus merging two prominent political dynasties within the colonies. Auchmuty, a lawyer in his own right who had been schooled at Kings College—which became Columbia College following the Revolution—also descended from Judge Robert Auchmuty. As a young man, he had served as a volunteer in the British army during the Revolutionary War and was Commissioner of Claims for the British government until that office was dissolved. His father, the Rev. Dr. Samuel Auchmuty, was an Anglican minister and rector of New York City's prestigious Trinity Church, a major center of British authority in the colony. By the time that the Revolutionary War was concluded, many of Auchmuty's fellow Tories had left America's shores for England, although Robert Nicholls Auchmuty and his future wife remained to participate in building the new nation.   CEM

References

Johnson, Allen, and Dumas Malone, eds. *Dictionary of American Biography.* Vol. 1:420–22. New York: Charles Scribner's Sons, 1927; rpt. 1964.

73
Rachel Gratz Etting (Mrs. Solomon Etting)

(1764–1831)

John Wesley Jarvis (1780–1840)
Baltimore, c. 1810–12
Oil on panel
Framed: 34 ¼ × 26 ¼ in.; 87 × 66.68 cm
The Maryland Historical Society.
Gift of Eleanor S. Cohen

The spirited Rachel Gratz Etting was born in Philadelphia on October 9, 1764, the daughter of pioneer merchant-trader Barnard Gratz (Plate 10, cat. 49) and Richea Myers-Cohen. A member of the important Gratz-Etting clan of Philadelphia and Baltimore, she was the niece of Michael Gratz (cat. 54) and the first cousin of Frances Gratz Etting (cat. 64) and Rebecca Gratz (Plate 7, cats. 39, 40). On October 26, 1791, Rachel became the second wife of Solomon Etting (Plate 12, cat. 74); at this time her widowed father moved with her to Baltimore. She later became the mother of eight children, among them Kitty Etting who married Benjamin I. Cohen, the brother of Mendes I. Cohen (Plate 14, cat. 84) and Jacob I. Cohen (cat. 61). The Etting-Cohen heirs are responsible for a multitude of fine and decorative arts objects given to the Maryland Historical Society.

John Wesley Jarvis probably did not paint the portraits of Mr. and Mrs. Solomon Etting at the same time, nor did he conceive of them as pendant pairs that interact with each other; the icon-like quality of this portrait clearly negates the pendant-pair theory. Rather Rachel's frontal pose, direct gaze, and half smile almost flirt with the viewer; she appears about to speak, which gives the work a pleasant sense of immediacy. The forty-six-year-old woman wears a white-lace cap festooned with ribbons cascading over one shoulder that sets off her olive complexion and almost covers her dark brown hair. Also quite properly, her décolletage is modestly covered and secured with a jeweled pin. A lacy white shawl is wrapped around the ample figure of this good-natured singular woman.   ELC

References

London, Hannah R. *Portraits of Jews by Gilbert Stuart and Other Early American Artists.* Rutland, Vt.: Charles E. Tuttle Company, 1969. Illus. 133.

Stern, Malcolm H. *First American Jewish Families: 600 Genealogies, 1654–1988.* Baltimore: Ottenheimer Publishers, 1978.

73 *Rachel Gratz Etting (Mrs. Solomon Etting)*

74 *Solomon Etting*

74

Solomon Etting

(1764–1847)

John Wesley Jarvis (1780–1840)
Baltimore, c. 1810–12

Oil on panel
Framed: 34 ³⁄₁₆ × 26 ⅛ in.; 86.83 × 66.36 cm
The Maryland Historical Society.
Gift of Eleanor S. Cohen

Solomon Etting (see Plate 12) was the second son of Indian trader Elijah Etting and Shinah Solomon Etting (cat. 50); born in York, Pennsylvania, he was also a brother of Reuben Etting (cat. 65) and Sally Etting (cat. 75). In 1783 he married Reyna Simon, who died seven years later, leaving the twenty-six-year-old a widower with four small children. On October 26, 1791, in Philadelphia, he married Rachel Gratz (cat. 73), the daughter of his former mentor, Barnard Gratz (cat. 49); they had eight more children.

This powerful Jarvis portrait depicts Solomon at age fifty-six gazing at the viewer with kindly blue eyes. The artist captures the sitter's strength and energy; holding pen in hand and seated at a desk laden with books and papers, he is represented as a vigorous man of affairs and achievement. A gold watch-fob peeks out from under his conservative dark suit topped with a lustrous white stock and collar cut low at the chin.

Moving from Pennsylvania to Baltimore in about 1792, Solomon Etting maintained a hardware store on Calvert Street and became a director of the Union Bank in which his family also invested. In 1796, he gave up his emporium and became involved in large-scale shipping and commerce. He helped establish the Baltimore Water Company, the Baltimore East India Shipping Company, and became director of the Baltimore and Ohio Railroad, America's first. President George Washington was notified of Solomon Etting's disapproval of the Jay Treaty. Solomon was wounded at the Battle of Fort McHenry, near Baltimore, during the War of 1812.

Solomon Etting had many social, cultural, and religious interests. Sympathetic to the abolitionist cause, he worked for the resettlement of Baltimore blacks and assisted German immigrants in the city. Also a religious man, he worshipped privately in his home and maintained connections to his Philadelphia synagogue, Mikveh Israel. But he assisted with the purchase of a Jewish burial ground in Baltimore.

His most memorable achievement was the championing of civil rights for Jews. The passage of the bill giving Jews the right to hold public office and practice law was his personal triumph; from his unsuccessful petition to the Maryland House of Delegates in 1797, he persevered until the issue was resolved. This was not just a local or federal issue; people were involved around the world. In England, Mendes I. Cohen (Plate 14, cat. 84) petitioned his mother to send him copies of the speeches concerning "the Jewish Bill." Several months after the bill was passed in 1826, Solomon Etting was elected to the City Council.   ELC

References
Fein, Isaac M. *The Making of an American Jewish Community: The History of Baltimore Jewry from 1773 to 1920.* Baltimore: The Jewish Historical Society of Maryland, 1985.
London, Hannah R. *Portraits of Jews By Gilbert Stuart and Other Early American Artists.* Rutland, Vt.: Charles E. Tuttle Company, 1969. Illus. 135.

75

Sally Etting
(1776–1863)
Thomas Sully (1783–1872)
1808
Oil on canvas, 30 × 25 in.; 76.2 × 63.5 cm
The Jewish Museum, New York.
Gift of the William Wolman Foundation, F4610

76   *Solomon Isaacs*

75   *Sally Etting*

The life of Sally Etting remains a mystery; yet we know that she had great fashion sense and remarkably good foresight in the choice of her portraitist.

Sally is dressed in the height of fashion for 1808; the thirty-two-year-old woman chose a simple white neoclassical gown just coming into fashion in Philadelphia during the Federal period. Her hair is drawn up in ringlets that crown her head, not unlike the aristocratic women depicted by Jacques-Louis David in neoclassical France.

In 1808 Thomas Sully, not twenty-five years old, had just arrived in Philadelphia from New York; his register indicates that he had completed seventy portraits to date and had received more than three thousand dollars. The following year Sully would leave for London where he would study with Benjamin West and fall under the influence of Thomas Lawrence. In later years Sully would receive commissions to paint important full-length, Grand Manner portraits of the Marquis de Lafayette and Queen Victoria. The artist enjoyed a long life and prosperous career in Philadelphia. This splendid early portrait gives many indications of his future success.

77 *George Griffin*

78 *Lydia Butler Griffin (Mrs. George Griffin)*

Sally Etting also lived into her late eighties and came from a successful family. She was the daughter of the Indian trader Elijah Etting and Shinah Solomon (cat. 50) who had lived in Lancaster and York, Pennsylvania. After her father's death, her mother brought Sally and her four young siblings to Baltimore; somehow the family managed to thrive under difficult circumstances. Two of her brothers, Reuben Etting (cat. 65) and Solomon Etting (Plate 12, cat. 74), prospered in business.   ELC

76

Solomon Isaacs

(1786–1855)
John Wesley Jarvis (1780–1840)
Date unknown, Oil on canvas
28 ¼ × 26 ⅝ in.; 71.76 × 67.64 cm
The Jewish Museum, New York.
Museum Purchase; Gift of Mr. and Mrs. Jacob D. Shulman
and the J. E. and Z. B. Butler Foundation,
by exchange; with funds provided by the estate of Gabriel and
Rose Katz; and gift of Kallia H. Bokser, by exchange, 1996–6

Solomon I. Isaacs (Plate 13) was born in 1786, the son of Justina Brandly Lazarus (cat. 59) and Joshua Isaacs (cat. 58), who was president of the New York Jewish community in 1790. Solomon was a confirmed bachelor until he was forty-four years old when he met and married Elkalah Kursheedt, daughter of Israel Baer Kursheedt, a distinguished Jewish scholar who had emigrated from Frankfurt. Solomon and Elkalah had ten children. The family lived in New York City where Solomon became an active member of Shearith Israel, eventually serving as *parnas*, or president, of the congregation.

As a young man Solomon was apprenticed to Harmon Hendricks (cats. 79, 80), the husband of his sister Frances (cat. 60). Solomon served his apprenticeship in the Hendricks copper manufactory, the first in the nation. He prospered and became a devoted and valued partner to his brother-in-law; when he was not in residence near the Soho Copper Works in New Jersey, he lived with the Hendricks family and their many children. In the trade, Solomon was known as "Steamboat" Isaacs; he provided copper boilers for Robert Fulton's steamboats and dealt directly with Paul Revere's manufactory in Massachusetts. He supervised the mill, and understood the copper business from mining to rolling to nailing on the hull of a ship. He also managed people well; and at the precocious young age of twenty-nine, he knew more about brazier copper than most. Harmon Hendricks could count on Solomon to represent him in all matters; their partnership continued until the young Hendricks boys were old enough to be apprenticed into the business.

John Wesley Jarvis has used his familiar sparkling watch fob, bamboo cane, and details on the diagonally-turned open armchair to draw the viewer's attention to the picture plane. With his customary ingenuity, the artist imparts an immediacy to his portrait by creating the illusion of direct eye contact between the sitter and the viewer. Solomon Isaacs wears buff trousers, dark vest and coat, with a white ruffled shirt and stock. The artist appears to have had some difficulty with the sitter's right hand, which disappears into his vest; only a tiny triangle of flesh and some white cuff reaffirm the existence of a hand. The rich, deep palette provides a superb red background that perfectly suits the piercing black eyes and dark, curly hair of this successful, young gentleman of Sephardic heritage. Solomon appears to be in his late twenties, which would give the work a date of approximately 1813. Perhaps the portrait celebrates his new partnership in the Hendricks copper manufactory.   ELC

References
Stern, Malcolm H. *First American Jewish Families: 600 Genealogies, 1654–1988*. Baltimore: Ottenheimer Publishers, 1978.
Whiteman, Maxwell. *Copper for America: The Hendricks Family and a National Industry 1755–1939*. New Brunswick, N.J.: Rutgers University Press, 1971.

77

George Griffin

(1778–1860)
Samuel L. Waldo (1783–1861) and William Jewett (1789/1874)
New York, 1827
Oil on canvas
33 × 26 in.; 83.82 × 56.04 cm
The New-York Historical Society.
Bequest of Mrs. Robert Jaffray

This portrait was included in the 1827 annual exhibition at the American Academy of the Fine Arts. In this powerful character study, George Griffin, one of New York City's pre-eminent attorneys, appears thoughtful and self-assured.

George Griffin graduated from Yale in 1797 and became a member of the bar two years later. He began his law practice in Pennsylvania in 1801; five years later he moved to New York City where he prospered. Following the financial panic of 1837, he retired to devote himself to the writing of religious texts.

Samuel L. Waldo and William Jewett enjoyed a long, profitable artistic partnership from 1818 to 1854. Their most successful portrait type, as in the portrait of Mr. Hendricks (cat. 79), features the solitary, volumetric figure carefully placed in space and rendered in a painterly manner. The artists have placed George Griffin in a traditional pose and conservative dark suit that act as foils for his crisp white stock that leads the viewer's eye directly to the sitter's face. He sits before a marvelous bank of wispy clouds, providing a contrast to the power visible in his strong hands that grasp his documents and perfectly echo the dichotomy of his powerful yet sensitive expression.   ELC

Reference
Portraits in the New-York Historical Society. New Haven: Yale University Press, 1974.

78

Lydia Butler Griffin (Mrs. George Griffin)

(1778–1860)
Samuel L. Waldo (1783–1861) and William Jewett (1789/90–1874)
New York, c. 1827
Oil on canvas
33 × 26 in.; 83.82 × 66.04 cm
The New-York Historical Society.
Bequest of Mrs. Robert Jaffray

Lydia Butler Griffin was the daughter of Phebe Haight and Zebulon Butler, an officer in the British Army during the French and Indian Wars. She married George Griffin in 1801 in Pennsylvania.

The portraits of George Griffin (cat. 77) and his wife are a pendant pair because they are of similar size; they also face each other, simulating an interaction between the couple. Although both portraits were exhibited at the 1827 annual exhibition at the American Academy of the Fine Arts, they were not hung as pendants because Waldo and Jewett have given each portrait a different rhythm.

Like her husband, Lydia Butler Griffin appears confident and gracefully poised, but there is an ineffable difference between the pendants. Thematically they both are compatible and have Northern Baroque sources, but one is a march and the other a waltz. Her patrician features, her slender tapering fingers, the delicacy of her lacy double collar, the sumptuousness of her cashmere shawl, and the curvilinearity of her chair are Van Dyckian; she could have stepped out of one of his Genoese aristocratic portraits. Yet the source for her husband's portrait is Rembrandt's stolid Dutch burgher.   ELC

Reference
Portraits in the New-York Historical Society. New Haven: Yale University Press, 1974.

79 *Harmon Hendricks*

even made an offer to the government to help finance the war with the British in 1812.

Harmon Hendricks was one of ten surviving children born to Uriah Hendricks and Eve Esther Gomez, and the great-grandson of Chaim Hendricks who had emigrated from Holland. Harmon married Frances Isaacs (cat. 60) on June 4, 1880, and they left thirteen surviving children. An important part of their family life, her brother Solomon Isaacs (Plate 13, cat. 76) also played a vital role in the copper business. President of Shearith Israel and a leading philanthropist, Harmon joined the prestigious Union Club, thereby establishing his family socially in New York.

We are fortunate to be able to include examples of the New York artists Waldo and Jewett in this exhibition. Samuel Waldo studied in London at the Royal Academy and was befriended by John Singleton Copley and Benjamin West. He established a studio in New York City and made his apprentice, William Jewett, his partner in 1818. This powerful Waldo and Jewett portrait depicts an extraordinarily successful man of affairs, almost fifty years old with eleven children, impeccably dressed as an upper-class gentleman in a dark suit, white waistcoat, shirt and stock complete with the ubiquitous gold watch-fob. But what gives this work such powerful dynamism is the confident and forthright gaze of the sitter. The portrait has descended directly in the Hendricks family; it is part of the Ruth Hendricks Schulson collection.   ELC

References
Stern, Malcolm H. *First American Jewish Families: 600 Genealogies, 1654–1988.* Baltimore: Ottenheimer Publishers, 1978.
Whiteman, Maxwell. *Copper for America: The Hendricks Family and a National Industry 1755–1939.* New Brunswick, N.J.: Rutgers University Press, 1971.

79

Harmon Hendricks
(1771–1838)
Samuel L. Waldo (1783–1861) and
William Jewett (1789/90–1874)
New York, c. 1820
Oil on canvas
32 ½ × 25 ¼ in.; 82.55 × 64.14 cm
Collection of Ruth Hendricks Schulson

Harmon Hendricks (cats. 79, 80) exemplifies the successful man of affairs and patriotic citizen who would commission a public portrait during the Federal period. An early American industrialist, Hendricks was committed to his large family, his religion, and his country. He had commercial dealings with the colonial patriot Paul Revere; it is more than likely that the steeple bells chiming in the old cities of Boston, New York, or Philadelphia were made by Paul Revere of Hendricks copper. Even Old Ironsides from the War of 1812, tied up today in Boston harbor, was probably lined originally with copper rolled at the Hendricks Mill in Belleville, New Jersey, the first copper-rolling mill in the country. Robert Fulton also used Hendricks-manufactured copper boilers in his steamships. A patriotic American, Hendricks

80

Harmon Hendricks
(1771–1838)
John Wesley Jarvis (1780–1840)
New York, c. 1808
Miniature; watercolor and ink on parchment
3 ⅛ × 3 in.; 7.94 × 7.62 cm
Collection of Ruth Hendricks Schulson

John Wesley Jarvis's lively pen-and-ink profile miniature of Harmon Hendricks depicts a bright, ambitious young industrialist sporting fashionably long curving sideburns; he is thirty-seven years old with five children, and in his business is struggling with shipping problems between Britain and America. Bravely he assumed the mantle of leadership when he spoke out against the inertia of the American Congress to protect the American merchant-shipper in 1808, the approximate date of this portrait.

80 *Harmon Hendricks*

portrait of Samson Levy, Jr. (cat. 18) and James Sharples's portrait of Samuel Hays (cat. 34), both done in 1802. Jarvis's profile portrait of Harmon Hendricks follows in this tradition, but the size is considerably smaller than the Saint-Mémin and the Sharples works. More comparable in size to a tiny, oval American miniature like James Peale's Reuben Etting (cat. 65), the miniature portrait in the first decade of the nineteenth century becomes somewhat larger and rounder with a heavier frame. The Hendricks miniature is an anomaly of that worn by Sally Sanford Perit (Mrs. Job Perit) (cat. 51); Frances Isaacs Hendricks (cat. 60) might keep her husband's intimate portrait near her but would never wear it.

ELC

References

London, Hannah R. *Miniatures and Silhouettes of Early Jews.* Rutland, Vt.: Charles E. Tuttle Company, 1970.

Stern, Malcolm H. *First American Jewish Families: 600 Genealogies, 1654–1988.* Baltimore: Ottenheimer Publishers, 1978.

Whiteman, Maxwell. *Copper for America: The Hendricks Family and a National Industry 1755–1939.* New Brunswick, N.J.: Rutgers University Press, 1971.

The history of the small profile portrait originates in classical antiquity with the Imperial Roman coin and is revived in the neoclassical era. In this exhibition the profile portrait can be observed in Charles Balthazar Julien Févret de Saint-Mémin's

81 *Abraham Rodriguez Brandon*

81
Abraham Rodriguez Brandon
(1766–1831)

John Wesley Jarvis (1780–1840)
c. 1824
Oil on canvas
30 ¼ × 25 in.; 76.84 × 63.5 cm
Museum of the City of New York.
Gift of Julian Clarence Levi, 38.216

Abraham Rodriguez Brandon and his future wife, Sarah Esther Lopez, were both born on the Caribbean island of Barbados. In the second half of the eighteenth century, when Abraham and Sarah were growing up, approximately one hundred Jewish families lived on the island. They all shared the same synagogue, Congregation Nidhe Israel in Bridgetown, where dues and donations could be made in currency or in sugar. The congregation blended Jewish tradition with their Caribbean surroundings. For example, in the absence of standard ingredients, the Jewish islanders concocted Passover *charoset* using raisins, almonds, coconuts, and bananas.[1]

The dates of Abraham and Sarah's wedding and subsequent move to New York are unknown. However, since the couple's seven children were all born in Barbados, the family could not have traveled to America before 1801. Shearith Israel records a donation of a large brass chandelier from Abraham in 1819. The New York congregation further records the death of Sarah in the midst of a spring blizzard during March of 1823.[2] Abraham died eight years later amid sugar and sun in Barbados.

Jarvis most likely painted this portrait of Abraham during the latter part of the Brandon family's sojourn in New York. In the portly, middle-aged sitter, the artist has captured the wrinkles of experience that characterize a mature man of substance and that also attest to his life by the sea in the tropics.   JWZ

Notes
1. Jacob Rader Marcus. *The Colonial American Jew, 1492–1776* (Detroit: Wayne State University Press, 1970), 134.
2. David de Sola Pool, *Portraits Etched in Stone: Early Jewish Settlers, 1682–1831* (New York: Columbia University Press, 1952), p. 128.

References
Pool, David de Sola. *Portraits Etched in Stone: Early Jewish Settlers, 1682–1831*. New York: Columbia University Press, 1952.
Stern, Malcolm. *First American Jewish Families: 600 Genealogies, 1654–1978*. Cincinnati: American Jewish Archives, and Waltham, Mass.: American Jewish Historical Society, 1978.

82 *Abraham Touro*

82
Abraham Touro
(1777–1822)
Artist unknown
c. 1795
Miniature; watercolor on ivory
1 ¾ × 2 ¼ in.; 4.45 × 5.72 cm
The Newport Historical Society (1890.2)

Purchased by twenty–six anonymous donors and presented to the Newport Historical Society, this handsome miniature shows Abraham Touro at eighteen years of age. He wears a dark blue coat, his waistcoat has a diaper pattern of golden-brown on cream, and his stock is tied in a bow. He has long brown curly hair, prominent eyebrows, and brown eyes. The simple frame is gold on a base metal, crowned by a loop; the glass is not original. The verso of the miniature has "A T" inscribed in gold on glass over braided hair.

Not surprisingly, the miniature has an extensive publication history that includes two exhibitions curated for the American Jewish Historical Society: the 1980 exhibition, "On Common Ground: The Boston Jewish Experience, 1649–1980"; and the 1990 exhibition, "'A Most Valuable Citizen': Moses Michael Hays and the Establishment of Post-Revolutionary Boston," at the Bank of Boston.[1] There was also the 250th Anniversary exhibition, in 1980, at Congregation Shearith Israel in New York.   ELC

Note
1. These two exhibitions were curated by Ellen Smith for the American Jewish Historical Society.

Reference
London, Hannah R. *Miniatures of Early American Jews*. Springfield, Mass.: The Pond-Ekberg Company, 1953. Illus. p. 101.

83
Abraham Touro
(1777–1822)
Gilbert Stuart (1754–1828)
Date unknown
Oil on canvas
27 × 22 in.; 68.58 × 55.88 cm
Massachusetts General Hospital

Hannah R. London selected this magnificent portrait as the frontispiece for her landmark book *Portraits of Jews by Gilbert Stuart and Other Early American Artists*. In this painting, one of Stuart's finest works, the artist uses the neutrality of the background and the traditional male apparel merely as foils to bring out his sitter's facial expression, which was everything to Stuart. The unfinished quality of Stuart's work disturbed many sitters; the artist has admitted as much himself, stating that he paints God's work and leaves the clothing to the mantua makers and tailors. Even his contemporary artists corroborate that no one nails a face to a canvas like Stuart. In this masterpiece, he does indeed nail the face to the canvas, finishing it with elegance.

Abraham Touro was born of Portuguese descent in Newport, one of four children of Reyna Hays and Isaac Touro, who made his way to Newport from Holland by way of Jamaica, where he arrived in 1760. In 1763, Isaac Touro officiated at the dedication of the famous Touro Synagogue, Jeshuat Israel, which he served as spiritual leader. But the Jews of Newport supported the Revolution, and they evacuated the city when the British

83 *Abraham Touro*

buried in the Jewish Cemetery in Newport. Renowned for his philanthropy, Abraham Touro left ten thousand dollars in his will to the Massachusetts General Hospital and fifteen thousand dollars in trust for the State of Rhode Island for the preservation of the Touro Synagogue in Newport and the upkeep of its cemetery; both institutions venerate him to this day.   ELC

Notes
1. Morris A. Gutstein, "The Jews of Newport in Pre-Revolutinary Days." *Touro Synagogue of Congregration Jeshuat Israel,* (Newport, Rhode Island: The Friends of Touro Synagogue, 1948), 16–23.
2. Ellen Smith, "Strangers and Sojourners: The Jews of Colonial Boston." *The Jews of Boston,* ed. Jonathan D. Sarna and Ellen Smith (Boston: Combined Jewish Philanthropies of Greater Boston, 1995), 41–42.

References
London, Hannah R. *Portraits of Jews by Gilbert Stuart and Other Early American Artists.* Rutland, Vt.: Charles E. Tuttle Co, 1969. Illus. frontispiece.
Smith, Ellen. "Strangers and Sojourners: *The Jews of Boston.*" In *The Jews of Boston,* ed. Jonathan D. Sarna and Ellen Smith. Boston: Combined Jewish Philanthropies of Greater Boston, 1995. Illus. p. 40.

84
Mendes I. Cohen
(1796–1879)
Artist unknown
1832
Oil on paperboard
Framed: 12 $\frac{7}{16}$ × 9 $\frac{3}{4}$ in.; 31.59 × 24.77 cm
The Maryland Historical Society.
Bequest of Harriet Cohen Coale

invaded. The community never regained its prominence after the war.[1]

After the British left Newport, the family moved back to Jamaica where Isaac Touro died. They then left Jamaica for Boston to live with Mrs. Touro's brother, Moses Michael Hays. Seven years later the mother died, and Hays was left to alone raise the children, including Abraham's brother, the future New Orleans merchant, ship owner, and philanthropist Judah Touro.

Abraham lived in Boston and Medford, Massachusetts, working as the Boston agent for his brother Judah, and developing his own business interests as a merchant-trader and a shipbuilder. He also helped to finance the construction of bridges and roads, even a theater, in the Boston area. Touro Streets in Newport and Medford are named for Abraham Touro.[2]

The Touro mansion in Medford, outside Boston—the site of Touro's shipyard—was close to the canals where Abraham Touro could observe his ships that regularly plied between Boston and the West Indies. Abraham died in an accident when he was forty-five years old. As he was viewing a parade in Boston from his chaise, his horse became alarmed; Touro leaped or fell from his vehicle and broke his leg. He died from the trauma and was

In 1832, when Colonel Mendes I. Cohen (see Plate 14) traveled down the Nile River from Damietta, Egypt, his small craft proudly flew the burgee of the United States of America, the first American sailing vessel to display our colors on the river. The thirty-six-year-old adventurer, one of the unmarried sons of Judith Solomon Cohen (Mrs. Israel I. Cohen) (cat. 85), was the sixth child and fifth son in the family, which also included his brother Jacob I. Cohen (cat. 61); he had served in the military and in family enterprises before he left on his six-year adventure in 1829. His trip is documented in hundreds of letters written to his mother and brothers as he traveled to England, France, Germany, Austria, Switzerland, Russia, Poland, Bulgaria, Turkey, Syria, Palestine, and Egypt. These papers and letters, now part of the manuscript collection of the Maryland Historical Society,[1] colorfully record the third decade of the nineteenth century as observed through the eyes of an adventurous world traveler.

The various portraits of Mendes Cohen also represent the radically different facets of his life. The portrait in this exhibition presents an "orientalist" image of the sitter in exotic dress. His

84 *Mendes I. Cohen*

85 *Judith Solomon Cohen (Mrs. Israel I. Cohen)*

full untrimmed beard and mustache, turban, and colorful costume in the guise of a nomadic desert tribesman, with double
daggers tucked into his polychrome sash, symbolize his six years
of adventurous travel. Upon his return to Baltimore in 1835
Mendes is almost unrecognizable as depicted by Rembrandt
Peale in a portrait on view at the Arthur Ross Gallery of the
University of Pennsylvania in Philadelphia. There he appears as a
man of affairs, clean-shaven and dressed in dark, conservative
banker's clothing. For the remaining forty-four years of his life,
Mendes devoted himself to the family business, directorships of
major industries, benevolent societies, politics, community
affairs, and religious associations.   ELC

Note
1. Mendes I. Cohen's Egyptian artifact collection is at Johns Hopkins University.

References
Fein, Isaac M. *The Making of an American Jewish Community: The History of Baltimore
Jewry from 1773 to 1920.* Baltimore: The Jewish Historical Society of Maryland, 1985.
London, Hannah R. *Portraits of Jews By Gilbert Stuart and Other Early American Artists.*
Rutland, Vt.: Charles E. Tuttle Company, 1969.

85

Judith Solomon Cohen (Mrs. Israel I. Cohen)

(1766–1837)
Artist unknown
Baltimore, c. 1830–35
Oil on canvas
Framed: 30 × 28 ⅛ in.; 76.20 × 71.44 cm
The Maryland Historical Society.
Bequest of Harriet Cohen Coale

Like Shinah Solomon Etting (cat. 50), Judith Solomon Cohen
moved to Baltimore as a young widow with many young children in tow. These matriarchs founded the most prominent Jewish
dynasties in Baltimore; and the women survived to see their
progeny reap great financial and professional success.

Judith Solomon was born in Liverpool, England. She married
Israel I. Cohen—who was born in Oberdorf, Bavaria—in Bristol,
England, and settled with her husband in Richmond, Virginia, in
1784. Israel's firm of Cohen and Isaacs, the largest Jewish-owned
business in Richmond, employed Daniel Boone as a land sur-
veyor. The family lived in Richmond until Israel's death in 1803.
Judith gave birth to ten children; among the seven surviving into
adulthood were Jacob I. Cohen (cat. 61), Mendes I. Cohen,

(Plate 14, cat. 84), and Benjamin I. Cohen who consolidated the two families when he married Solomon Etting's (cat. 74) daughter Kitty. Their direct descendant, and generous benefactor of the Maryland Historical Society, Eleanor Septima Cohen (1858–1937), concluded her 1937 account of her illustrious Cohen-Etting ancestors with the mournful sentence, "I am the only survivor."[1]

Mrs. Cohen, probably in her sixties at the time of this portrait, presents almost an iconic or frontal image, seated modestly attired in a black dress adorned simply with a jeweled pin at the neckline. The rose, cherry, and moss green braid of her white shawl carries the eyes up to the tour de force of the portrait, her indescribably lacy and beribboned bonnet. While she is not a handsome woman, the artist has captured her compassionate eyes and her "no nonsense" air; in short, she has presence.   ELC

Note

1. Helen Burman Sollins, "Eleanor Septima Cohen (1858–1937)," Special Exhibit: The Etting/Cohen Connection, Third Annual Maryland Antiques Show and Sale, February 12–15, 1981.

References

Fein, Isaac M. *The Making of an American Jewish Community: The History of Baltimore Jewry from 1773 to 1920.* Baltimore: The Jewish Historical Society of Maryland, 1985.

London, Hannah R. *Portraits of Jews by Gilbert Stuart and Other Early American Artists.* Rutland, Vt.: Charles E. Tuttle Company, 1969.

Stern, Malcolm H. *First American Jewish Families: 600 Genealogies, 1654–1988.* Baltimore: Ottenheimer Publishers, 1978.

Conclusion

86

Moses Judah

(1778–1831)

William Dunlap (1766–1839)

1818

Oil on canvas

49 ½ × 41 ½ in.; 125.73 × 105.41 cm

Cincinnati Art Museum.

The Edwin and Virginia Irwin Memorial, 1970.20

William Dunlap painted his magnificent portraits of Mr. and Mrs. Moses Judah (see also Plate 15, cat. 87) in 1818, the year that the Romantic artist Washington Allston returned to America from his triumphs in England, where Sir Thomas Lawrence continued to create his portraits with their restless sparkle captured so beautifully by Thomas Sully in his later works. But William Dunlap looked to a Europe infused with the Byronic spirit in their post-Napoleonic era, specifically to Jacques-Louis David, now in exile in Brussels.

David's portrait of Emmanuel-Joseph Sieyes, dated 1817, depicts a former cleric who is seated in an open armchair wearing a long, dark blue-black coat and pants; he holds a tobacco box in his hands. The nondescript scumbling of the background creates the perfect spatial setting for the vital, volumetric figure placed in the foreground of the picture plane. This is a middle-class portrait, not the aristocratic portrait that David was forced to create cyclically during the political vicissitudes painfully experienced by him in France.

86 *Moses Judah*   87 *Hetty Sayre Judah (Mrs. Moses Judah)*

William Dunlap has also created a middle-class portrait of Moses Judah, age thirty-five, one of the nine children of David Judah and Esther Taylor of Westport, Connecticut. He was associated with the artist's family hardware business in New York.

Like David, Dunlap places his vigorous volumetric figure in the foreground picture plane. However, he has returned to the multitude of formulaic attributes for his portrait of a man of affairs holding a document in his hands. The artist has placed the sitter on a side chair, near a table; the background is also non-specific, a somewhat formulaic river view through a window. Like David, Dunlap has prominently signed and dated the work. Both sitters present large areas of dark blue-black color with their costume. Moses Judah wears a double-breasted coat with gold buttons and high stock that perfectly set off his dark eyes and black hair. His gold watch-fob leads the viewer's eye to the hat that he holds on his lap, not unlike the tobacco box held by David's cleric.

For both the American and French artists, the age of revolution and the era of the aristocratic portrait had ended and a new egalitarian era had begun. In America, William Dunlap would live long enough to experience the first flowering of the Jacksonian age.   ELC

References

Coad, Oral Sumner. *William Dunlap: A study of His Life and Works and of His Place in Contemporary Culture*. New York, 1917.

Dunlap, William. *History of the Rise and Progress of the Arts of Design in the United States*. New York, 1843.

Elam, Charles H. "The Portraits of William Dunlap and a Catalogue of his Works," M.A. Thesis, New York University, 1952.

Stern, Malcolm H. *First American Jewish Families: 600 Genealogies, 1654–1988*. Baltimore: Ottenheimer Publishers, 1978.

87

Hetty Sayre Judah (Mrs. Moses Judah)

(Life dates unknown)
William Dunlap (1766–1839)
1818
Oil on canvas
49 ½ × 41 ½ in.; 125.73 × 105.41 cm
Cincinnati Art Museum.
The Edwin and Virginia Irwin Memorial, 1970.21

William Dunlap may have looked to one of Jacques-Louis David's most elegant female portraits for the source of this sparkling depiction of the graceful Hetty Sayre Judah from Fairfield, Connecticut; this pendant portrait painted at the height of the Romantic era probably celebrated her marriage on February 11, 1817, to Moses Judah.

Like Vicomtesse Vilain XIV and her daughter, Mrs. Judah (Plate 15) is placed in a domestic interior; she has a deep blue curtain trimmed in gold fringe at right, which echoes the palette in Moses Judah's portrait. Sitting on elaborate classical chairs, both women wear dark velvet dresses with their décolletages framed by double layers of extraordinary lace setting off their dark hair and eyes. However, the Vicomtesse, wife of a local dignitary in Brussels, probably purchased her lace from the Brussels lace-makers, whereas Hetty is making lace herself. The white of the lace contrasts handsomely with the light-blue support beneath.

The Vicomtesse's aristocratic elegance is completely without personal adornment; on the other hand, Hetty Judah adds her eye-catching lace resting on an elaborate pedestal table, sumptuous pendant earrings and brooch, as well as a chatelaine, a satchel carried by ladies at home containing keys, scissors, thimble, thread, spoon, and other necessities.[1] The quantity of personal adornments and accessories that she has chosen to display removes her portrait from the realm of aristocratic elegance, making it more of a middle-class or mercantile portrait that is transitional to the Jacksonian era.

William Dunlap was born in New Jersey to a prosperous Northern Irish family that later moved to New York for political reasons. The artist studied with Benjamin West in London and, surprisingly, that experience yielded a consuming interest in the theater. The artist was briefly involved in the American Academy of Fine Arts, and founded the National Academy of Design; later he wrote the history of the American theater and the seminal account of the arts of design in America.   ELC

Note

1. The National Museum of American Jewish History, Philadelphia, owns a gold and mother-of-pearl chatelaine formerly used by Rebecca Gratz (Plate 7, cats. 39, 40).

References

Coad, Oral Sumner. *William Dunlap: A Study of His Life and Works and of His Place in Contemporary Culture*. New York, 1917.

Dunlap, William. *History of the Rise and Progress of the Arts of Design in the United States*. New York, 1843.

Elam, Charles H. "The Portraits of William Dunlap and a Catalogue of his Works." M.A. Thesis, New York University, 1952.

Stern, Malcolm H. *First American Jewish Families: 600 Genealogies, 1654–1988*. Baltimore: Ottenheimer Publishers, 1978.

Chronology:
Highlights of Early American Jewish History, 1585–1830

1585
Joachim Gaunse (Ganz) lands on Roanoke Island.

1654
Twenty-three Jewish refugees from Recife in Brazil arrive on the *Ste. Catherine* and settle in New Amsterdam.

1655
• Jews establish burial ground in New Amsterdam.
• Abraham de Lucena, a Sephardic merchant from Amsterdam, brings the first Torah scroll to America for use by the New Amsterdam Jewish community.

1664
British seize Dutch colonies in North America; New Amsterdam is renamed New York, and Jews in North America come under British rule.

1678
Newport Jews, who arrived sporadically beginning about 1658, purchase a cemetery. No permanent community develops until the mid-eighteenth century.

1695–1703
• Jewish public worship is inaugurated in America with the renting of a building on Mill Street in New York for Congregation Shearith Israel; Saul Pardo serves as its first *hazzan* (lay religious leader of worship). No "ordained" rabbis arrive in America until the 1840s.
• Jewish settlement begins in Charleston, South Carolina.

1728
Shearith Israel purchases land for a new cemetery and for building a synagogue.

1730
New York Jews complete and dedicate the first colonial synagogue, Shearith Israel, known as the Mill Street Synagogue.

1733
Jewish community is established in Savannah, Georgia, but does not become permanent until the 1790s.

1735
• *A Grammar of the Hebrew Tongue,* by Judah Monis, the first Hebrew-language book published in North America, is produced in Boston with Hebrew type imported from England, and becomes a required textbook at Harvard University through 1760.
• Shearith Israel establishes a school for teaching the Hebrew language.

1740
• The British Plantation Act offers Jews a limited form of citizenship.
• Threat of Spanish invasion causes dispersal of the Savannah Jewish community.
• A Jewish cemetery is established on Spruce Street in Philadelphia.
• Joseph Simon, the principal merchant and Jewish landowner in the Pennsylvania Dutch country, settles in Lancaster, Pennsylvania, in the early 1740s.

1745
Portuguese ceases to be used in the official records of Shearith Israel in New York.

1749
Congregation Beth Elohim is established in Charleston, South Carolina.

1750s
Newport develops an organized Jewish community.

1755
First Jewish day school is established at New York's Shearith Israel; Hebrew, Spanish, English, writing, and mathematics are taught by the *hazzan* (leader of worship) at no cost to poor students and for a fee to children of wealthier families.

1760s
• Philadelphia organizes a Jewish community.
• Montreal establishes a Jewish community.

1760
The Form of Prayer Which was Performed at Jews Synagogue in the City of New-York, composed by D. R. Joseph Yesurun Pinto—the first Jewish prayer service published in North America—is printed in New York.

1761

The first volume of prayers printed in English for use on the Jewish holidays is published in North America: *Evening Service of Rosh-Hashana and Kippur,* compiled and translated by Isaac Pinto, and printed in New York.

1763

Jeshuat Israel, later known as the Touro Synagogue, designed by architect Peter Harrison in a Georgian Revival style, is dedicated in Newport.

1766

Expanded form of *Prayers for Shabbath, Rosh-Hashanah, and Kippur* is compiled and translated by Isaac Pinto and printed in New York.

1768

Gershom Mendes Seixas, a native of New York City, is hired as the *hazzan,* or leader of worship, of Shearith Israel, making him the first native-born Jewish religious leader in America.

1771

A Jewish synagogue, which would later become Congregation Mikveh Israel, is established in rented quarters in Cherry Alley in Philadelphia.

1773

The first published Jewish sermon printed in America, "A Sermon Preached at the Synagogue In Newport, Rhode-Island," by Rabbi Haijm Isaac Karigal of "Hebron, near Jerusalem, in the Holy Land," is printed in Newport. The sermon was delivered in Spanish and translated into English by Abraham Lopez.

1776

• The British colonies in North America become the United States of America.
• Gershom Seixas and several Shearith Israel families take Torah scrolls and other congregational belongings and flee to Stratford, Connecticut, for four years in advance of the British invasion of New York. Philadelphia also receives Jewish refugees fleeing British occupation.

1777

New York's state constitution grants freedom of religion; other state constitutions adopt similar clauses over the next four and a half decades.

1780s

An organized Jewish community is established in Richmond, Virginia.

1780

Gershom Seixas becomes *hazzan* of Philadelphia congregation.

1782

Mikveh Israel, the oldest congregation in Philadelphia, is formally organized and a synagogue building is dedicated; its governing document is called a constitution.

1783

Philadelphia Jewry establishes the first immigrant aid society in the United States.

1787

The Northwest Territory Act offers Jews equality in all future territories and states.

1788

• The U.S. Constitution, adopted by a majority of the states, grants full civil rights to Jews. However, state laws are not required to do the same.
• Mickve Israel, Savannah's first permanent Jewish congregation, is established.

1790

George Washington writes the Jewish congregation in Newport, assuring them that "the government of the United States ... gives to bigotry no sanction, to persecution no assistance."

1791

The Bill of Rights is ratified, including the First Amendment guaranteeing freedom of religion.

1794

Beth Elohim synagogue is built and dedicated in Charleston.

1796

The first Jew to serve in a state legislature is Dr. Levy Myers of Georgetown, South Carolina.

1800s

Sephardic and Ashkenazic groups begin to segregate into separate congregations and other organizations.

1801

The Jewish population of Charleston surpasses that of New York City in the early 1800s.

1802

Rodeph Shalom, the first Ashkenazic synagogue in the United States, is established in Philadelphia.

1819

Rebecca Gratz initiates the founding of the Female Hebrew Benevolent Society in Philadelphia.

1820

Mickve Israel synagogue is dedicated in Savannah.

1822

The Hebrew Benevolent Society, the first charitable organization unaffiliated with a congregation, is founded in New York to assist new immigrants.

1824

• Charleston Jewry establishes the Reformed Society of Israelites, the first American attempt to liberalize Judaism, foreshadowing the later Reform movement.

• The first American Jewish periodical, *The Jew,* is published in New York.

• The first Jewish congregation west of the Alleghenies is founded in Cincinnati.

1825

• Mordecai Manuel Noah proposes the founding of Ararat, a Jewish colony on Grand Island in upstate New York.

• Congregation Bnai Jeshurun, an Ashkenazic synagogue, is established in New York by members who secede from Shearith Israel.

1826

Maryland passes the "Jew Bill" granting the Jews of Maryland the right to hold state office.

1828

Congregation Shanarai-Chasset is organized in New Orleans.

1829

German-born Isaac Leeser, who has been called the father of American modern Orthodoxy, becomes the *hazzan* of Congregation Mikveh Israel in Philadelphia.

1830s

German and Central European Jews begin immigrating to the United States.

Sources:

Faber, Eli. *A Time for Planting: The First Migration, 1654–1820.* Baltimore: The Johns Hopkins University Press for the American Jewish Historical Society, 1992.

Marcus, Jacob Rader. *The American Jew, 1585–1990: A History.* Brooklyn, N.Y.: Carlson Publishing, 1995.

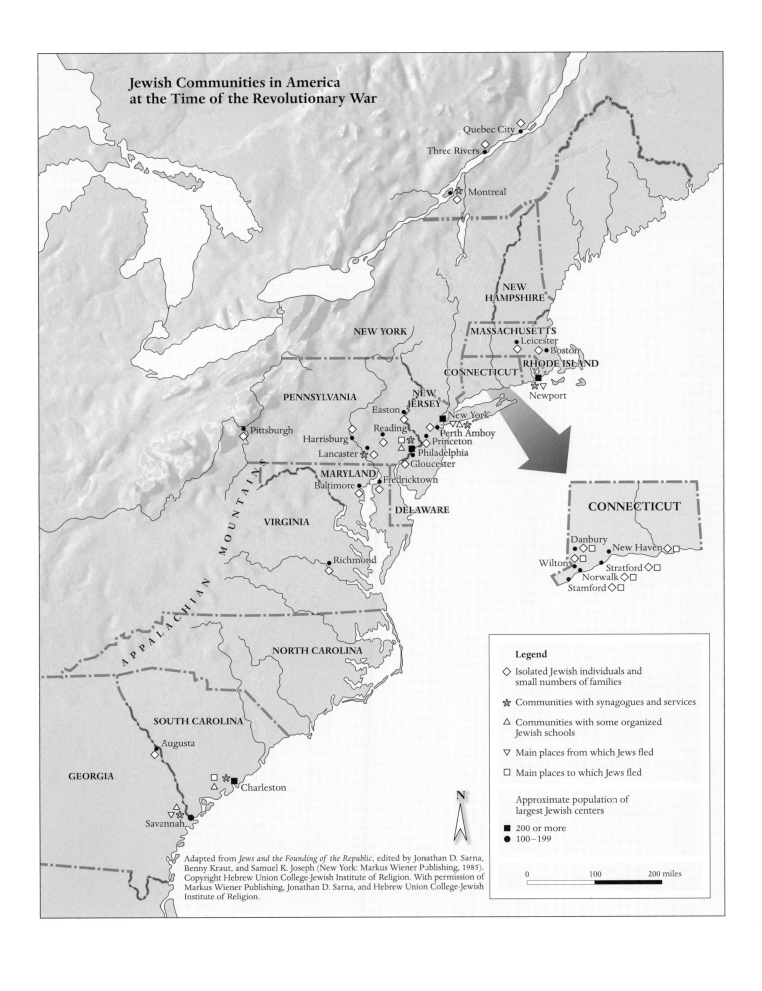

Jewish Communities in America at the Time of the Revolutionary War

Quebec City

Three Rivers

Montreal

NEW HAMPSHIRE

NEW YORK

MASSACHUSETTS

Leicester
Boston

CONNECTICUT

RHODE ISLAND

Newport

PENNSYLVANIA

NEW JERSEY

Easton

New York

Reading

Perth Amboy

Pittsburgh

Harrisburg

Princeton

Lancaster

Philadelphia

Gloucester

MARYLAND

Baltimore

Fredricktown

DELAWARE

VIRGINIA

CONNECTICUT

Danbury

New Haven

Wilton

Stratford

Norwalk

Stamford

Richmond

NORTH CAROLINA

SOUTH CAROLINA

Augusta

Charleston

GEORGIA

Savannah

Legend

◇ Isolated Jewish individuals and small numbers of families

✳ Communities with synagogues and services

△ Communities with some organized Jewish schools

▽ Main places from which Jews fled

☐ Main places to which Jews fled

Approximate population of largest Jewish centers

■ 200 or more
● 100–199

N

Adapted from *Jews and the Founding of the Republic*, edited by Jonathan D. Sarna, Benny Kraut, and Samuel K. Joseph (New York: Markus Wiener Publishing, 1985). Copyright Hebrew Union College-Jewish Institute of Religion. With permission of Markus Wiener Publishing, Jonathan D. Sarna, and Hebrew Union College-Jewish Institute of Religion.

0   100   200 miles

ESTIMATED JEWISH POPULATION OF THE UNITED STATES, 1654–1830

Year	Estimated Jewish Population[1]	Total U. S. Population	Percentage Jewish Population
1654	23		
1660	50		
1654–1700	c. 462		
1700	c. 200–300		
18th century	never more than 500 households		
1776	1,000	2,780,369	0.04
1790	1,300–1,500	3,929,214	0.04
1800	2,000	5,308,483	0.04
1812	c. 3,000		
1820	2,600–3,000[2]	7,239,881	0.03
1830	4,000[3]	12,866,020	0.03

Notes

1 Early population statistics are sporadic, and should be seen as trends as much as precise numbers. The first U. S. Census was taken in 1790.
2 In 1820, two-thirds of the Jewish population lived in Charleston, S.C., Philadelphia, New York City, and Richmond, Va.
3 U. S. cities with populations over 10,000 that had 5 or less Jewish households recorded in 1830: Boston, Mass.; Albany, N.Y.; Washington D.C.; Brooklyn, N.Y., Louisville, Ky.

Sources

Marcus, Jacob Rader. *To Count a People: American Jewish Population Data, 1585–1984.*
   Lanham, Md.: Universtity Press of America, 1990.
Rosenswaike, Ira. "An Estimate and Analysis of the Jewish Population of the United States in 1790."
   Publications of The American Jewish Historical Society 50 (1860–61): 23–67.
Rosenswaike, Ira. "The Jewish Population of the United States as Estimated from the Census of 1820."
   American Jewish Historical Quarterly 53 (1963–64): 131–78.
Rosenswaike, Ira. *On the Edge of Greatness: A Portrait of American Jewry in the Early National Period.*
   Cincinnati: American Jewish Archives, 1985.

LEVY-FRANKS FAMILY

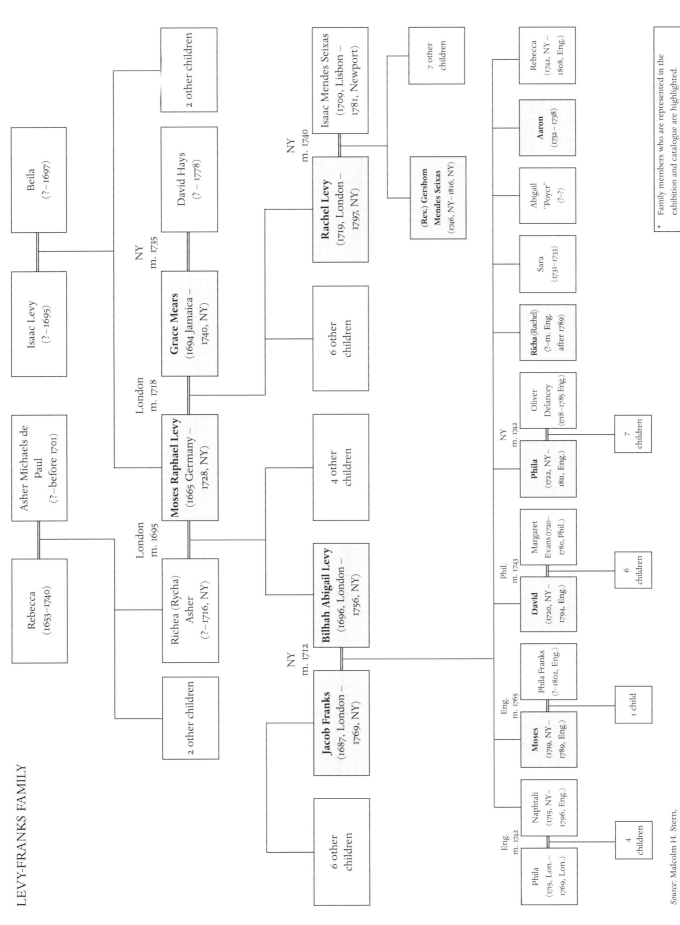

Source: Malcolm H. Stern,
First American Jewish Families: 600 Genealogies, 1654–1988.
Third edition, revised and updated. Baltimore: Ottenheimer Publishers, 1991.

* Family members who are represented in the exhibition and catalogue are highlighted.

* Horizontal double lines indicate a married couple.

Beila
(?–1697)

Isaac Levy
(?–1695)

2 other children

David Hays
(?–1778)

NY
m. 1735

Grace Mears
(1694 Jamaica –
1740, NY)

London
m. 1718

Moses Raphael Levy
(1665 Germany –
1728, NY)

6 other
children

4 other
children

Asher Michaels de
Paul
(?–before 1701)

Rebecca
(1653–1740)

London
m. 1695

Richea (Rycha)
Asher
(?–1716, NY)

2 other children

Isaac Mendes Seixas
(1709, Lisbon –
1781, Newport)

7 other
children

NY
m. 1740

Rachel Levy
(1719, London –
1797, NY)

(Rev.) Gershom
Mendes Seixas
(1746, NY–1816, NY)

Abigail
"Poyer"
(?–?)

Sara
(1731–1733)

Aaron
(1732–1738)

Rebecca
(1742, NY –
1808, Eng.)

Bilhah Abigail Levy
(1696, London –
1756, NY)

NY
m. 1712

Jacob Franks
(1687, London –
1769, NY)

6 other
children

Phila
(1722, NY –
1811, Eng.)

NY
m. 1742

Oliver
Delancey
(1718–1785 Eng.)

7
children

Richa (Rachel)
(?–m. Eng.
after 1789)

David
(1720, NY –
1794, Eng.)

Phil.
m. 1743

Margaret
Evans (1720–
1780, Phil.)

6
children

Moses
(1719, NY –
1789, Eng.)

Eng.
m. 1765

Phila Franks
(?–1802, Eng.)

1 child

Naphtali
(1715, NY –
1796, Eng.)

Eng.
m. 1742

Phila
(1715, Lon.–
1769, Lon.)

4
children

ETTING/GRATZ FAMILIES

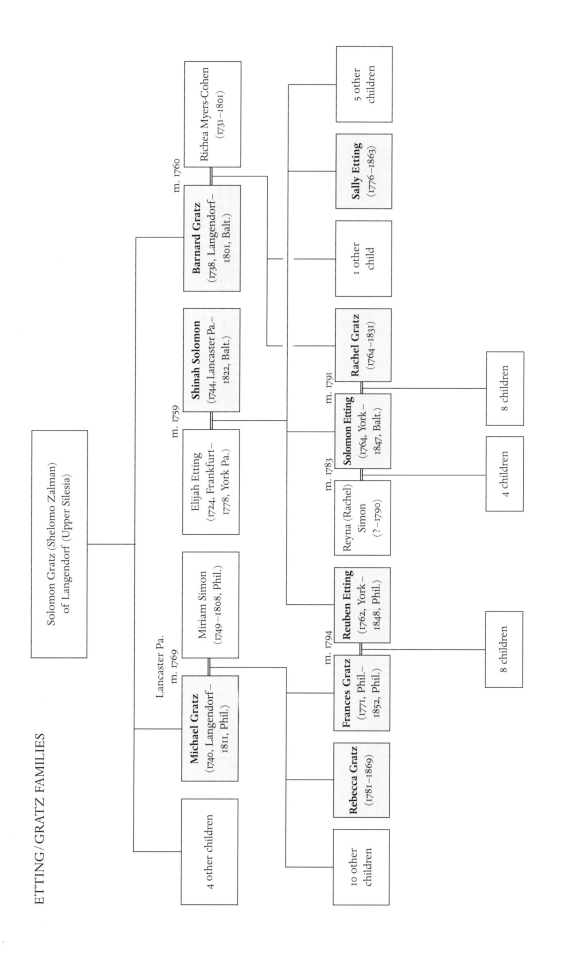

Source: Malcolm H. Stern,
First American Jewish Families: 600 Genealogies, 1654–1988,
Third edition, revised and updated. Baltimore: Ottenheimer Publishers, 1991.

* Family members who are represented in the exhibition and catalogue are highlighted.
* Horizontal double lines indicate a married couple.

Selected Bibliography:
Early American Portraiture

Bayley, Frank William. *Five Colonial Artists of New England: Joseph Badger, Joseph Blackburn, John Singleton Copley, Robert Feke, John Smibert.* Boston: Privately printed, 1929.

Benes, Peter, ed. *Painting and Portrait Making in the American Northeast.* Boston: Boston University, 1995.

Biddick, Kathleen. "'Paper Jews': Inscription/Ethnicity/Ethnography." *Art Bulletin* 78 (1996): 594–99.

Black, Mary. "Aspects of American Jewish History: A Folk Art Perspective." In *The Jewish Heritage in American Folk Art,* ed. Norman L. Kleeblatt and Gerard C. Wertkin. New York: Universe Books, 1984.

Brilliant, Richard. *Portraiture.* Cambridge, Mass.: Harvard University Press, 1991.

Caldwell, John, and Oswaldo Rodriguez Roque et al. *American Paintings in the Metropolitan Museum of Art.* Vol. I. New York: Princeton University Press, 1994.

Craven, Wayne. *Colonial American Portraiture: The Economic, Religious, Social, Cultural, Philosophical, Scientific, and Aesthetic Foundations.* Cambridge, Eng.: Cambridge University Press, 1986.

———. "John Wollaston: His Career in England and New York City." *American Art Journal* 7, no. 2, (1975): 19–31.

Danley, Susan. *Facing the Past: Nineteenth-Century Portraits from the Collection of the Pennsylvania Academy of Fine Arts.* Philadelphia: 1992.

Early American Jewish Portraiture. Exhibition catalogue. New York: The American Jewish Historical Society, 1952.

Flexner, James Thomas. *America's Old Masters: Benjamin West, John Singleton Copley, Charles Willson Peale and Gilbert Stuart.* New York, 1967.

———. *History of American Painting.* Vol. 1, *The Colonial Period: First Flowers of Our Wilderness.* New York: Dover Publications, 1969 (1947). Vol. 2, *1760–1835: The Light of Distant Skies.* New York: Dover Publications, 1969 (1954).

Groce, George C., and David H. Wallace. *The New-York Historical Society's Dictionary of Artists in America, 1564–1860.* New Haven: Yale University Press, 1957.

Hirshler, Erica E. "The Levy-Franks Family Colonial Portraits." Exhibition brochure. Boston: Museum of Fine Arts, 1990.

———. "The Levy-Franks Family Portraits." *The Magazine Antiques* (November 1990): 1020–30.

Kayser, Stephen S., and Isidore S. Meyer. "Early American Jewish Portraiture." *Publications of the American Jewish Historical Society* 41 (1952): 275–94.

Kleeblatt, Norman L., and Gerard C. Wertkin. *The Jewish Heritage in American Folk Art.* New York: Universe Books, 1984.

Kornhauser, Elizabeth M. *Ralph Earl: The Face of the Young Republic.* New Haven: Yale University Press, 1991.

London, Hannah R. *Miniatures of Early American Jews.* Springfield, Mass.: The Pond-Ekberg Company, 1953.

———. *Portraits of Jews by Gilbert Stuart and Other Early American Artists.* New York: William Edwin Rudge, 1927; reprint Rutland, Vt.: Charles E. Tuttle Company, 1969.

———. *Shades of My Forefathers.* Springfield, Mass: The Pond-Ekberg Company, 1941.

Melucci, Alberto. *The Playing Self.* Cambridge, England: Cambridge University Press, 1996.

Miles, Ellen G. *American Painting of the Eighteenth Century.* Washington D.C.: National Gallery of Art, 1995.

———. "The Great American Profile: Folk Portraiture Reconsidered." *Art Journal* (1980): 279–81.

———. *Saint-Mémin and the Neoclassical Profile Portrait in America.* Washington D.C.: The Smithsonian Institution Press for The National Portrait Gallery, 1994.

Miles, Ellen G., ed. *The Portrait in Eighteenth-Century America.* Newark: University of Delaware Press, 1993.

Miles, Ellen G., and Leslie Reinhardt. "'Art conceal'd': Peale's Double Portraits of Benjamin and Eleanor Ridgely Laming." *Art Bulletin* 78 (1996): 57–74.

Miller, Lillian B. *In Pursuit of Fame: Rembrandt Peale: 1778–1860.* Seattle: The University of Washington Press, 1992.

Ockman, Carol. "Two Large Eyebrows à l'Orientale: Ethnic Stereotyping in Ingres's *Baronne de Rothschild.*" *Art History* 14 (1991): 521–39.

Quick, Michael, et al. *American Portraiture in the Grand Manner: 1720–1920.* Los Angeles: Los Angeles County Museum of Art, 1981.

Quimby, Ian M. G. *American Painting to 1776: A Reappraisal.* Charlottesville: The University of Virginia Press, 1971.

Ragussis, Michael. "Representation, Conversion, and Literary Form: Harrington and the Novel of Jewish Identity." *Critical Inquiry* 16 (1989): 113–43.

Rubens, Alfred. *Anglo-Jewish Portraiture.* London: The Jewish Museum, 1935.

Rumford, Beatrix T., ed. *American Folk Portraits: Paintings and Drawings from the Abby Aldrich Rockefeller Folk Art Center.* Boston: New York Graphic Society for the Colonial Williamsburg Foundation, 1981.

Saunders, Richard H., and Ellen G. Miles. *American Colonial Portraits: 1700–1776.* Washington D.C.: The Smithsonian Institution Press for the National Portrait Gallery, 1987.

Strawson, Galen. "The Sense of the Self." *London Review of Books,* April 18, 1996, 21–22.

Weekley, Carolyn, and Stiles Tuttle Colwill et al. *J. Joshua Johnson: Freeman and Early American Portrait Painter.* Williamsburg, Va., and Baltimore: The Colonial Williamsburg Foundation and Maryland Historical Society, 1987.

Selected Bibliography:
Early American Jewish History

GENERAL

Blau, Joseph L., and Salo W. Baron. *The Jews of the United States, 1790–1840: A Documentary History*. 3 vols. New York: Columbia University Press, 1963.

Chyet, Stanley F. *Lopez of Newport: Colonial American Merchant Prince*. Detroit: Wayne State University Press, 1970.

———. "The Political Rights of the Jews in the United States: 1776–1840." *American Jewish Archives* 10 (1958): 14–75.

Daniels, Doris G. "Colonial Jewry: Religion, Domestic and Social Relations." *American Jewish Historical Quarterly* 66 (1976–77): 375–400.

Daughters of the American Revolution Museum. *The Jewish Community in Early America, 1654–1830*. Exhibition catalogue. Washington, D.C.: Daughters of the American Revolution Museum, 1980.

Faber, Eli. *A Time for Planting: The First Migration, 1654–1820*. Vol. 1 of *The Jewish People in America*, ed. Henry L. Feingold. Baltimore: The Johns Hopkins University Press, for the American Jewish Historical Society, 1992.

Freund, Miriam K. *Jewish Merchants in Colonial America*. New York: Behrman's Jewish Book House, 1939.

Hershkowitz, Leo. "Some Aspects of the New York Jewish Merchant and Community, 1654–1820." *American Jewish Historical Quarterly* 66 (1976–77): 10–34.

———. *Wills of Early New York Jews, 1704–1799*. New York: American Jewish Historical Society, 1967.

Hershkowitz, Leo, and Isidore S. Meyer, eds. *Letters of the Franks Family (1733–1748)*. Waltham, Mass.: American Jewish Historical Society, 1968.

Huhner, Leon. "Daniel Gomez, A Pioneer Merchant of Early New York." *Publications of the American Jewish Historical Society* 41 (1951–52): 107–25.

———. *The Life of Judah Touro (1775–1854)*. Philadelphia: Jewish Publication Society of America, 1946.

Marcus, Jacob Rader. *The American Jew, 1585-1990: A History*. Brooklyn, N.Y.: Carlson Publishing, 1995.

———. *American Jewry: Documents, Eighteenth Century*. Cincinnati: Hebrew Union College Press, 1959.

———. *The Colonial American Jew, 1492–1776*. 3 vols. Detroit: Wayne State University Press, 1970.

———. *Early American Jewry*. 2 vols. Philadelphia: Jewish Publication Society of America, 1951–53.

———. "Jews and the American Revolution: A Bicentennial Documentary." *American Jewish Archives* 27 (1975): 103–269.

———. "The Handsome Young Priest in the Black Gown: The Personal World of Gershom Seixas." *Hebrew Union College Annual* 40–41 (1969–70): 445–71.

———. *To Count a People: American Jewish Population Data, 1585–1984*. Lanham, Maryland: University Press of America, 1990.

Marcus, Jacob Rader, ed. *The Concise Dictionary of American Jewish Biography*. 2 vols. Brooklyn, N,Y: Carlson Publishing, 1994.

Pool, David de Sola. *Portraits Etched in Stone: Early Jewish Settlers, 1682–1831*. New York: Columbia University Press, 1952.

———. *An Old Faith in the New World: Portrait of Shearith Israel, 1654–1954*. New York: Columbia University Press, 1955.

Rezneck, Samuel. *Unrecognized Patriots: The Jews in the American Revolution*. Westport Ct.: Greenwood Press, 1975.

Rosenbloom, Joseph R. *A Biographical Dictionary of Early American Jews, Colonial Times through 1801*. Lexington: University of Kentucky Press, 1960.

Rosenswaike, Ira. "An Estimate and Analysis of the Jewish Population in the United States in 1790." *Publications of the American Jewish Historical Society* 50 (1960–61): 23–67.

———. "The Jewish Population of the United States as Estimated from the Census of 1820." *American Jewish Historical Quarterly* 53 (1963–64): 131–78.

———. *On the Edge of Greatness: A Portrait of American Jewry in the Early National Period*. Cincinnati: American Jewish Archives, 1985.

Sachar, Howard M. *A History of the Jews in America*. New York: Knopf, 1992; reprint New York: Vintage, 1993.

Sarna, Jonathan D. "The Impact of the American Revolution on American Jews." *Modern Judaism* 1 (1981): 149–60.

———. *Jacksonian Jew: The Two Worlds of Mordecai Noah*. New York: Holmes & Meier, 1981.

Sarna, Jonathan D., Benny Kraut, and Samuel K. Joseph, eds. *Jews and the Founding of the Republic*. New York: Markus Wiener, 1985.

Schappes, Morris U. *The Jews in the United States: A Pictorial History, 1654 to the Present*. New York: Citadel Press, 1958.

———. *A Documentary History of the Jews in the United States, 1654–1875*, 3rd ed., rev. New York: Schocken, 1971.

Schoenberger, Guido. "The Ritual Silver Made by Myer Myers." *Publications of the American Jewish Historical Society* 43 (1953): 1–9.

Stern, Malcolm H. *First American Jewish Families: 600 Genealogies, 1654–1988*. Baltimore: Ottenheimer Publishers, 1978. Third edition, updated and revised, 1991.

Whiteman, Maxwell. *Copper for America: The Hendricks Family and a National Industry, 1755–1939*. New Brunswick: Rutgers University Press, 1971.

Wischnitzer, Rachel. *Synagogue Architecture in the United States: History and Interpretation*. Philadelphia: Jewish Publication Society of America, 1955.

COMMUNITY STUDIES

Berman, Myron. *Richmond's Jewry, 1769–1796*. Charlottesville: University Press of Virginia, 1979.

Brener, David. *The Jews of Lancaster, Pennsylvania: A Story with Two Beginnings*. Lancaster: Congregation Shaarai Shomayim and the Lancaster County Historical Society, 1979.

Elzas, Barnett A. *The Jews of South Carolina, from the Earliest Times to the Present Day*. Philadelphia: Jewish Publication Society of America, 1950.

Ezekiel, Herbert T., and Gaston Lichtenstein. *The History of the Jews of Richmond from 1769 to 1917*. Richmond: Herbert T. Ezekiel, 1917.

Fein, Isaac M. *The Making of an American Jewish Community: The History of Baltimore Jewry from 1773 to 1920*. Baltimore: The Jewish Historical Society of Maryland, 1985.

Grinstein, Hyman B. *The Rise of the Jewish Community of New York, 1654–1860*. Philadelphia: Jewish Publication Society of America, 1947.

Gutstein, Morris Aaron. *The Story of the Jews of Newport: Two and a Half Centuries of Judaism, 1658–1908*. New York: Block Publishing Co., 1936.

Hagy, James William. *This Happy Land: The Jews of Colonial and Antebellum Charleston*. Tuscaloosa, Ala.: The University of Alabama Press, 1993.

Hershkowitz, Leo. "New Amsterdam's Twenty-three Jews—Myth or Reality?" In *Hebrew and the Bible in America: The First Two Centuries*, ed. Shalom Goldman, 171–83. Hanover, N.H.: University Press of New England, 1993.

Morgan, David T. "Judaism in Eighteenth-Century Georgia." *Georgia Historical Quarterly* 58 (1972–73): 41–54.

Reznikoff, Charles, and Uriah Z. Engelman. *The Jews of Charleston: A History of an American Jewish Community*. Philadelphia: Jewish Publication Society of America, 1950.

Rosenswaike, Ira. "The Jews of Baltimore to 1810." *American Jewish Historical Quarterly* 64 (1974–77): 291–320.

———. "The Jews of Baltimore, 1810 to 1820." *American Jewish Historical Quarterly* 67 (1977–78): 101–124.

Rubin, Saul J. *Third to None: The Saga of Savannah Jewry, 1733–1983*. Savannah, Ga.: S.J. Rubin, 1983.

Sarna, Jonathan D., and Ellen Smith, eds. *The Jews of Boston*. Boston: Combined Jewish Philanthropies of Greater Boston, 1995.

Shargel, Baila R., and Harold L. Drimmer. *The Jews of Westchester: A Social History*. Fleischmanns, N.Y.: Purple Mountain Press, 1994.

Wolf, Edwin 2nd, and Maxwell Whiteman. *The History of the Jews of Philadelphia from Colonial Times to the Age of Jackson*. Philadelphia: Jewish Publication Society of America, 1957.

BIBLIOGRAPHICAL TOOLS

Index to the Publications of the American Jewish Historical Society: Numbers 1–20. Publications of the American Jewish Historical Society, 1914.

An Index to Publications of the American Jewish Historical Society: Volumes 21–50 (1913–1961). Prepared by the American Jewish Historical Society. Brooklyn, N.Y.: Carlson Publishing, 1994.

An Index to American Jewish Historical Quarterly/American Jewish History: Volumes 51–80 (1961–1991). 2 vols. Prepared by the American Jewish Historical Society. Brooklyn, N.Y.: Carlson Publishing, 1995.

Index to the American Jewish Archives, Volumes 1–24 [1948–1972]. Compiled by Paul F. White. Cincinnati: American Jewish Archives, 1979.

Kaganoff, Nathan M. *Judaica Americana: An Annotated Bibliography of Publications from 1960 to 1990*. 2 vols. Brooklyn, N.Y.: Carlson Publishing, 1995.

Rosenbach, A.S.W. *An American Jewish Bibliography Being a List of Books and Pamphlets by Jews or Relating to Them Printed in the United States … Until 1850*. Publications of the American Jewish Historical Society 30 (1926): iii-486.

Singerman, Robert. *Judaica Americana: Bibliography of Publications to 1900*. 2 vols. New York: Greenwood Press, 1990.

Index of Portrait Subjects

Page numbers in *italic type* refer to the portraits or other illustrations.

Index of Artists

Board of Trustees of The Jewish Museum

Contributors

Richard Brilliant is Professor of Art History and Archaeology and Anna S. Garbedian Professor in the Humanities at Columbia Unversity. He is the author of numerous books, including *Portraiture* (1991).

Ellen Smith is Curator of the American Jewish Historical Society and a member of the Luce Foundation "Visual Culture of American Religions" project. Her most recent publications include *The Jews of Boston,* co-edited with Jonathan D. Sarna (1995), and entries in *American Jewish Women: An Historical Encyclopedia* (1997).

Elizabeth Lamb Clark is a doctoral candidate in Art History at the City University of New York. She has been a researcher for several museum exhibitions, including *John Singleton Copley in America* at the Metropolitan Museum of Art.

Joellyn Wallen Zollman is a doctoral candidate in American Jewish History at Brandeis University. She also serves as Registrar for the collection of material culture at the American Jewish Historical Society.

Charlotte Emans Moore is a doctoral candidate in the American and New England Studies Program at Boston University. She is co-author of *American Paintings in the Museum of Fine Arts, Boston, An Illustrated Summary Catalogue* and *Folk Art's Many Faces: Portraits in the New York State Historical Association,* among other publications.

Photo Credits